Kerygmatic Hermeneutics

Kerygmatic Hermeneutics

Formulating a Pentecostal-Charismatic Practice
of Reading Scripture in the Spirit in Community

SWEE SUM LAM
Foreword by Mike Higton

◆PICKWICK *Publications* • Eugene, Oregon

KERYGMATIC HERMENEUTICS
Formulating a Pentecostal-Charismatic Practice of Reading Scripture in the Spirit in Community

Copyright © 2021 Swee Sum Lam. All rights reserved. Except for brief quotations in critical publications or reviews, no part of this book may be reproduced in any manner without prior written permission from the publisher. Write: Permissions, Wipf and Stock Publishers, 199 W. 8th Ave., Suite 3, Eugene, OR 97401.

Pickwick Publications
An Imprint of Wipf and Stock Publishers
199 W. 8th Ave., Suite 3
Eugene, OR 97401

www.wipfandstock.com

PAPERBACK ISBN: 978-1-6667-0144-9
HARDCOVER ISBN: 978-1-6667-0145-6
EBOOK ISBN: 978-1-6667-0146-3

Cataloguing-in-Publication data:

Names: Lam, Swee Sum, author. | Higton, Mike, foreword.

Title: Kerygmatic hermeneutics : formulating a pentecostal-charismatic practice of reading Scripture in the Spirit in community / Swee Sum Lam; foreword by Mike Higton

Description: Eugene, OR: Pickwick Publications, 2021 | Includes bibliographical references.

Identifiers: ISBN 978-1-6667-0144-9 (paperback) | ISBN 978-1-6667-0145-6 (hardcover) | ISBN 978-1-6667-0146-3 (ebook)

Subjects: LCSH: Bible—Hermeneutics. | Pentecostalism. | Bible—Theology. | Bible—Christian Church. | Hermeneutics—Religious aspects—Pentecostal churches.

Classification: BX8762 L36 2021 (print) | BX8762 (ebook)

For all who desire to flow in the Spirit

CONTENTS

List of Figures xi
Foreword xiii
Preface xv
Acknowledgments xvii

1 INTRODUCTION 1
   1.1 Motivation of Research 5
      1.1.1 A practice of praying in the Spirit in search of a theology 6
      1.1.2 A theology to refine practice in scriptural reading
          in the Spirit 11
   1.2 Research Problem, Research Question and Thesis Statement 12
   1.3 Methodology 13
   1.4 Definitions of Terms 16
   1.5 Structure of Research 20

2 LOCATING THIS PROJECT 23
   2.1 Within the Theological Interpretation Movement 24
   2.2 Reading Scripture with the Spirit 27
      2.2.1 Emphasis on the immediate experience
          of the Spirit through Scripture 28
      2.2.2 Emphasis on the work of the Spirit in the church 29
      2.2.3 Emphasis on the Spirit's work in the world
          beyond the church 30
   2.3 A Review of Three Voices 31
      2.3.1 Nicholas Lash 33
      2.3.2 Stephen Fowl 36
      2.3.3 Clark Pinnock 39
      2.3.4 Discussion 42
   2.4 Conclusion 44

3 THE HOLY SPIRIT: FORMULATING THE MARKS OF THE SPIRIT 46

- 3.1 The Holy Spirit and His Work 47
  - 3.1.1 Spirit and Trinity 48
  - 3.1.2 Spirit and Creation 51
  - 3.1.3 Spirit and Jesus Christ 53
  - 3.1.4 Spirit and Church 55
  - 3.1.5 Spirit and Transformation 59
- 3.2 Discerning the Marks of the Spirit 63
  - 3.2.1 Intoxication: Bond of love in communion 63
  - 3.2.2 Life: Mediating new life and co-creating 65
  - 3.2.3 Participation: Ongoing knowing, becoming and proclaiming 66
  - 3.2.4 Revelation of truth: Conviction of sin and correction of error 69
- 3.3 Locating Kerygmatic Hermeneutics 72
- 3.4 Conclusion 73

4 KERYGMATIC HERMENEUTICS: A THEOLOGY 74

- 4.1 Preamble 75
- 4.2 A Theology of Kerygmatic Hermeneutics 79
  - 4.2.1 The Spirit uses Scripture's otherness 80
  - 4.2.2 The Spirit enables a reader to read Scripture 87
  - 4.2.3 Kerygmatic hermeneutics is ordered three ways 90
- 4.3 An Epistemology of Kerygmatic Hermeneutics 98
  - 4.3.1 Spirit epistemology 104
  - 4.3.2 Apprehension and reception 109
- 4.4 Conclusion 115

5 KERYGMATIC CRITICISM 116

- 5.1 Theological Characterization 127
  - 5.1.1 Christology 128
  - 5.1.2 Spirit 131
  - 5.1.3 Logos 132
- 5.2 Reader Dispositions 134
- 5.3 Community Habits 136
  - 5.3.1 Bible reading and meditation 139

5.3.2 Prayer and contemplation 141
5.3.3 Proclamation and witness 145
5.4 Community Practices 146
5.4.1 Praying in the Spirit 147
5.4.2 Interpreting Scripture in the Spirit 150
5.4.3 Proclaiming Christ in the Spirit 151
5.5 Community Outcomes 152
5.5.1 Characterization of a kerygmatic reader 153
5.5.2 Characterization of a kerygmatic community 155
5.6 Community Impacts 157
5.7 Conclusion 160

6 KERYGMATIC HERMENEUTICS: A PRACTICE 162
6.1 Preamble 166
6.2 Praying in the Spirit 168
6.2.1 Attending and listening to the Spirit 169
6.2.2 Learning and correction in the Spirit 173
6.3 Interpreting Scripture in the Spirit 177
6.3.1 Pre-PAL Scriptural Interpretation Program 183
6.3.2 PAL Scriptural Interpretation Program 185
6.4 Theological Integrity 192

7 CONCLUSION 197
7.1 Contributions of this Research 200
7.1.1 A theology of a Spirit-led hermeneutics 202
7.1.2 A practice of a Spirit-led hermeneutics 203
7.1.3 A criticism of a Spirit-led hermeneutics 204
7.2 Implications for Epistemology and Theology 205
7.3 Directions for Future Research 207

Bibliography 211

List of Figures

Figure 1 | 161
Exhibit 1 | 171
Figure 2 | 182

Foreword

SCRIPTURE IS A GIFT of God, given by the hand of the Holy Spirit. It is a gift that we unwrap only as our hands are guided by the same Spirit. By means of this text, the Spirit leads us to the feet of Jesus, and to the foot of the cross. By means of this text, the Spirit teaches us how to place our own feet in the walk of discipleship.

The receiving, unwrapping, and using of this gift do not take place primarily as we walk alone. The Spirit gives this gift to the church, to the Body of Christ that the Spirit animates and guides. As members of the Body, by the Spirit's grace, we receive this gift from each other's hands—our own reading enriched, challenged, redirected by the reading of others. As members of the Body, by the Spirit's grace, we receive this gift as our feet walk the world—our reading interrupted, excited and transformed by the people we meet and the situations we encounter.

Reading scripture well is therefore never simply a matter of our own effort, our own diligence and responsibility. It depends upon the Spirit's work. If we would read well, we must wait upon the Spirit and be open to the Spirit. We must stay awake, listening for the voice of the Spirit calling to us through the voices of all those around us.

Swee Sum Lam is a theologian who takes the role of the Spirit in our reading of scripture with unusual seriousness. For her, it is not enough to urge individual believers to cultivate a disposition of openness, vital though such a disposition is. Rather, a church's communal practices and its polity need to be shaped around such openness—arranged around a space in which it is trusted that the Spirit will speak.

You will find in these pages a discussion of the marks of the Spirit's work in general, and you will find a discussion of the Spirit's work specifically in scriptural interpretation. You will also find, however, an original, detailed and challenging proposal for how a church can wait upon the

Spirit in its reading practices. It is a proposal for a form of reading buoyed up by prayer, energized by multiple voices, and steered by a deliberate and painstaking discernment.

The proposal is certainly a demanding one, but it is made with a striking confidence that the Spirit has spoken, is speaking, and will speak. God's people have not been left on their own with scripture—and, as Swee Sum knows, that makes all the difference.

Mike Higton
Professor of Theology and Ministry
Durham University

Preface

READING SCRIPTURE IN THE SPIRIT is a revised version of my doctoral dissertation that was written at the School of Theology and Religion, Durham University. I was gratified to have passed my viva without corrections.

Upon reflection, I find this enriching journeying with the Spirit in those 31 months quite unlike writing my first doctoral dissertation in finance at the University of Washington, Seattle. In this enriching journeying with the Spirit, there was a deep engagement of desires, emotions, and spirit, beyond that of the mind. There was clarity over the main idea and the claims made to address the research question throughout the journeying. This was not me. There was a growing awareness of the deep darkness in the wide expanse within me. I learnt to attend to the voice of the Spirit as he directs my writing. I have also learned to attend to the voices of my supervisors, Professors Mike Higton and Walter Moberly, as they guided me through the readings. The final formulation of the main idea and claims of *Reading Scripture in the Spirit* has not changed substantially from its conception at the proposal stage. Yet, the main idea and claims have found expression in evolving form and shape as my thoughts crystallize with reading and praying in the Spirit. All remaining errors are mine.

This book documents a church in search for a theology for its practice of praying in the Spirit. This theology, in turn, yields a practice in scriptural interpretation in the Spirit in a community of faith. This book is also a sequel to a documentation of the history of this church in Seah's doctoral dissertation, "A Spirituality Approach to Organizational Transformation." This journeying in theological education that culminates in the writing of this book is a response to the Spirit's call to document the history of this church. This call came to me in an inaudible voice one day as I was walking along the Blue Ridge Mountains in Virginia in the summer of 1996. This voice came in the otherness of the Spirit but it was met with inaction for many years. This confession testifies to the work of grace in one as undeserving as I.

Swee Sum Lam
Asian Pastoral Institute, Singapore

Acknowledgments

FIRSTLY, I WISH TO express my thanks to Dr. David Jeremiah Seah, Senior Pastor of The Tabernacle Church and Missions, for the continuous guidance and encouragement in my pursuit of theological education and research and, in particular, the germination of this project.

I thank both my supervisors, Professor Mike Higton and Professor Walter Moberly of Durham University, for their skilful guidance in tooling me up for the work of theological research. Professor Mike Higton gave me constructive comments and guided me meticulously in the preparation of this work for publication. I am especially grateful that he has written such a gracious foreword to this book.

Lastly, I appreciate my examiners, The Revd Professor William Kay of Wrexham Glyndŵr University and Professor Pete Ward of Durham University for their encouragement that led to the publication and dissemination of this work.

Swee Sum Lam
Asian Pastoral Institute, Singapore

1

INTRODUCTION

PENTECOSTAL THEOLOGY EMPHASIZES THE immediate experience of the Spirit in the present. Harvey Cox points to experience as a distinctiveness recognizable at Pentecostalism's origin and early stages of growth; Pentecostals give primacy to the immediate experience of the Spirit.[1] Here, I want to draw attention to some aspects of this focus on experience that are relevant to this research.

First, there has been a recent emphasis on an immediate experience of the Spirit speaking through Scripture. In the 1990s, scholarly work on Pentecostal hermeneutics became extensive. Most of that work emphasized the way that the Spirit speaks through Scripture or shapes the interpretation of Scripture. Similar themes and approaches also appeared outside circles that may be directly associated with Pentecostalism, in diverse charismatic contexts and beyond. New voices included Kenneth Archer, Timothy Cargal, Gordon Fee, Stephen Fowl, Richard Israel, Daniel Albrecht, Randall McNally, Clark Pinnock, Roger Stronstad, Theodore Stylianopoulous, and N. T. Wright.[2] Kevin Spawn and Archie Wright, in a project that explores pneumatic hermeneutics, bring together seven other scholars to address the Spirit's role in biblical hermeneutics: Mark Boda,

---

1. In contrast, fundamentalists ascribe unique authority to the letter of Scripture. Together with many other Christian groups, fundamentalism has its beliefs and practices formalized in theological systems and doctrines (Cox, *Fire from Heaven*, 15).

2. See, e.g., Archer, "Pentecostal Hermeneutics," 63–81; Archer, *Spirit, Scripture and Community*; Cargal, "Pentecostals and Hermeneutics," 163–87; Fee, "Hermeneutics and Historical Precedent," 83–104; Fowl, *Engaging Scripture*; Israel et al., "Pentecostals and Hermeneutics," 137–61; Pinnock, "Holy Spirit in Hermeneutics," 3–23; Pinnock, "Perspective," 157–71; Stronstad, "Pentecostal Experience and Hermeneutics," 14–30; Stylianopoulous, *Orthodox Perspective*; Wright, "Authoritative," 7–32.

Ronald Herms, John C. Thomas, Mark Cartledge, Craig Bartholomew, James Dunn, and Walter Moberly.[3] Besides taking a biblical theological approach that explored how Scripture described the work of the Spirit, scholars also applied an inductive approach in understanding how the interpretation of Scripture evolved in the first century church after the outpouring of the Holy Spirit.[4] They were looking at the interpretive practice of first-century readers who understood themselves to be filled with and guided by the Spirit.

Second, there has within this work often been a focus on the multiple messages the Spirit might use a text to convey, in different circumstances. The early Pentecostal scholars in the 1980s, like French Arrington, Mark McLean, and William Menzies, advance Pentecostal hermeneutics as that which focuses on experience informing scriptural interpretation, and this inevitably opens up the text so the same text can speak differently in multiple contexts.[5] The development of this theme in formal Pentecostal hermeneutics coincides with the era when theological interpretation was developing, with Anthony Thiselton as one of its main protagonists, to move hermeneutics beyond the horizons of the author, and the text, to embrace the horizon of the reader as well.[6] That is, Thiselton's move would be consistent with this emphasis on the multiple messages the Spirit might use a text to convey, in different circumstances.

---

3. This project brings together scholars to present ideas on the role of the Spirit in hermeneutics. Among other issues that were raised concerning pneumatic hermeneutic in the present renewal (Pentecostal-charismatic) movement, the discourse also discussed attempts to comment on the way the New Testament writers read their Scripture, the Hebrew Bible/LXX or the Old Testament. There also appears to be an agreement among the respondents and authors that the discernment of false claims to speak in the Spirit has "not been sufficiently addressed by the renewal tradition and a pneumatic hermeneutic, or for that matter the academy in general" (see, e.g., Spawn and Wright, *Spirit and Scripture*, 178).

4. See Thomas, "Women," 41–56, for an example in inductive approach to reading Acts 15. Thomas lets the event, experience and field data speak for themselves to generate possible understanding of the scriptural text, as compared to reading what the text meant from its own context in historical criticism. Grey, *Three's A Crowd*, gives another account of how the Old Testament may be read in Pentecostal communities. Fowl also read Acts 10–15, not for an exegetical account of the text, but with a view of learning from the apostolic account what "practical social structures, practices and habits" were at work there that enabled the apostles and community "to recognise, interpret and enact the work of the Spirit" (Fowl, "How the Spirit Reads," 350).

5. See Arrington, "Hermeneutics," 382–84; McLean, "Pentecostal Hermeneutic," 35–56; Menzies, "Methodology of Pentecostal Theology," 1–14.

6. See Thiselton, *Two Horizons*; Thiselton, *New Horizons*.

Third, one of the things that lingers in this discourse is the persistent general question of discernment and testing. Among the diverse senses of what 'experience' may inform an interpretation of Scripture, there appears to be a leaning toward considering how corporate (rather than simply personal) experience can generate a fresh reading. That is, this discernment has to do with the way a community can help guard against individual waywardness. Moreover, there has been discussion of how any fresh reading has to cohere with the canonical text to be a valid reading.[7] Fee analyzes the problem bluntly: "it is probably fair—and important—to note that in general the Pentecostals' experience has preceded their hermeneutics. In a sense, the Pentecostal tends to exegete his or her experience."[8] By focusing on the work of the Spirit in relation

---

7. According to Arrington, a characteristic of classical Pentecostal hermeneutics is the dialogical role of experience in interpretation and the multiplication of paradigmatic meanings. He argues that "personal and corporate experience inform[s] the Pentecostal hermeneutical process" (Arrington, "Hermeneutics," 383–84). In fact, he goes beyond to say that experiential revelation "can unlock previously undiscovered scriptural truths." This represents a push beyond what Menzies and McLean have articulated in a Pentecostal hermeneutic. The former seeks to restrict the role of experience to verifying the accuracy of the interpretation (Menzies, *Methodology of Pentecostal Theology*, 12–14). McLean seeks a somewhat balanced view. McLean contends that a Pentecostal hermeneutic that reads Scripture with the Spirit is not only "a vital necessity if we are to have an effective ministry to our 'modern' world, it is inescapable." On the other hand, this Pentecostal hermeneutic does not just incorporate the 'rhema' word, "the personal revelation of the Holy Spirit to the individual which transcends the plain sense of the written canonical text." This Pentecostal hermeneutic has in fact to be "a well articulated, canonically based expression of normative Christianity" (McLean, *Pentecostal Hermeneutic*, 36). Dunn adds that the New Testament canon norms a diversity of readings and hermeneutical practices. He says, "All this is to underlie the fact that the New Testament canon canonizes diversity—diversity of interpretation and practice. And if that is so then the only appropriate response of different Christians and individual churches (which respect the New Testament as canon) is to recognize, acknowledge and respect those whose reading of the New Testament is different from theirs but which can be shown to be as equally (or more) valid as theirs. The New Testament, with its focus so entirely on Jesus Christ as Lord, is indeed the key unifying bond of Christians and Christian churches. But it only truly unifies when it engenders acceptance and full respect for those who seek equally to conform to the norm of the New Testament but hear it differently" (Spawn and Wright, *Spirit and Scripture*, 159).

8. Fee, *Hermeneutics and Historical Precedent*, 86. Fee concludes that the presupposition of Pentecostal hermeneutic appears to be—One who has been filled with the Spirit or has ministered in the Spirit is likely to make a better scriptural interpreter than one who has no such experience. I agree that a Pentecostal experience does not substitute for the need for good hermeneutical principles and practices. However, it makes good sense that a scholar's openness to the Pentecostal reality will help in

to the interpretation of Scripture, in thinking in particular about how the Spirit can generate multiple readings of the same text, and in seeking to acknowledge and answer the question about discernment, my work aligns with these trends.

Outside the developed Western world, Allan Anderson studies global Pentecostal movements in Africa and Asia and advances a taxonomy in reading these with multidisciplinary lenses.[9] Similarly, William Kay and Anne Dyer observe that Pentecostal-charismatic engagements in missions, migration, globalization and all facets of public life show up the Spirit's work in fast growing churches in, say, Latin America, Africa, and Asia in myriad visible ways.[10]

In this research, I speak, to varying extent, into these discourses in Pentecostal-charismatic theology. I speak into the Spirit's working from Singapore, an Asian gateway that offers a unique blend of the east and the west in religious and secular thoughts and practices. I come from an evangelical contemplative charismatic community in Singapore. It has four church congregations worshiping out of two locations in Singapore, and missionary churches in Philippines, Thailand, and Myanmar. Each church congregation is structured to hold no more than 300 members. There are many charismatic communities in Singapore, many of which have remained within the traditional Christian denominations including the Catholic church. Among the independent charismatic communities, notably dominated by four or five mega-churches, we have the rare distinction of being contemplative and charismatic at the same time. A journey that started in 1975 with extremely charismatic and ecstatic experiences has evolved into the current blend of contemplative charism. I have personally experienced this evolution since 1977. We practice healings and deliverances, pray and sing in the Spirit, work signs and wonders, exercise the charismatic gifts, and do all good.[11] Yet we also can be contemplative in prayer, meditation, and quiet in devotional worship

---

his/her making good theology because s/he has experienced that reality that needs explaining.

9. See Anderson, "Varieties, Taxonomies and Definitions," 13–29.

10. Kay and Dyer, *Pentecostal and Charismatic Studies*.

11. "Signs and wonders" is a standard way of naming, in the Pentecostal-charismatic church context, the supernatural and miraculous element in ministry. I acknowledge that people, including Christians, have different opinions about what signs and wonders are, and do. Here, I am writing from a church context in which the assumption that this miraculous element in ministry is possible and expected is widely held, even if in the general case it is subject to suspicion.

in the pursuit of God and faith, hope and love in Christian living. In this research, I am exploring how Scripture can and should be read in a Pentecostal-charismatic community like this, whether in the developed western world or the developing south and east.

I next explain my motivation for this research. In section 1.2, I lay out the research problem, research question, and thesis statement. Section 1.3 explains my methodology in using a constructive theological approach to formulate this account. Section 1.4 lists some of the terms formulated in this research and their definitions. Finally, section 1.5 gives the structure of this research.

1.1 Motivation of Research

This research springs from my experience in this church community; nevertheless, this is not a study of this church community. I am motivated in particular by a specific practice of Christian spirituality that has been developed in this church, which aims at realigning individuals, ministries, practices, and structures for sustainable transformation of the church community. This practice involves praying in the Spirit and listening to the Spirit. It trains discernment for learning, correction, and transformation under the guidance of the Spirit. This practice provides the inspiration for my account of how a Pentecostal-charismatic community like this might also read Scripture in the Spirit. I seek to answer questions raised from this experience. It is hoped that my research would feed back into this practice and speak to a wider Pentecostal-charismatic community.

After giving an account of the renewal movement since the 1970s, Stibbs argues for "a betrothal of academic theology and the pneumocentric spirituality of charismatics and Pentecostals."[12] Consistent with the present work of the Spirit in the church and the world, "there is a responsibility on the part of Pentecostal and charismatic church leaders to embrace a more critical, theological emphasis in their ministries."[13] This project is consistent with a call for a renewal of Pentecostal-charismatic theology that critically discerns the Spirit's work in creation and the world.[14]

---

12. Stibbe, "Theology of Renewal," 74.
13. Stibbe, "Theology of Renewal," 79.
14. See also Stibbe, "This is That," 181–93; Moltmann, *Spirit of Life*; Moltmann,

1.1.1 A practice of praying in the Spirit in search of a theology

A practice of praying in the Spirit is fluid and can take diverse forms and modes. This could take place in small groups at one level, or at church-wide prayer meetings at another.

Prayers can be silent, in patient waiting on the Spirit. This involves being in attentive waiting upon the Spirit for him to speak. Prayers can also be vocalized in the Spirit (i.e., in 'tongues') or in the vernacular. Vocalized praying in the Spirit calls for simple trust as one willingly flows where the Spirit leads and that the Spirit will give 'words' when one opens one's mouth, not knowing specifically what one is going to saying. Here, the mind is silenced and does not control the tongue. These 'words' can come in the form of a spiritual language, not learnt, or any language or dialect in the vernacular, at the Spirit's direction. *Charismata*, such as the gifts of prophecy, knowledge, and discernment, may also be exercised during prayers under guidance of the leadership.

Praying in the Spirit is God-speak. Unlike a conventional understanding of prayer where human beings speak to God in confession, petition, intercession, thanksgiving, or praise, praying in the Spirit is Spirit-breathed communication by human beings, directed by God's agency. This praying in the Spirit is orderly. Such praying is done with seriousness and awe, and members hold one another to account for their own lives and decision-making. Each member is fully conscious and can choose to participate or refrain at any time. That is, one may choose to interrupt one's flow in the Spirit as God speaks.

This practice of praying in the Spirit has been used to develop a church's vision and mission. It has also been used for ministry realignment as well as small group learning. Consistent with the uncharacterizable working of the Spirit, there is a wide range of ways in which such praying has been practiced. For example, this practice has been used to train discernment in reading the Spirit: that is, in learning to pay attention to what the Spirit is saying and doing to me, other members of the community and the wider world. It also involves actively listening to what the Spirit may be directing me or others to say, do or make a decision on.

For illustration, I can describe what I have experienced of this attending to the Spirit. Members are assigned to a small group of four or

---

"God in the World, " 369–81; Yung, "21st Century Reformation," 32–33. Moltmann argues that the Christian theology has to embrace the work of God, in his Spirit, in creation and the world that is beyond the church (Moltmann, *Spirit of Life*, 8, 10).

five, either randomly or systematically. Each small group is under the charge of a trained facilitator. Praying in the Spirit in each small group may take the following format. Each takes a turn to pray in tongues, one after another. Members can decide to pass at any point. Throughout the time when members take turns to pray in tongues, each member listens silently and attentively for the Spirit to give an interpretation of a member's tongue as it is being spoken. An interpretation of a tongue can come in an inaudible voice, a vision, a thought, or an emotion. Members are free to keep their eyes open, close their eyes, pen down what they 'hear' for a particular member, or just remember what has been revealed to them by the Spirit.

This is followed by small group sharing on members' interpretation in the Spirit. Starting with any member, s/he shares his/her interpretation of his/her own tongue first, then followed by others one after another sharing their interpretations of that same member's tongue. Here, there is no specific requirement of coming to a group agreement in the interpretation of any person's tongue. A member may choose to share more of what the listening and interpreting means to him/her in his/her specific context. The outcome is a learning of discernment through iterative practices in discriminating the voice of the Spirit from other voices. It is a form of devotion that involves listening to the Spirit in a community.[15]

The work of reflecting on and providing resources for this practice of Christian spirituality has already begun in the work of David Jeremiah Seah. Seah documents a case study of a church community as it embarked on developing a fresh vision and a sense of mission for a sustainable transformation.[16] He addresses the research question: *What can harness and release the subconscious creative potentials of people for responsible organizational transformation of a church?*[17] Given that Seah was studying a religious organization, he argues for an approach

---

15. This practice of praying in the Spirit can be very different from what many Christians, including possibly Pentecostal-charismatics, may understand it to be. It is characterized not so much by extended time and passion, or earnest crying to God to meet our deepest needs or answer our petitions. It also does not have to be loud and boisterous. This praying comes in the flow of a desirous spirit longing after God, what he is saying or doing, where the self has been silenced in sweet contentment of his presence. This praying is not about self at all. It is all about God. This is not to say that a church community does not also practice conventional praying where human speaks to God in confession, petition, intercession, thanksgiving or praise.

16. Seah, "Spirituality Approach," 23–26.

17. Seah, "Spirituality Approach," 3.

grounded in religious spirituality, and formulates a theory based on an integrative psychological and theological perspective on transformation.

As part of the exploratory study on organizational transformation, the incumbent leadership of the church community was invited to participate. Participants were sampled from several levels of male/female leadership across every ministry. These were all people who had adequate grasp of Scripture, were relatively spiritually mature, and were able to relate to the Spirit. Seah formulated what he called a Participatory Active Listening (PAL) Prayer Method that he believed would be capable of transforming both individuals and the community through praying in the Spirit, which I will be describing in more detail in chapter 6.[18] This prayer method was put into practice and was then evaluated over a two-year period for its organizational transformation effects.[19]

As appropriate for documentation of a journey in religious spirituality, Seah used mixed methods in qualitative and quantitative research. Qualitative research methods are appropriate to uncover perceptions, emotions, and the spirituality of individuals in a community. Quantitative research methods, on the other hand, can render some subjective qualities observable and measurable. These then become capable of being evaluated. Weekly transcribed data of the two-year PAL prayer program provided robust evidence of learning, relearning and unlearning, with a conviction of sin and correction of error in individuals. Participants relearn the same scriptural truth when different contexts plausibly call

---

18. 61 leaders responded and started the PAL program in July 1996. 16 new leaders were inducted when they joined the leadership, and ten incumbent leaders ceased participation at various stages. Towards the end of the PAL program, 67 leaders participated in the PAL sessions regularly. Except for public holidays and the extended holiday season in December, a PAL session was scheduled weekly over a two-year period. Participants would sit in free-forming small groups of no more than four persons. This approach randomized the group mix and avoided group polarization. This process preserved focus on the Spirit of God. In PAL, participants utilized much of their senses. They saw words/messages in their mind, felt meanings by way of touch and emotions, heard the inaudible divine voice, sensed an impression and saw pictures like a clip. Often participants interfaced Scripture texts with all of the above to give scriptural meanings to each experience or to provide fresh insights to a text.

19. Unlike the example of praying in the Spirit in a small group that trains a member's discernment in reading the Spirit, this PAL prayer method—as will be explained more fully in chapter 6—necessarily brings a convergence in sensemaking in reading the Spirit. This method is appropriate for community purposes like reading the Spirit for a fresh visioning and missioning of a church community as in Seah's work, or a fresh reading of scriptural truth for a community's theological self-understanding as in my research.

for their proclamations to take different shapes and therefore different expressions and acts. Participants may also have to unlearn as they learn to discard ideas and patterns of thoughts about God's truth that prove unhelpful. Seah used quantitative analysis to abstract, validate, and distil a fresh development of a vision and mission of the community in the Spirit. As Seah's evaluative work had a particular focus on its organizational transformation effects, he drew on organizational studies in management to help frame his evaluation.

What came out of this patient yet active listening in the Spirit over the two years was a statement of vision and mission for the community, with its core values.[20] This fresh envisioning of a witness to the world helped realign personal dispositions and disciplines, and community practices and structures, to build identity. That is, individuals were being drawn together as one people of God growing together to bear God's presence. The mission statement (comprising three goals) represented the community's consensus that it should embrace spiritual discipline, disciple-making, and accountability for a charismatic witness to Jesus Christ. This has translated into behavioral norms of people in this community committing "to win souls, make disciples, raise leaders, grow churches, and extend the borders of missions." The four core values that surfaced from this two-year discourse were commitment, trust, community, and joy. Therefore, one outcome of this two-year praying in the Spirit was the consensual setting of norms for which members pledged accountability to leadership.

Moreover, Seah reported both observable and statistically significant attitudinal changes for the PAL participants for all seven mission goals and core values, as well as statistically significant behavioral changes for most of the mission goals and core values.[21] Interestingly, there had also

---

20. The vision is to become a community of God's people that bears the presence of God to fulfill the great commission through discipleship, church planting, and missions. The mission (or goals) is to train and equip every believer in the community so that each one will demonstrate the strong presence of God through the disciplined exercise of the fruit and gifts of the Holy Spirit, evidence spiritual growth by doing every good work, and prove discipleship through the winning of souls and their enfolding as responsible members of the community.

21. Some of the key findings are abstracted for easy reference: "Respondents of all three samples: PAL, NO PAL and the Church organization have more positive attitudes in July 1998 compared to a year ago with respect to the seven core values and goals of the Church . . . PAL respondents have more positive behaviors in July 1998 compared to a year ago with respect to six out of the seven core values and goals of the Church (with the exception of 'strong presence of God') . . . Just like the NO PAL

been statistically significant attitudinal changes in the wider church community (including those who did not participate in the PAL program) for all seven mission goals and core values. However, behavioral changes in the wider church community were less significant across the goals and values. This is expected, as behavioral changes tend to lag attitudinal changes in any re-ordering of life's priorities and activities. This empirical evidence therefore suggests that the Spirit was directly transforming participants in their interiority, and that there had been some unanticipated spill-over effects on those who did not participate. This suggests that leadership potentially can play a key role in bringing about sustainable organizational transformation of a church through its interaction with the community.

For the purpose of my research, I re-read Seah's findings with a theological lens. His pioneering work in empirically reading the Spirit and documenting his work in a church community was impressive and significant. While Seah's work was primarily at the organizational level of a church, what I am going to explore here could be understood as a theological reading of this account, and an extension of it, that can speak to a wider Pentecostal-charismatic community. Upon initial scrutiny, his work seemed to me to suggest the following. In all the fluidity of praying in the Spirit, the Spirit was unveiling participants' emotional and cognitive struggles and disquiet, which may have been hidden in their subconscious.[22] The Spirit made explicit what was implicit and tacit in their interiority. Participants then expressed to one another their struggles and disquiet over competing agendas and priorities in the proclamation of Jesus Christ. Through this discourse, participants got to know more about themselves and one another, and learnt to discern truth from lies, spirituality from self-deception, and light from darkness. There was an openness to confess sins and errors one to another, without needing to conform to uniformity. It came with an openness and attending to the Spirit and one another. In all this development of knowledge of self and

---

sample, the Church organization has more positive behaviors in July 1998 compared to a year ago with respect to two out of the seven core values and goals of the Church: 'joy' and 'qualitative growth' . . . The PAL respondents are significantly more positive in behavioural changes than the non-PAL respondents (at the 5% significance level for a one-tailed test) with respect to all seven core values and goals of the Church" (Seah, "Spirituality Approach," 382–83). Also, see abstracts of Seah's qualitative analysis in chapter 6 that inform on a practice of praying in the Spirit.

22. See, e.g., Cole, "Taking Hermeneutics to Heart," 264–74; Coulter and Yong, *Spirit, the Affections*.

another in community, there was a growth in personal coherence, yet also in communion with others.

It is therefore Seah's evidence-based reading of the Spirit and his working in all his fluidity that inspired me to explore a theology of the Spirit in his transforming of human desire, volition, and disposition in a community.[23] I am particularly concerned to see what role the reading of Scripture could play in this work of the Spirit. This leads us to the second motivation.

1.1.2 A theology to refine practice in scriptural reading in the Spirit

My project is driven by a hunch that a similar practice of praying in the Spirit could possibly be of value in the reading of Scripture. I call this practice "kerygmatic interpretation" and my account of it "kerygmatic hermeneutics." I have encountered a claim, which is perhaps not always clearly articulated, that Christians can and should read in the Spirit. I have experienced something of that, even though the practice has sometimes not been what it should be. This research on kerygmatic hermeneutics is therefore an attempt to develop and refine ideas about reading Scripture in the Spirit and, based on the theology being developed, to make recommendations about the practice.

The crucial element of this attempt to develop a theology of scriptural reading in the Spirit is an attempt to dig much deeper into pneumatology—because claims about the work of the Spirit are central to

---

23. This brings theologians and biblical scholars who seek understanding in systematic theology and practical theology into a deeper conversation that reveals more of God in the ordinary. For a discussion of how practical theology interacts with social sciences, see, e.g., Kay, "Philosophy and Developmental Psychology," 267–78. Spiritual experiences are usually transforming because they bring about change in one's interiority. While spiritual experiences may be articulated, they are subjective representations and are subject to human deception as well as the limitations of oral communication. Moreover, even when these are communicated visually, much room remains for one's interpretation as to what exactly is happening in one's interiority. Therefore, evidence-based experience in the Spirit may be one way that Christians may come into conversation with the world and particularly social scientists. These tend to demand evidential support for faith-based arguments. Such evidence-based experience is open to interrogation and validation by external evaluators in humanities and social sciences like history, anthropology, and organizational science. There is one caveat though: that is, one cannot fully make explicit an experience in the Spirit unless one has also been touched by the Spirit.

the whole development. Yet, pneumatology is an elusive subject. This is because the Spirit is elusive. He is probably the least understood or the most misunderstood of the Trinitarian communion. Since the Spirit does not speak of himself but always of Jesus Christ, his work is often mistaken for that of Jesus. Thus, it is sometimes asked: What does the Spirit do that the Son does not do better?[24] Moreover, the Spirit is also fluid and unpredictable in all his moves. He works differently with different people in different contexts. Therefore, what is needed critically then is a theology that acknowledges the Spirit's unique role in the Trinitarian communion.

These twin motivations lead us next to articulate the research problem, research question and our thesis statement for kerygmatic hermeneutics.

1.2 Research Problem, Research Question and Thesis Statement

In ways that I will explain in more detail later—the overall theological frame for my account is that the Spirit is at work in believers, individually and corporately, forming them to be an embodied witness to Jesus Christ in the world. My project is an attempt to understand something of *how* the Spirit does this. The foregoing discussion has set out the research problem of understanding *how* the Spirit forms an embodied witness to Jesus Christ. This involves critically identifying the role of the Spirit in God's *revelation* in hermeneutics. Through God's *revelation*, the Spirit *speaks to God's people* so as to form them into an embodied witness to Jesus Christ. This research aims to understand how God speaks to his people in this way through Scripture—and so to understand *how God's people should read Scripture* to hear God's speech. And, specifically, this research seeks to understand *the role the Spirit plays in this process*—in order to understand *how God's people should read Scripture "in the Spirit"* in order to hear what God is saying to them and be formed into an embodied witness to Jesus Christ. With this understanding, I seek to develop and critically evaluate the kind of spiritual practice that I have described taking place in my church context.

While Scripture, according to Luke, John, and Paul, portrays the Spirit as active in God's revelation, and in the giving and receiving of Scripture, the key challenge is that of discernment, interpretation, and

---

24. See Rogers, *After the Spirit*.

attribution. On one hand, we say there are characteristic ways in which the Spirit acts. On the other hand, we also say that the Spirit acts differently for different individuals, and in different contexts. Therefore, the Spirit is characteristically uncharacteristic. The substantive research problem then revolves around questions of *How?* For example, *how* does one discern where the Spirit is working, what the Spirit is doing and saying? *How* does the Spirit interpret Scripture? *How* does one make an attribution of one's interpretation to him?[25]

This primary hermeneutical problem raises other secondary questions. In asking *how* an individual or a community discerns what the Spirit is saying to them through Scripture, I am also asking what role is being played in their interpretation by the voices of multiple people in a community, the voices of other Christians in the present, the voices of other Christians in the past (i.e. tradition), and the voices of scholars and theologians.

By focusing on pneumatology in addressing these theological and epistemological challenges in contemporary Christian living, kerygmatic hermeneutics makes a truth-claim about the centrality of the role of the Spirit. Specifically, the thesis statement is: *A Spirit-led process is the proper context for an interpretation of Scripture that makes for an embodied witness to Jesus Christ.*

In this research, I demonstrate that one can read the Spirit in spite of the associated discernment, interpretation, and attribution challenges surrounding his elusive, fluid, and unpredictable working.

1.3 Methodology

In formulating a theology and practice of kerygmatic reading, I apply an approach and the research methods that match its elements: The work of the Spirit in *the making of an embodied witness to Jesus Christ,* Spirit-led scriptural interpretation, the Spirit's working in and through the complexity of human attitudes and behavior in the community, and the community's self-critical reading of the Spirit, his marks, and working.

---

25. That is, *how* can one discern and refute hermeneutical claims purportedly made in the Spirit? Alternatively, *how* does one discriminate words and actions that are not only human but also of God?

My approach to this account in the *making of an embodied witness to Jesus Christ* is constructive theology.[26] This is a process of making theology that is open to the Spirit's work in bringing the ongoing learning, the constant freshness, and the self-criticism that is appropriate to his work. Here, I mean a constructive theological approach to be one that re-reads Scripture and tradition in the light of the Spirit's work in the present in a specific context, discovering how the abiding truth of God's revelation can be seen afresh, and perhaps surprisingly, in that context. Since the Spirit's work of revealing the mystery of God is nestled in the ordinariness of a life being transformed, I also blend this account with practical theology that looks into concrete desires, volitions, dispositions, habits, and practices of believers that make this embodied witness. These include practices of devotion, scriptural interpretation, and Christian witness.

I argue that a constructive theological approach is appropriate to this account in the following senses.

First, constructive theology is premised on the belief that knowing God and his complex working—in hearing what God is saying as he works with us in *making* us into *an embodied witness to Jesus Christ*—is not primarily achieved by the hand of theologians in a theology to be communicated to believers. Instead, this knowledge of God is discovered by God's people as they live out their lives together in the world. The theologian only seeks to support this constructive process to guard it against potential problems. Toward this end, I hope to paint a compelling picture of how the Spirit works so a reader may know where to look and what to look for in discerning the Spirit and his work in such a community. Moreover, I hope that painting this big picture will help guide concrete practices of spiritual devotion, reading, and discernment. Nevertheless, neither in painting the big picture nor in proposing concrete practices will I be able to render the subject matter controllable and predictable. This is because the Spirit never fails to surprise, and his work is marked by a constant freshness and unpredictability.

---

26. See McFarland on "Systematic Theology" and "Constructive Theology" in McFarland et al., *Cambridge Dictionary*, 114, 491–93. In the conventional sense, constructive theology is more often used, especially by some North American theologians, in a nuance to express a "concern that the metaphor of a theological 'system' fails to attend to the inherently open-ended and dialogical character of the discipline" (McFarland et al., *Cambridge Dictionary*, 491). Otherwise, many scholars understand both categories to be undifferentiated.

Second, this embodied witness to Jesus Christ necessarily *speaks into the world*. We know that God speaks into the world concretely through Jesus. God also speaks concretely into the world through the witness of his apostles, and now through the speech and acts of Christians, and the church in the particularities of day-to-day interactions. What speaks to the world is specific to each context. Such speech and acts are concrete rather than abstract or propositional. Therefore, there is a limit to what systematic theology can do to speak into the world effectively. In this sense, constructive theology emphasizes the relevance and accessibility of a theology to a Christian who seeks in his/her concrete life to speak into the world.

Third, constructive theology makes operational *a process of making theology* that is open to the Spirit's work in bringing ongoing learning, constant freshness, and the self-criticism that is appropriate to his work. This process attends to how the Spirit interprets Scripture, drawing significance from the text in the light of what he is doing in a specific context. Here, the Spirit of truth is free to illumine or inspire afresh from the living Word. Constructive theology reads the Spirit's interpretation in the light of the scriptural truth that is already given in systematic theology. This process is therefore open to a fresh reading of God that allows for any surprise from the Spirit. Constructive theology and systematic theology are hence held in tension in this process of making theology.

Fourth, constructive theology is *open to the Spirit's work* in revealing the *mystery* of God that is nestled in the ordinariness of a transforming life. He is unconstrained by any human system of philosophical thought, the making of theology, dogma or doctrine, or hermeneutics. This approach avoids a reductionist formulation that force-feeds into pre-determined categories, thus missing out on any of the mystery that is God himself.

Last and perhaps most significantly, constructive theology can address the discernment challenges of *self-critically* reading the Spirit, his marks, and working. Its attentiveness to the Spirit whose work is bound up in complex ways with the attitudes and behaviors of the people of God means it needs to be open to the forms of *self-criticism* that is appropriate to that work. This also means it is open to the use of evaluative methods in humanities, social sciences, and organizational science in management. These can give the external confirmation of claims about what is attributable to the Spirit's work and its outcomes.

In the next section, I abstract the definitions and explanations for some of the terms commonly used in this research. I will be exploring more fully all the key ideas introduced below in the body of the work.

1.4 Definitions of Terms

Bible reading	a vocalization of scriptural reading by a kerygmatic reader as s/he flows in the Spirit in kerygmatic devotion.
Co-creation	*a Spirit-empowered lived-out interpretation of scriptural truth that is life giving.* The Spirit's revelation of scriptural truth is incarnate in a reader. In created grace, a reader calls into being signs and wonders, healings and deliverances in doing all good in the contingency of the particular.
Contemplation	a practice of being freed of self so that one may embody God. This practice is akin to Saint John of the Cross's praying prayer of loving attention, where intellect and emotions (mind and heart) are stilled, and volition alone is drawn in a desiring after God in patient attention. It is a journey, not away from one's humanity, but in fulfilment and perfection of humanity.
Found theology & givenness	Given theology is the exposition of what we already understand of what we have received—the faith handed down to us. Found theology is the re-thinking of what we have received in the light of new experiences, new discoveries. We see what we have been given (the deposit of the faith; the Scriptures; the tradition) in new ways as our understanding is opened up and changed by what we find.[27]
Hermeneutical gap	the "distance" between what speech (vocalized *kerygma*) and patterns of action (performed *kerygma*) should be when the Body of Christ transforms into Christ's likeness and radiates

---

27. See Quash, *Found Theology*.

	the Father's glory, and, what speech and patterns of action actually are in the reader's world.
Illumination	a *fresh and timely interpretation* of scriptural truth as the Spirit leads readers to read a text differently in each new situation—to hear what the given word is saying in that situation. The Spirit's illumination opens up a text to give different significance to different persons at the same time, or different significance to the same persons at different times.
Inspiration	a *fresh* Spirit-breathed *revelation* of scriptural truth being found in a prophetic elucidation of God's ongoing work in creation.
Kerygma	the proclamation of the gospel of Jesus Christ according to a kerygmatic reader or community. This proclamation is vocalized, lived out, and performed in the Spirit in speech, life, and power.
Kerygmatic community	a local assembly of kerygmatic readers that is characterized by a unified identity, faith, and witness in the Spirit yet without need for uniformity in communal life.
Kerygmatic criticism	the name I give to the discerned testing and reasoned evaluation of the realist claims about the work of the Spirit in reader dispositions, community habits, practices, outcomes, and impacts. Kerygmatic criticism draws from theologically driven discernment of the marks of the Spirit; it also uses empirical enquiry for its evaluation. Testing and evaluation make attributions to the presence and activity of the Spirit in his working in the world.
Kerygmatic devotion	a kerygmatic community's daily spiritual disciplines practiced in moments of reading, meditation, praying, contemplation, and proclamation in the Spirit. It presumes readers have been baptized in the Spirit.
Kerygmatic hermeneutics	the account of an interpretation of scriptural truth in the lives of believers who are being caught up by the Spirit to become living proc-

	lamations of Jesus Christ. That is, this is an account of a Spirit-led scriptural interpretation that helps form people to be an embodied witness that proclaims Jesus Christ to the world.
Kerygmatic reader	born as a new creation in Christ and flows in the Spirit as *logos* enfleshed to proclaim the gospel of Jesus Christ in speech, life, and power.
Kerygmatic theology	the theology underlying kerygmatic hermeneutics.
Logos enfleshed	flesh becoming word (*logos*) in the Spirit, so that human beings can participate in divinity. *Logos* enfleshed represents a union of humans and Christ in the flesh. The exemplar of Jesus, the Word incarnate, demonstrates that it is possible for one who is fully human to be sinless, and to be fully united to divinity. A believer, born of the seed of God who cannot sin, therefore has every potentiality of not sinning when that divinity is unleashed in Spirit possession.
Marks of the Spirit	are the characteristics of the Spirit's presence and working that may be described by nouns and verbal nouns. These marks—intoxication, life, participation, and revelation of truth—bear signature to the Spirit's working. They are also qualities that the Spirit shares with those he gives life to in Jesus Christ.
Meditation	a continuous activity of reflection, study, and meditation on Scripture that forms a reader as *logos* enfleshed.
Praying in the Spirit	vocalizing God-speak in the Spirit. It is Spirit-talk to God, self, or other hearers, all in the flow of the Spirit. It is the pivotal moment in kerygmatic devotion that transposes a reader from the earthly realm to speak from the heavenly realm.
Proclamation	a vocalized witness to one's encounter with Jesus Christ that flows naturally from an experience of life in the Spirit. More broadly, it is a life in

	which the Spirit catches humans up continuously into an encounter with Jesus so that we may witness to him.
Reading the Spirit	involves paying attention to what the Spirit is doing in the world in general, *and* what the Spirit is saying through the scriptural text. It involves actively listening to what the Spirit may be directing oneself or others to say, do or make a decision on.
Scriptural truth	the whole of the knowledge of God that God imparts to the world by means of Scripture—an abundant whole that the people of God endlessly discover as they go on living out their lives in the world, in all the contexts into which the Spirit leads them.
Sensegiving	the ongoing communication of the meaning that one has deciphered and made sense of to the world, through one's articulation and performance.
Sensemaking	the ongoing making of meaning by fitting new experiences into one's existing plausibility structure, and any consequent adjustment of that plausibility structure. This is often done collaboratively in a community or organization because sensemaking is context-dependent.
Spirit possession	a spiritual state in which humans are so attuned to the Spirit's work that their actions can be understood as the Spirit's actions working through them. This comes with an infilling and outflowing of the Spirit that catches humans up in participation in divinity. Such a created causal order suggests both human volition and divine mercy; and if humans willingly flow in created grace of desiring God, then the entire work of Spirit possession is God's work in the Spirit. That is, only God can deify humans. This theology underlies the transformation that the Spirit engenders in humans through kerygmatic hermeneutics.

Spiritual discernment	the capacity of readers to read the Spirit and to interpret Scripture in the Spirit. It involves discerning the marks of the Spirit, so readers may make attributions to the Spirit and identify his working.

1.5 Structure of Research

This research seeks to understand *how* the Spirit forms an embodied witness to Jesus Christ by means of Scripture. Therefore, it also seeks to understand *how* God's people should read Scripture *in the Spirit* in order to hear what God is saying to them and be formed into an embodied witness to Jesus Christ.

Chapter 2 aims to position my propositions on a Spirit-led interpretation of Scripture in relation to existing work in theological interpretation, and particularly, in hermeneutical work that focuses on the work of the Spirit. I argue that this research can be located within theological interpretation. I also argue that this research bears the characteristics of hermeneutical work that focuses on the Spirit's work that draws mainly from Pentecostal-charismatic hermeneutics. Centrally, I look at how this work addresses discernment challenges in relation to scriptural interpretation, when Scripture is read within a community of faith and within the purposes of God with the church. Readers need to discern if such a reading is in fact self-serving and self-deceiving. To push in the direction that I want to go in this research—that is, to interpret Scripture with the Spirit—I interact with three authors whose work come close to this and have them interact with each other. This push establishes how far their projects have developed, and how much further this research will have to go.

I position a Spirit-led interpretation of Scripture as a hermeneutic that is lived out or performed in the ordinariness of life. My account of kerygmatic hermeneutics therefore involves a form of practical theology: a theology of the extraordinary manifest in the ordinariness of life. The Spirit works in and through visible things. In this world, the Spirit's working and its outcomes are therefore not closed to evaluation. There is nevertheless the challenge of discerning what is not only human but also of the Spirit. In this research, I propose that a community of faith that performs Scripture in the Spirit would also have been transformed to discern the Spirit and his working.

Chapter 3 takes up the discernment challenges of interpreting Scripture in the Spirit, by providing a more general theology of the Spirit's work and noting its identifying features. I paint a broad picture of the Spirit and his working that connects with the Trinity, creation, Jesus Christ, the church, and transformation. This broad picture gives a fuller understanding of what the Spirit does with Scripture. This aptly locates kerygmatic hermeneutics within the Spirit's revelatory and transformative work. From this broad picture, I also draw out the marks of the Spirit that give his work a visible signature. These marks can thus help us to discern critically when and to what extent a performance of Scripture is taking place in the Spirit, as the Spirit forms an embodied witness to Jesus Christ.

In chapter 4, I introduce kerygmatic hermeneutics—an account of a Spirit-led interpretation of Scripture that helps form an embodied witness to Jesus Christ. I formulate an underlying theology that is founded on the *otherness* of Spirit and Scripture. My claim is that kerygmatic hermeneutics is capable of yielding a critical reading of Scripture—a reading that can stand over against and challenge a community of faith, even when the practice of reading is located firmly within a community of faith. This underlying theology of kerygmatic hermeneutics yields a set of propositions about *how* the Spirit makes use of Scripture's otherness to form the church into an embodied witness to Jesus Christ. The power and efficacy of the Spirit's agency to do this is closely related to the power and efficacy of readers' Spirit-led agency to appropriate scriptural truth—truth concerning God and his ways with the world. Therefore, the power and efficacy of kerygmatic reading is predicated on readers learning to read Scripture in the Spirit in community.

In chapter 5, I close this theological account with kerygmatic criticism. I propose that kerygmatic hermeneutics subjects realist claims about the work of the Spirit in the community to criticism, looking for his graduated transformative work displayed in the concrete life of the community, with visible expressions of the dispositions, habits, practices, outcomes, and impacts of such a learning church community. While chapter 4 gives an account of *what the Spirit does with Scripture* in the revelation of truth, I now focus on *what the Spirit does with readers in community* in the making of this embodied witness to Jesus Christ. I show that the marks of the Spirit can enable us to make attributions to the Spirit. This addresses the discernment challenge that is central in *performing Scripture in the Spirit*. Kerygmatic hermeneutics, because of this self-critical strand that can test and confirm claims about the Spirit's presence and working in the world, is one account of *how* the world may hear and see God.

In chapter 6, I apply this theology to refine a practice of kerygmatic interpretation for a church community. I first show in more detail what a practice of praying in the Spirit in a church community looks like. This account yields empirical evidence of the Spirit's correction of errors, community confession, and learning from the Spirit and one another that guided community purpose, goals, and actions. Flowing from the theology that underlies kerygmatic hermeneutics and that I have explored in the previous two chapters, I demonstrate what the practice of kerygmatic reading may look like. I narrate how readers in a community may read Scripture in the present situation in relation to a history of interpretation of specific text(s). I claim that this practice of kerygmatic interpretation—with its habits, processes, and structures—located in a church community can lend itself also to socio-scientific empirical enquiry and evaluation. Such empirical evidence can corroborate readers' theologically driven spiritual discernment in a process of testing and evaluation. I suggest that a community can periodically evaluate to what extent this performance of Scripture in the Spirit is forming ever more fully an embodied witness to Jesus Christ.

Chapter 7 concludes this research. I have adopted a constructive theological approach, stepping back from a church community's practice of praying in the Spirit to contemplate the underlying theology. This account was predicated on an account of the Spirit's agency forming in each specific place the one holy catholic apostolic church, the true Christian church of all times and all places. I then drew on this theology to refine the habits, practices, and structures involved in the interpretation of Scripture, proposing kerygmatic hermeneutics as a form of Spirit-led interpretation of scriptural truth that would make sense for such a community. This form of interpretation involves a strong element of self-criticism, which includes both theologically driven discernment and empirical enquiry in a process testing and evaluation. I draw out the key contributions made in my research and highlight its limitations and some directions for future research.

2

LOCATING THIS PROJECT

THE INTERPRETATION OF SCRIPTURE is one of the means by which the Spirit catches people to become living proclamations, forming an embodied witness to Jesus Christ. The purpose of this chapter is to position my propositions in relation to existing work in theological interpretation, and in particular in relation to hermeneutical work that focuses on the work of the Spirit.

I look to the relevant literature that asks or comes close to asking the same question as I about *how* one may interpret Scripture with the Spirit. In section 2.1, I show that this research is an example of theological interpretation. That is, it belongs broadly with those other works that argue that an interpretation of Scripture should be located within a community of faith and within the purposes of God with the church. Moreover, I locate this account of theological interpretation with those that take seriously Scripture's otherness.

In section 2.2, I characterize the hermeneutical work that focuses on the work of the Spirit, most of which is drawn from Pentecostal-charismatic hermeneutics.[1] I note that this research bears a specific relation to those hermeneutical works that focus on the work of the Spirit. In fact, I will be pushing this work on hermeneutics forward to answer my question about *how* one may interpret Scripture with the Spirit.

---

1. I owe a great debt for my learning to many scholars in biblical, theological, and Pentecostal-charismatic hermeneutics, some of whose writings are cited throughout this research. However, there could also be many others that I may have inadvertently omitted given the constraints of this research. I express my gratitude to all scholars and theologians who have gone ahead to give us such treasures in the pursuit of the knowing of God and his truth in Scripture.

In section 2.3, I examine three sample authors who share the direction that I want to go in this research—that is, to interpret Scripture with the Spirit. I then bring these three authors into interaction with each other. This examination of the three authors is for the purpose of clarifying how far they have gotten, and how much further I want to push.

Concluding this chapter in section 2, I emplace scriptural reading firmly in the context of a community of faith in a move that is broadly aligned with the recent focus of theological interpretation. This is a focus on the purposes of God with the church. This teleological account springs from the Spirit's giving of life everlasting in his calling and forming of the one holy catholic apostolic church. I therefore position this interpretation of Scripture with the Spirit within the purposes of God with the church. This teleology gives us the thesis statement: *A Spirit-led process is the proper context for an interpretation of Scripture that makes for an embodied witness to Jesus Christ.*

Reason and discernment in testing and evaluation, even a hermeneutic of suspicion, may be safeguarded in communities of faith as much as in the academy. A Spirit-led scriptural interpretation acknowledges the otherness of God and Scripture. Scripture stands over and against a reader's problematic and distorted attitudes and responses—not so much to distance itself from the reader's situatedness, but to allow itself to interrupt and question that life. Therefore, an account of a Spirit-led interpretation of Scripture is firmly founded on Scripture's otherness and over-againstness.

2.1 Within the Theological Interpretation Movement

This research asks the question: *How* may God's people read Scripture with the Spirit in order to hear what God is saying to them, so as to be formed into an embodied witness to Jesus Christ? In this section, I look to the relevant literature that asks or comes close to asking the same question about *how* God's people may interpret Scripture with the Spirit.

This research is an example of theological interpretation. That is, it belongs broadly with those other works that argue that an interpretation of Scripture should be located within a community of faith and within the purposes of God with the church. Recent proponents of theological interpretation have seen themselves as recovering an older sense that interpretation belongs in the community of faith, after a period dominated (in the West) by forms of reading that belong in the secularized academy.² These proponents argue against locating scriptural interpretation solely or primarily within the historical-critical project of uncovering the sense the text had in its original contexts. Theological interpretation attempts to recover the authority of scriptural interpretation. For so many centuries in the pre-modern period, Scripture had always been read in communities of faith as part of guiding, correcting, and worshiping in an ongoing struggle for God's people to live faithfully before him. Yet, theological interpretation still seeks to be informed by historical-critical insights.

Stephen Fowl is a prominent example of this "theological interpretation"; he focuses firmly on reading Scripture within and for the life of the church.³ Fowl argues for this move of the locus of scriptural reading from mainly the academic community to communities of faith by making a modern-postmodern argument—suggesting that the rise of postmodernism has made it easier to argue that modern forms of scriptural reading are not the only rationally justifiable approaches to scriptural interpretation.⁴

2. Mather, in her review and critique of relevant literature concerning the renewal movement, addresses the question, "How does the Holy Spirit work to communicate with us as we engage with scripture?" (Mather, *Interpreting Spirit*, 1). Even within the renewal movement, and among those who identify with the renewal movement, there is a distribution of scholars who prioritize community approaches versus those who prioritize historico-grammatical approaches (Mather, *Interpreting Spirit*, 11–12). See, e.g., Green, *Practicing Theological Interpretation*; Johns, "Grieving, Brooding and Transforming," 141–52; Johnson and Moore, "Soul Care," 125–52; Johnson, *Pneumatic Discernment*; Moore, "Altar Hermeneutics," 148–59; Oliverio, *Theological Hermeneutics*; Seitz and Richards, *Brevard S. Childs*; Spawn and Wright, "Pneumatic Hermeneutic," 191–98; Stronstad, "Some Aspects," 32–58; Tesafaye, *Pneumatic Hermeneutics*; Vanhoozer, *Meaning*; Waddell and Althouse, "Editorial Note," 123–25.

3. Fowl introduces theological interpretation of Scripture as "a reading aimed at shaping and being shaped by a community's faith and practice . . . That is, theological interpretation of scripture will take place primarily within the context of the church and synagogue, those communities that seek to order their common life in accord with their interpretation of Scripture" (Fowl, *Theological Interpretation of Scripture*, xix).

4. In *Theological Interpretation of Scripture*, Fowl demonstrates how to read Scripture theologically with a rich variety of views that constitute theological interpretation. For each of the four chosen texts, he included an example of patristic interpretation, an example of medieval or reformation interpretation, and then three contemporary voices. This follows from the recognition in theological interpretation that a reader's context informs and is informed by a reading of Scripture. The dominant practice of historical criticism in biblical scholarship, on the other hand, recognizes only one particular context—the historical one. This has resulted in the separation of biblical

John Webster is another example—one who focuses even more firmly on the positioning of reading within the purposes of God.[5] However, Webster is less interested in whether prevailing intellectual currents made this move plausible. In fact, Webster criticizes some other theological interpretation work for leaving their accounts of the role of Scripture too captive to postmodern epistemology (and, I could add, to the life of the church). Webster raises concerns that this move risks re-imprisoning theological interpretation within another general epistemology, which may not align with scriptural truth.[6]

Instead, Webster provides a theological account of the authority of Scripture. He argues that this central move to re-locate Scripture is what is demanded on theological grounds of an interpretation of Scripture. He observes that some theological hermeneuticians, just like the biblical scholars whom they criticize, are also not doing enough to acknowledge the otherness or over-againstness of Scripture.[7] Such an acknowledgment would demand our recognizing Scripture as the dynamic and living Word of God. That is, Scripture is the text that becomes an instrument of divine action that speaks of God. This living voice is often contrary to human will and demands active listening and ready compliance. Webster's positive account is that Scripture is an instrument given and used by God in the overcoming of sin and the sanctification of God's people.[8]

In this research, I want to do justice to both sides: I want to position scriptural reading within the church, and, within the purposes of God

---

scholarship in its historical reconstruction from its theologically significant ends (Fowl, *Theological Interpretation of Scripture*, xiii, xxi).

5. See Webster, *Word and Church*; Webster, *Holy Scripture*.

6. Webster's concerns about inadvertently subjecting theological interpretation to another epistemology indeed appeared in the shape of certain experience-led practices in hermeneutics. See, e.g., Cox, *Fire from Heaven*.

7. Webster observes, "The problem, that is, is not the affirmation that the biblical texts have a 'natural history', but the denial that texts with a 'natural history' may function within the communicative divine economy, and that such a function is ontologically definitive of the text. It is this denial—rather than any purely methodological questions—which has to form the focus of dogmatic critique" (Webster, *Holy Scripture*, 19).

8. Webster argues that what is needed is a "reintegration of the authority of Scripture into the doctrine of God" (Webster, *Holy Scripture*, 54). This has the effect of decisively redrawing the character of the church's affirmation of Scripture's authority. He contends that this removes that affirmation from the sphere of ecclesial politics and restricts the church's office to a pedagogical one—confessing or attesting that Scriptures' authority flows from its place in God.

with and for the church. I also want to do justice to the otherness or over-againstness of Scripture.

These moves, incidentally, leave open the question of how scriptural reading within the church and the purposes of God relates to historical criticism and to critical readings (i.e., readings that operate with a hermeneutics of suspicion). Whereas historical criticism interprets Scripture to recover the sense it made in the context of its first production and reception (when understood as a human product in that context), theological interpretation reads the text in the context of God's ongoing work in a community of faith. This is one of the general questions facing theological interpretation. In this research, I am looking for a form of theological interpretation that is serious about the location of the text in God's present work in a community, but that acknowledges that the text that God is using to guide and shape this community is one that can be clarified by historical criticism.

Moreover, whereas critical readings ask in what ways scriptural texts encode and convey problematic and distorted attitudes (for example, patriarchy, slavery), this account of theological interpretation asks how Scripture stands over-against readers' problematic and distorted attitudes. That is, this account of theological interpretation is interested in Scripture's otherness, not in order to distance it from the current life of readers, but to allow it to interrupt and question that life. As a corollary of this other main point, this leaves open the question of how theological interpretation relates to the question of problematic tendencies in the text itself (for example its under-determinateness, which possibly allows the text to support multiple valid readings). This is also another general question facing theological interpretation, which I will also attempt to address in this account. This account is serious about allowing Scripture to speak with the authority and otherness of God into the current life of readers, such authority and otherness that may be discerned in testing and evaluation, in and by a community of faith.

2.2 Reading Scripture with the Spirit

In this section, I attempt very briefly to locate this research in relation to scholars who focus on the work of the Spirit in general and on how one may read Scriptures with the help of the Spirit.[9] Much of this scholarship

---

9. Lee Roy Martin presents a chronological and thematic documentation of the

is drawn from Pentecostal-charismatic theology, of which there is now a substantial tradition.[10] Before formal Pentecostal-charismatic theology came into being, Pentecostalism used to have its theology embedded mainly in experiences articulated in oral testimonies and ecstatic speech, practices like praise and worship, and collaterals like evangelistic pamphlets.[11] Cox observes, "But it *is* a theology, a full-blown religious cosmos, an intricate system of symbols that respond to the perennial questions of human meaning and value."[12] It is, however, only a recent phenomenon that Pentecostals have started writing books of formal theology. Pentecostalism is growing in scholarship.

I locate and characterize extant scholarship in three ways: an emphasis on the immediate experience of the Spirit through Scripture, an emphasis on the work of the Spirit in the church, an emphasis on the Spirit's work in the world beyond the church. I then draw out the relation that this bears to my research.

2.2.1 Emphasis on the immediate experience of the Spirit through Scripture

I introduced this research with an annotated review of the recent emphasis on the immediate experience of the Spirit in the present. This includes the emphasis on the immediate experience of reading Scripture with the Spirit in diverse communities of faith.[13] Here, we recall the call

---

history of Pentecostal hermeneutics by collating articles in the *Journal of Pentecostal Theology* since its first issue in the fall of 1992. This collection draws contributions from himself and scholars like Rickie D. Moore, Jackie David Johns, Cheryl Bridges Johns, John W. McKay, John Christopher Thomas, Robert O. Baker, Kenneth J. Archer, Scott A. Ellington, Robby Waddell, Clark H. Pinnock, and Andrew Davies that together gives a representation of the theory and practice of Pentecostal hermeneutics over the last three decades (see Martin, *Reader*).

10. In growing an understanding of Pentecostal-charismatic theology in the last decade, Kenneth Archer and William Oliverio brought Pentecostal hermeneutics into conversation with other disciplines: philosophy, biblical theology, anthropology, social and physical sciences (Archer and Oliverio, *Constructive Pneumatological Hermeneutics*).

11. See, e.g., Boone, "Pentecostal Worship and Hermeneutics," 110–24.

12. Cox, *Fire from Heaven*, 15.

13. Mather's concern is with pneumatic interpretation—or the role of the Spirit in scriptural interpretation —over, in, and through all such human approaches. She argues that where focus on the two interpretive frameworks—community versus historico-grammatical—increased, "*attention to the Spirit actually decreased*" (Mather,

for criticism—a discernment in testing and evaluation—by scholars from diverse persuasions, including those who identify with or are open to the Pentecostal-charismatic tradition. This emphasis gives me further support to locate this research in theological interpretation.

2.2.2 Emphasis on the work of the Spirit in the church

The first thing to say, quite simply, is that there is a strong emphasis on the work of the Spirit in scholarship both inside and outside the Pentecostal-charismatic tradition. Kay and Dyer give a comprehensive account of the diversity of experiences of and accounts of the Spirit's working across the Pentecostal-charismatic and mainline denominational contexts from the perspective of scholars from the English-speaking countries in the Western hemisphere.[14] Adding to this diversity, Cecil Robeck and Amos Yong draw together scholarship that points to what the Spirit is saying and doing in regional studies across Latin America, Africa, and Asia, besides North America and Europe.[15] This research, by focusing squarely on the Spirit's work in the life of believers and in the church, can be understood in relation to this burgeoning scholarship.

Interpreting Spirit, 14). Mather stresses that "the Spirit works personally in the life of the person engaging in relationship with God via scripture but this is also not a 'how to' work, instead purposefully asking about the Spirit's interpretive nature and reflecting some of these aspects in approach and style" (Mather, *Interpreting Spirit*, 19). In a sense, this project may be seen to extend Mather's discourse in formulating a "how to" framework in a practice of pneumatic interpretation although this project was completed before I read Mather's comprehensive critique.

14. Kay explains this diversity. He observes that the "charismatic movement was distinct from the Pentecostal movement of the 1920s and 1930s in the sense that the existing ecclesiastical structures and terminologies of the mainline denominations were left intact." Moreover, he notes that a "general description of the charismatic movement is an over-simplification because different denominations and different parts of different denominations reacted to preserve the impact of the outpoured Spirit in different ways. Moreover the impact of the charismatic movement within the United States, when coupled with burgeoning Christian broadcasting, helped to enlarge potential audiences and raise the profile of charismatic and Pentecostal Christianity in complicated new ways" (Kay and Dyer, *Pentecostal and Charismatic Studies*, xxii-xxiii).

15. On the diversity of the Spirit's work both inside and outside the Pentecostal-charismatic tradition, Robeck and Yong argue, "In short, Reed's chapter can be read as providing parallel depiction, even commentary, on Robeck's and McClymond's chapters in ways that illuminate the (contested) origins, growth, and development of Pentecostalism while also showing why diversity has been a central part of these narratives from the very beginning" (Robeck and Yong, *Cambridge Companion*, 4).

2.2.3 Emphasis on the Spirit's work in the world beyond the church

Archer notes the Spirit may be experienced not only in his work in a community of faith but also in the world—he is active in the lives of people even before any missionary may arrive.[16] Such a focus on the present work of the Spirit beyond the church prompts the natural response of seeking to discern what the Spirit might then be saying to believers from outside the church community, or as the church community engages with the world.

We can also observe this emphasis on the present work of the Spirit in the world through scholarship, in disciplines other than theology. Robeck and Yong draw from multiple disciplines—historical, economic, political, cultural, anthropological, and sociological—to provide an overview of the ways in which Pentecostal and charismatic Christians engage in multiple ways in the world, and understand that work to be a context in which they are impelled by the Spirit and encountering the Spirit.[17] Of particular interest are the Spirit's working in relation to missions and power evangelism, social concerns and drug addiction, demon possession and exorcism, healings and miracles, etc.[18] These scholarly works

---

16. Archer, *Spirit, Scripture and Community*, 247–51. Archer observes, "[T]he Spirit does speak and has more to say than just Scripture . . . For this reason, the voice of the Spirit cannot be reduced to simple recitation of Scripture, nonetheless, it will be connected to and concerned with Scripture" (Archer, *Spirit, Scripture and Community*, 248).

17. See Robeck and Yong, *Cambridge Companion*. Contributions in Part III on Disciplinary Perspectives include "The Politics and Economics of Pentecostalism: A Global Survey" by Calvin Smith, "Cultural Dimension of Pentecostalism" by André F. Droogers, "Sociological Narratives and the Sociology of Pentecostalism" by Michael Wilkinson, and "Pentecostal Mission and Encounter with Religion" by Veli-Matti Kärkkäinen, etc.

18. In the Pentecostal-charismatic parlance, "miracles" include signs and wonders, healings and deliverances. See "Miracles," in *Christian Classics Ethereal Library*, for examples of scriptural accounts of miracles; also Bonk, *Encyclopedia of Missions and Missionaries*, for accounts of "Miracles" in missions; Gardner, "Miracles of Healing," 1927–33. Philosophical challenges include questions like what constitutes a miracle, and whether an attribution may be made to the Creator and Lord of nature. On this debate, see, e.g., Archer, "Miracles as Law-Violations," 83–98; Castelo, "If Miracles Don't Happen?" 236–45; Geisler, *Signs and Wonders*; Hume, *Human Understanding*; Johnson, *Hume, Holism and Miracles*; Kay and Dyer, *Pentecostal and Charismatic Studies*; Keener, *Miracles*; Lewis, *Miracles*; Synan, *Century*; Tennant, *Miracle: Three Lectures*; Tillich, *Systematic Theology*; Torr, *Anti-Theodicy*; Twelftree, "Historian," 199–217; Van Inwagen, *God, Knowledge and Mystery*; Wright, *Resurrection*.

point to the church's immediate experience of the Spirit in her concrete and impactful interactions with the world. My own focus on the way in which engagement with the world can provide one of the main contexts in which Christians can re-read Scripture in the Spirit, also aligns with this broader scholarship.

Concluding this section on reading Scripture with the Spirit, I locate my research in relation to the work of all scholars who focus on the work of the Spirit (both in and with the church as well as in the world) in the interpretation of Scripture. Although this research is exploring familiar themes (which have become prominent especially in Pentecostal-charismatic hermeneutics, but also more widely in theological hermeneutics), my claim is that extant scholarship does not go far enough to be sufficiently clear as to *how* Scripture is to be read in the Spirit: what concrete structures, dispositions, disciplines, and practices would be involved, especially the concrete practices of discernment in testing and evaluation. There is a need for a coherent theology that may inform concrete practices of reading Scripture with the Spirit, and to push beyond a generalized account to lay out in detail a corporate process of reading Scripture in its otherness.[19] In the next section, I will illustrate these claims by examining three sample authors who push in the direction I want to go, but who do not go far enough.

2.3 A Review of Three Voices

In this section, I explore in greater depth three sample accounts that speak of *how* Christians should read Scripture with the help of the Spirit. Given the constraints of this research, I could only review some of the key voices in recent literature that are most directly relevant. This does not mean ignoring the many other scholars who have written about reading Scripture with the help of the Spirit in one way or another over the centuries. I reviewed a wide range of theological and Pentecostal-charismatic hermeneuticians that come close to this question. Of the authors I explored, three authors came closest to my concerns, and in the most interesting ways, that interact. I do not claim that these sample authors are representative of the whole field, but simply that they are relevant and

---

19. I formulate kerygmatic theology in chapter 4. I next articulate its self-criticism in kerygmatic criticism in chapter 5. See also chapter 6 for what a practice of kerygmatic interpretation may look like.

significant voices. While they do not go far enough, I will attempt, in the ensuing discussion, to have the three voices interact to provide an initial sketch of a Spirit-led interpretation of Scripture that forms an embodied witness to Jesus Christ.

A Spirit-led interpretation of Scripture can take on multiple nuances that can potentially be wider than what being a *charismatic* can mean, in that there are ways of thinking about a Spirit-led interpretation that may not be recognizably charismatic.[20] This is because understanding what 'Spirit-led hermeneutics' means (just as with understanding what 'charismatic' means) can be elusive as it involves reading the working of the Spirit in all his multiphonic expressions in human beings, both in the church and the world. That is, Spirit-led hermeneutics can take multiple different forms. Therefore, an account of Spirit-led hermeneutics has to do justice to the variety of forms it takes. A good account will include these multiple forms.

To help us gain greater clarity on what a Spirit-led interpretation of Scripture involves, I build on my brief overview of Pentecostal-charismatic hermeneutics from the last section.[21] Spirit-led hermeneutics involves readers paying attention to the Spirit to discern what he is up to in the church and in the world, and what he is saying through the scriptural text in the present (what we will call "reading the Spirit" here).[22] This

---

20. This highlights the challenge of discerning the mysterious work of the Spirit, not merely in and with the church but also in and with the world. Therefore, this discerning is even more complex than merely recognizing his charisms in a church community. The latter is somewhat mitigated because the Spirit gives charisms for the common good of the church, that include the gift of discernment, for effectuation precisely for her edification. Nonetheless, there remains a discernment challenge, for his charisms are so varied and each may be manifested in so many different ways in different contexts of community life (1 Cor 12: 4–11, 27–31).

21. Apart from our review in section 2.2, Craig Keener names "Spirit hermeneutics" as "an approach that humbly recognizes that it is God's voice, rather than our own, that we must hear in his Word" (Keener, *Spirit Hermeneutics*, 288). Keener argues for a Spirit-led scriptural interpretation because what he calls Christian hermeneutic, a hermeneutic of hearing in Scripture the God who is revealed in Jesus Christ, is no less than a Spirit hermeneutic. He argues that scriptural reading in the Spirit is simply a Christian hermeneutic from the vantage of Pentecost. He maintains that this is "not a dismissal of the old, textual one; it simply submits to the Spirit's leading and affirms application by analogy, which we seek to do with the Spirit's guidance" (Keener, *Spirit Hermeneutics*, 117–18). Likewise, Yong argues that a Pentecostal hermeneutics is Christian hermeneutics, one that is intrinsic to any Trinitarian theological interpretation (Yong, *Hermeneutical Spirit*).

22. "Read the Spirit" is a shorthand that Fowl uses for attending to and discerning

includes a focus on an experience of the Spirit's work in the present, on receptivity to what the Spirit is doing *and* saying, on the multiple messages the Spirit might use a text to convey in different circumstances, and on God speaking through Scripture in the present, by the Spirit. This reader reads the Spirit in his working not only in a community of faith but also in the world.

Next, I bring Nicholas Lash, Stephen Fowl, and then Clark Pinnock into conversation with my concerns. These inform my project as they write from different traditions and contexts. Lash is an English Roman Catholic theologian who writes from a secular university context. Fowl and Pinnock are Anglican and Baptist respectively, and they write from a non-secular context. I also attempt to show how they interact in interesting ways.

2.3.1 Nicholas Lash

In *Performing the Scriptures*, Lash argues for an interpretation of Scripture that pushes beyond exegesis of the text to penetrate to the subject matter.[23] For Lash, the Christian practice of interpretive action consists in the *performance* of texts, rendering the truth of God revealed in human history. Lash argues that performance is the ultimate form of interpretation. That is, Lash reformulates the creative act of interpretation as taking place in its concrete performance.

Central in such an interpretative performance of this living text in the history of humanity, both existentially and experientially, is the role of the church community. That is, scriptural interpretation is a corporate act and individuals are multiple players in this interpretative performance— a performance that is woven into the harsh realities of daily living, often interspersed with suffering, oppression, temptation, persecution, and fears. Lash thus makes a stand for theological interpretation by locating his account of scriptural interpretation in a community of faith and within the purposes of God.

Lash allows for multiple ways the story of a text may be performed without losing its integrity. Lash summarizes his proposition: The

---

what the Spirit is doing. He uses this short-hand because it gives a nice play of words in the title of his work—"How the Spirit Reads and How to Read the Spirit." In this research, I use "reading the Spirit" to mean paying attention to *both* what the Spirit is doing and saying through scriptural text.

23. See Lash, "Performing the Scriptures," 467–74.

fundamental form of scriptural interpretation is the life, activity, and organization of the Christian community, representing the performance of biblical text at the level of the individual and the body corporate. Even if the meaning of the text evolves across time and space and we tell the story differently, what is constraining is that for the same text we do not tell a different story. Christian interpretation needs to recognizably tell the story of the central character of the New Testament, this Jesus of Nazareth, and to point to the mystery of divine action in his life. Nevertheless, in pushing for a performative interpretation of Scripture in a community of faith, Lash clearly admits that there can be different performances of a text in different contexts, all of which pay faithful attention to the text's central story.

Lash attempts to address the question of how scriptural reading within the church and the purposes of God relates to historical criticism and to critical readings. He explains, "The fundamental form of the interpretation of Beethoven consists in the performance of his texts. The academics have an indispensable but subordinate part to play in contributing to the quality and appreciation of the performance."[24] Nevertheless, just as with a musical score, there might be all sorts of things to be said about a text, but it is not truly being read until someone actually plays the music in some particular way. In Lash's hermeneutics, therefore, there is a kind of "division of labor" in the sense that the academics play a critical yet subordinate role for the ultimate production of the performance.

Lash measures the quality of a scriptural performance by the quality of humanity of individual players in a community. He asserts that an interpretation of Scripture is better performed as true to Christ when individual players grow in their humanity. Yet, Lash notes that this humanity is hidden in the mystery of God and is not directly observable.[25] Lash's comments that the quality of this humanity tends to be general; it is not easy to see how this growth in humanity could be evaluated or tested, as a means of testing the authenticity of the interpretation. Though Lash maintains that a performance must be true to the fact and significance of the divine action, he does not explore in any detail in his project how such performing would translate into concrete practices.

Lash, in his later project on *Believing Three Ways*, alludes to a life-giving divine action, but he does not draw any link between the two

24. Lash, *Performing the Scriptures*, 470.
25. Lash, *Performing the Scriptures*, 473–74.

projects.[26] Of the third article, Lash speaks of the Spirit who gives life everlasting to the holy catholic church, a people summoned out of the world to common life and communion in God.[27] Through God's gift of the Spirit, humankind learns to see, hear and do the Word uttered in Jesus Christ.[28] The holy catholic church comes into being when we read the life-giving Spirit in these ways.

What I may draw from Lash's *Believing Three Ways* project then is this focus on the relationship between the Word and the Spirit, which forms the holy catholic church. For Lash, we are talking about the one activity of God that is, from one perspective, Word, and from another, Spirit. God gives all life that fuels every learning, word, and action; the Word, incarnate in Jesus Christ is 'the way' to life that we are called to follow, and the Spirit is the lively, vivifying energy that gives that life. The fullness of this life takes the form of the one holy catholic apostolic church in the world.

We can glimpse how Scripture fits into this picture for Lash: it plays a role within God's life-giving, Christ-focused work. It is in *reading Scripture in the Spirit* that humans learn to habituate God's message, the Word enfleshed in Jesus Christ. This is *how* humans can come to be related to the mystery of God in his divine action.[29] Lash did not explicitly link his account of *Performing the Scriptures* with this account of the Spirit; the elements are there, but they are not integrated. This is where Fowl's work represents an advance on Lash's work. I therefore review Fowl with specific reference to his work on reading the Spirit—that is, paying attention to *both* what the Spirit is doing *and* saying through the scriptural text.

---

26. Lash, *Believing Three Ways*.

27. Lash highlights the need to stand in constant tension between "the wholeness of the 'great' church . . . and . . . 'all legitimate local congregations [or gatherings] of the faithful' . . . Each community, suffering and striving and praying in its place, *is* the church of God, the catholic church" (Lash, *Believing Three Ways*, 87).

28. Lash reads the Spirit as God's self-gift, "the 'being-given' of God." Here, we can read the Spirit more fully in relation to God the Father, who gives the gift, and of the Word (God's utterance) enfleshed in Jesus Christ, his Son (Lash, *Believing Three Ways*, 96–99).

29. Lash observes, "It is in the utterance of the Word God is, and in donation of the Gift God is, that all things come to be, and come to be related to the mystery of God" (Lash, *Believing Three Ways*, 101).

2.3.2 Stephen Fowl

In my earlier discussion, I located my research in relation to theological interpretation. Fowl stands as a key proponent who is interested in how the text can be read in the church and within the purposes of God. Like Lash, Fowl insists that this does not mean finding the one meaning of the text. Instead, it is about discovering the different things it can mean in different contexts—without thinking it can mean whatever we want it to mean. He sees scriptural interpretation in any specific context as a matter of discernment, and so as Spirit-led.[30] However, he questions whether there are ways of acknowledging the hermeneutical significance of the Spirit in practice that go beyond paying lip service to his role. This leads to the question I am exploring here: *how* is the interpretation of Scripture Spirit-led?

In his book chapter, "How the Spirit Reads," Fowl argues for a more immediate discernment by reading the Spirit, having explored how fruitfulness of an interpretation might be judged in the long term. First, this is appropriate or necessary when contemporary interpretative disputes demand an immediate response.[31] Second, reading the Spirit is appropriate or necessary when there has been no precedent practice or decisions made on the same interpretive dispute in the community that may be open for revision. Yet, for all his concern for a more immediate discernment of the Spirit's work, Fowl appears quite dismissive of the possibilities of discernment by means of charisms, like signs and wonders, which may accompany the Spirit's working in the present.[32] Fowl argues from

---

30. Fowl observes that Christians probably agree that the interpretation and embodiment of Scripture should be Spirit-led. He cites, for example, the Westminster Confession (1646), which claims that the "Holy Spirit speaking in the Scripture" is the "Supreme Judge by which all controversies of religion are to be determined" (ch. 1 art. x). As well, the Vatican II document *Dei Verbum* (par. 23) refers the Church reading Scripture as the "Pupil of the Holy Spirit" (Fowl, "How the Spirit Reads," 348–49).

31. Fowl cites the Acts 5 account of Gamaliel's advice to the Sanhedrin as one discernment approach to read the work of the Spirit. That is, if what was reported and witnessed were God's work, it will outlast all efforts to snuff it out. However, he observes that such patient discernment to look for the long-term outcomes of purportedly the Spirit's work in Peter's witness of Jesus Christ may not be appropriate for many contemporary and interpretive and practical disputes that demand almost an immediate response (Fowl, "How the Spirit Reads," 349). In this research, I attempt to address the more immediate as well as the longer-term discernment needs in a Spirit-led scriptural interpretation.

32. Fowl limits the exploration of his discernment question to non-charismatic

the narrative of gentile inclusion in Acts 10–15 that the "miraculous verification of one's position is not a central element" for scriptural interpretation. He therefore rejects any objection that claims, "'signs and wonders' are the only reliable markers of the Spirit's activity."[33]

In addressing the question: *how* is interpretation to be Spirit-led? Fowl turns to an exegetical reading of the narrative in Acts 10–15 for an exemplar. He asked, "Can Christians in the midst of interpretive and practical disputes, like those Christians in Acts 10–15, recognize, account for, and interpret the Spirit's work in more immediate ways"? Fowl focuses on seeing the Spirit at work in the lives of those who are interpreting Scripture. He observes that discerning the Spirit at work in one another involves being close enough to one another to observe each other's lives. He then argues that "the formation of friendship is . . . crucial to a community's abilities to be wise hearers of testimony."[34] However, it also involves being trusting enough that we do not too quickly dismiss things that do not fit our existing expectations of where and how the Spirit might be at work. Fowl highlights that this is precisely what the Spirit first taught Peter in his seeking to read what God was doing with and for Cornelius and his household—that is, *not* to engage in hasty and dismissive judgment when things do not fit our existing expectations of where and how the Spirit might be at work.[35]

Fowl considers that his prescription of forming close friendships, drawn from this apostolic account, might be the only way to counter the privatizing tendencies of contemporary Western church life. Fowl concludes that communal structures, habits, and practices are needed to

---

categories, by saying, "It is more difficult, however, to account for the practical force of claims about the Spirit's role in scriptural interpretation. How, especially in the absence of miraculous signs, can an individual or a community discern Spirit-inspired interpretation and practice from more mundane varieties? Are there particular exegetical methods that will generate Spirit-inspired interpretation? How might we know this?" (Fowl, "How the Spirit Reads," 348–49)

33. Fowl, "How the Spirit Reads," 350.

34. Fowl, "How the Spirit Reads," 361.

35. I note, in the Acts 10–15 account, how instances in, e.g., Acts 10:28; 11:12, 17 indicate how Peter seriously considered his immediate experience of the Spirit through and beyond Scripture (i.e., visions and miracles) in living out his vocation faithfully for the purposes of God, especially when things did not fit his present reading of Scripture. In fact, Fowl himself concludes, "For Peter, the pouring out of the Spirit upon the Gentiles takes this matter out of his hands. It is the decisive point which convinces him that this is God's doing . . . For Peter's audience, testimony to the pouring out of the Spirit upon the Gentiles is convincing" (Fowl, "How the Spirit Reads," 354)

engender this transformative outcome. For example, communities that structure for close friendship and a mutual accountability are better able to witness to the Spirit's work in one another and therefore to discern the Spirit's guidance. These communities would have habits that patiently enfold visitors and members alike in building sustainable relationships. Moreover, there is a need for practices where members would be open to a mutual witness of one another's lives. This gives Fowl his thesis: that communal structures, habits, and practices are essential to support recognizing and interpreting the Spirit's guidance of the church's reading of Scripture, and that in the absence of these factors no amount of miracles could make up for the lack.[36] However, Fowl did not venture beyond this structuring for friendship to attend fully to discerning the Spirit and his working in such a Spirit-led interpretation of Scripture.

Fowl did attend to relating a Spirit-led interpretation of Scripture to the reading of the text in its historical context. The church in Acts discerned the Spirit working where they did not expect him to—among gentiles!—and, without the conditions they thought necessary to a Spirit-filled life. Fowl shows how such a discernment worked together with their reading of Scripture, to generate a Spirit-led interpretation. Fowl argues from James's entire speech that there are complex interactions between reading the Spirit's work in the present, and the Spirit's interpretation and application of Scripture to the immediate dispute. What happened was not an abandonment of Scripture, but a creative re-reading. James's judgment then became the basis for a communal consensus with the community reading the Spirit and his work in James.

Fowl's project is an attempt to read what the Spirit is doing and saying through Scripture to the Western churches about their

---

36. Fowl, "How the Spirit Reads," 349–57. It is interesting that, on one hand, Fowl looks to this apostolic account in Acts 10–15 as exemplar for an immediate discernment of the Spirit's hermeneutical leading in a community of faith. On the other hand, Fowl screens off, by the stroke of a pen, all the charismatic and present working of the Spirit in signs and wonders that were being witnessed to in the central message of multiple testimonies—of Cornelius, Peter, Paul, Barnabas, and James—that the conversion experience of the gentiles was a work of God that was also authenticated by signs and wonders. Here, Cornelius, Peter, Paul, Barnabas, and James are examples of those who experienced the Spirit and his working in the present through and beyond Scripture. These paid attention to what the Spirit was saying and doing, through signs and wonders performed at their own hands. These witnesses read the Spirit and Peter and James, in particular, re-read the Scripture in the Spirit. There was an active participation with the Spirit in his working in the present. Their communities could discern the apostolic participation with the Spirit by the attendant transformative outcomes.

reading of Scripture in decision-making on contemporary interpretive disputes. Fowl is concerned about the privatizing tendencies and self-authenticating behavior that secularization has brought into the North American churches in particular. While Fowl's project is located close to where I want to take this research, he did not go far enough to explore what such a practice of reading Scripture with the Spirit would look like, beyond the need to build sustainable friendships. Fowl also did not go far enough to attend to discernment challenges when multiple readings are conveyed from a single text that is meant to help resolve interpretive and practical disputes in a community.

For this, I turn to Pinnock. He is probably one of the first to formulate a Spirit-led hermeneutics, which includes Spirit-sensitive hermeneutical criteria intended to address the need for reasoned discernment in testing and evaluation of interpretations.

2.3.3 Clark Pinnock

Pinnock did venture, where Fowl did not, to embrace the role of charisms in the discernment of immediate experiences of the Spirit both through and beyond the Scriptures. Pinnock extends Pentecostal hermeneutics to what he calls *Spirit-hermeneutics*, with a view to discerning what the Spirit is saying to the churches now.[37] Like Arrington, Pinnock argues that a Spirit-inspired interpretation of Scripture could be as authoritative as the original Spirit-inspired form of the Bible, as they are breathings from the same Spirit.[38]

---

37. See Pinnock, "Perspective," 157–71. Pinnock does not explicitly distinguish Spirit-hermeneutics from Pentecostal hermeneutics except that here he goes beyond Luke's account of the Pentecost phenomenon in the Acts of the Apostles to build a biblical basis for Spirit-hermeneutics. Amos Yong names the Christian imagination in the reading and discernment of Scripture as "pneumatological imagination" (Yong, *Spirit-Word-Community*). Concerning imagination in spirituality, see also Wolfgang Vondey, *Beyond Pentecostalism*; Wolfgang Vondey, *Pentecostal Theology*; Mather, *Interpreting Spirit*).

38. See Pinnock, "Holy Spirit in Hermeneutics," 3–5, and Bruce, *Canon of Scripture*, 282. Specifically, Arrington observes that an interpreter may hold similar authority in the *inspiration* (and not *illumination*) of scriptural interpretation when the modern reader's experience of the Holy Spirit reenacts the apostolic experience of the Spirit. Yet, he stopped short of identifying who this modern reader is, what profile one such reader may have and how such an inspiration process may be re-enacted. He adds, "If the 'apostolic experience of the Spirit' is used to pre-qualify such a reader who may have the authority to inspire scriptural interpretation, one can quickly conclude that

Pinnock models Spirit-hermeneutics on the hermeneutical practices of Jesus in which he re-interpreted Scripture to bring currency and significance to his hearers. There were examples where Jesus provided striking new interpretations when the text was opened up to the present context.[39] This showed how Jesus, open to the Spirit and the living Word, opened up scriptural texts to let them speak significantly in the present. "And beginning from Moses and from all the prophets, he interpreted to them in all the scriptures the things concerning himself" (Luke 24:27). These texts remained texts concerning Moses and the prophets, but Jesus re-read them in the light of his own life, death and resurrection in the present to provide significant insight into how one ought to live in the future. Pinnock highlights the fact that central to Spirit-hermeneutics is the role of the Holy Spirit in bringing dynamism and leading the hearers into all truth. The Spirit "fuses the past and present horizons."[40]

Pinnock next addresses the question of discernment in testing: How do we know when we have interpreted the Bible well? "Interpretation involves testing and discerning" and not all interpretations are equally valid.[41] Firstly, Pinnock suggests the criterion of 'fruitfulness': "A fruitful interpretation is something that lets the text speak and lights up the faith of the community." Secondly, Pinnock advocates the use of safeguards in the authority of the charismatic community as well as the charismata, even when few 'lay' people are theologically trained. Charismata come with their own safeguards—for example, teaching can challenge a

---

this would disqualify the majority of the Pentecostal-charismatic communities which may have some experience of encountering God through the use of the spiritual gifts without necessarily having to pay a cost for apostleship or discipleship. For certainly, the apostles' positive experiences of spiritual encounters were also accompanied by the sufferings and persecutions in bearing the Cross of Jesus Christ" (Arrington, *Hermeneutics*, 383). Pinnock goes some way to respond to this challenge of forming readers who can thus re-read Scripture with the inspiration of the Spirit. Pinnock highlights these prerequisites for anyone to read the Spirit in his otherness: the need for one to be open to reproof, judgment, and correction in humility, to foster godly habits of the heart, a disposition of faith, patience, and obedience to the inspiration of God's word by the Holy Spirit in the present (Pinnock, "Holy Spirit in Hermeneutics," 22–23).

39. See Pinnock, "Perspective," 159–60. Pinnock reviews Jesus teachings on the Sermon on the Mount, e.g., Matt 5:38–48, that re-read the Hebrew Scripture. Yet Jesus, in the same sitting, affirmed that he did not come to destroy but to fulfil the law and the prophets (Matt 5:17–18).

40. Pinnock, "Perspective," 165.

41. Pinnock, "Perspective," 168.

prophecy, prophets may be subject to one another, and those with apostolic authority can lead a church in a crisis in bad teaching.

Finally, Pinnock was careful to explain that a genuine Spirit-led interpretation would have to look like 'the apostolic witness'.[42] Pinnock notes that one mark of the church is its apostolicity. Here, the testimony of the apostles and prophets that established the church remains valid as a norm for all times and places. That is, what the Spirit says today through scriptural text has to be coherent with this apostolic witness and teaching.[43] The Spirit brings a fresh reading that will not contradict what his witnesses had earlier said in Scripture. Thus, Pinnock adds reason to Spirit-hermeneutics by giving us some criteria for discernment and testing.

In an earlier project, Pinnock gives us some propositions about making a move from the original meaning to interpreting significance in the present.[44] Like Lash, Pinnock clarifies that the narrative of salvation in the Bible does not change while the Spirit continues to create significance in the present to lead readers into the future. To help readers keep focus on this central narrative then, Pinnock proposes the following guideposts for a fresh reading with the Spirit:

1. The focus is on the church community and not the individual.
2. The process is dynamic, and the framing is eschatological, while recognizing that we need the Spirit's direction to walk by faith.
3. The goal is to lead the church community in all sorts of truth, in thought, word, and deed (and not just intellectual truth) for growth.
4. The purpose is world mission, characterized by bold witness in power, in apostolic tradition, continuing in the tasks of sending and commissioning.

---

42. See Hollenweger, "Critical Exegesis," 7–18; Pinnock, "Perspective," 165.

43. Pinnock references the early church decision to use "apostolic witness" as the scriptural interpretation that norms any claim to purportedly speak for God in a fresh reading of scriptural text. He says, "The ecumenical consensus has always been that the Spirit continues to speak but that the criterion for knowing that it is the Spirit of God speaking is the light of normative revelation, a product of salvation history and located in the writings of the apostles." While Pinnock argues against the "liberal transformist theology of development where revelation is a dynamic experience lacking in specific content," set against "the biblical canon," he did not go further in this project to test this principle with difficult readings (Pinnock, "Holy Spirit in Hermeneutics," 12).

44. Pinnock, "Holy Spirit in Hermeneutics," 16–23.

5. The Spirit leads the church to recognize what God is doing in the present.

6. The Spirit, with witness of Scripture, stands in judgment and correction on the church's errors, corruption, and deception.

7. The Spirit restores the unity of the church in the interpretation of Scripture.

8. The Spirit opens up Scripture to transform individuals' dispositions, habits, and practices to enable them to know God experientially.

Pinnock emphasizes that discernment is central to Spirit-hermeneutics. His list of propositions focuses discernment on the Spirit's work. However, this review raises more questions concerning the practice and discernment of a Spirit-led interpretation of Scripture.[45] In the next section, I raise these remaining questions and sketch out how kerygmatic hermeneutics will go beyond the work of these three authors.

2.3.4 Discussion

Lash describes scriptural reading as a corporate performance of the life of God focally performed in Christ. However, despite his Trinitarian project, Lash does not link scriptural reading explicitly to the Spirit's work. Fowl does link scriptural reading to the Spirit, and he makes discernment of the Spirit's work central to the church's corporate interpretation of Scripture. However, Fowl does not talk much about what the work of the Spirit might look like in the concrete. Moreover, he is rather dismissive of the charismatic forms that discernment may take. Pinnock therefore comes into this conversation as the author who speaks most directly and comprehensively about discerning the Spirit's charisms and his work in the present, both in the church and in the world. Pinnock therefore supplements Fowl, going where he did not venture. And, Fowl supplements Lash, whose project did not explicitly speak of the Spirit's

---

45. Pinnock pushes his argument for a case of Spirit-hermeneutics that locates scriptural interpretation in a community of faith. He categorically lays out his criteria for discernment against self-serving and self-deceptive behavior in "Holy Spirit in Hermeneutics," 3–23, and "Perspective," 157–71. However, he did not speak explicitly of testing these hermeneutical principles with a difficult text. Pinnock also did not show the dynamics of how the Spirit mediates this move from the original meaning to interpreting significance in the present, and how discernment of these dynamics may help readers discriminate across different readings of a difficult text.

work in performing the Scripture. Nevertheless, even Pinnock does not go all the way that I need him to go in providing an account of how Christians can perform the Scripture in the Spirit.

In the light of this discussion, I can now offer an initial sketch of kerygmatic hermeneutics. I put Lash's two projects together and argue that performing the Scripture in the Spirit is one way that the Spirit forms the one holy catholic apostolic church—although Lash himself does not directly say that. I suggest that the mystery of God that transforms humanity as they are drawn to *perform the Scriptures* is the Spirit that is spoken of in *Believing Three Ways*. So one grows in humanity as an outcome of more fully performing the Scriptures in the Spirit. This gives me my thesis statement: *A Spirit-led process is the proper context for an interpretation of Scripture that makes for an embodied witness to Jesus Christ.*

Consistent with Fowl and Pinnock, I will model kerygmatic hermeneutics after apostolic teachings, seeking to read the whole Bible in something like the way that the first Christians read the Hebrew Bible—in a complex interaction between the community's narrative in its contemporary context and the scriptural text(s), yielding an application in the present.

I emphasize readers' attentiveness to the surprise and freshness of the Spirit as they *perform Scripture in the Spirit* in kerygmatic hermeneutics. Moreover, participating in his charisms is an integral part of this surprise and freshness that often do not fit our present expectations. To limit or to deny the Spirit's charisms is to restrict the life-giving work of the Spirit that can transform readers as they perform the Scripture. Kerygmatic readers seek to find new things in the Scripture without denying the existing referents of those texts.

Finally, kerygmatic hermeneutics will also address the remaining questions left open by Lash, Fowl and Pinnock. These questions include, *How* does one perform Scripture in the Spirit in the concrete? *What* are the dispositions, habits, and practices that form this embodied witness? *How* is this reader and community characterized? *How* is decision-making undertaken in this community of faith? *What* are the operational criteria for discernment, testing, and evaluation of this practice? *Who* tests and evaluates? Chapters 4 and 5 will develop the underlying theology of kerygmatic hermeneutics with its kerygmatic criticism that addresses these questions, but I will set out the concrete practice of kerygmatic interpretation in chapter 6.

2.4 Conclusion

Extant literature does give us accounts of how Christians should interpret Scripture with the help of the Spirit. However, these do not provide the clarity I am seeking about the concrete practices involved, especially the concrete practices of discernment, testing, and evaluation. These therefore do not provide me with the theological tools I need to respond to the needs of a church community seeking to read Scripture in the Spirit. This motivates me now to dig deeper into the underlying theology for a Spirit-led hermeneutics, in order to find further resources for that practical theological task. What I have uncovered by locating my project in relation to existing scholarship is an initial sketch of this theology for what I call kerygmatic hermeneutics, an account of a Spirit-led interpretation of Scripture that forms an embodied witness to Jesus Christ.

Kerygmatic hermeneutics is built on the axiom that the Spirit who first inspired Scripture continues to inspire its interpretation in the present with the same authority. Yet while kerygmatic hermeneutics draws substantially from the emphasis on the work of the Spirit in Pentecostal-charismatic hermeneutics, there is in fact a discontinuity, though this may not be readily discernible.[46] This discontinuity involves my focus on attending to the Spirit in his otherness. I will suggest that readers in community participate actively in attending to the ways in which the Spirit stands *against* them—for learning, correction, and growth in holiness. While this reading cannot avoid subjective participation, kerygmatic hermeneutics seeks to guard against self-deception and self-serving attitudes and behavior. It is a work of grace bestowed on a community of God's people—one that is disposed to and trained in reading the Spirit's work in one another's lives.

Kerygmatic hermeneutics places the interpretation of Scripture firmly in the context of a community of faith. This move makes it broadly aligned with the recent focus of theological interpretation. Yet, a similar discontinuity may be discerned here. First, theological interpretation need not be arbitrary, self-serving or self-deceiving (as some may construe); in fact, readers engage in spiritual disciplines when they read Scripture in the Spirit. This reading is used as God's instrument that reads

---

46. Pentecostal-charismatic hermeneutics tends to be driven by an immediate experience of the Spirit that informs scriptural interpretation. It allows a text to speak in diverse contexts. It admits diverse approaches and emphases at the choice of the reader. These could range from biblical theological to theological interpretation to inductive approaches.

Scripture *against* readers, for teaching, reproof, correction, and training in righteousness. Second, theological interpretation need not compromise on questions of truth (i.e., it upholds what scriptural truth for everyone is, rather than just my "truth" or your "truth"). Finally, a theological interpretation that is Spirit-led can even support critical reading (i.e., the ability to call into question particular interpretations in the light of critical scholarly inquiry).[47]

Kerygmatic hermeneutics, attending to the Spirit's otherness, relates to both theological interpretation and Pentecostal-charismatic hermeneutics; yet it is distinguished in its own category. This devotion to reading the Spirit's otherness is not an engagement in abstract polemics. It involves Christian individuals and communities in developing concrete dispositions, disciplines, practices, and structures. Therefore, this is also an exercise in practical theology as well. In reading the Spirit's otherness, kerygmatic hermeneutics makes ordinary and concrete the extraordinary and mysterious work of the Spirit. At the same time, it also makes apparent what is the extraordinary and mysterious in the ordinariness of human living. This lived-out performance of Christian witness speaks mysteriously to the world to call believers and the world alike to account.

Central to kerygmatic hermeneutics, therefore, is a discernment that is made critical in performing the Scripture in the otherness of the Spirit. Kerygmatic hermeneutics, when well-practiced may ironically make itself indistinct from a Christ-centred hermeneutic that makes the one holy catholic apostolic church. This outcome is consistent with the non-self-referential nature of the Spirit—he makes himself indistinct in the Trinitarian communion.

In the next chapter, I will draw from a broad picture of the Spirit and all his work the marks of the Spirit. The marks of the Spirit are also qualities that the Spirit shares with those he gives life to in Jesus Christ. I then locate my research within this broad picture because we need to know more about the Spirit and his work before we may fully understand what the Spirit does with Scripture. These marks then help us to discern critically the otherness of the Spirit and his work in catching people up as living proclamations of Jesus Christ, the forming of the one holy catholic apostolic church.

---

47. Chapter 6 lays out a practice of kerygmatic interpretation that incorporates testing and evaluation within its corporate processes. For early evidence of the Spirit reading over-against readers, documented in confession and repentance, see section 6.1 Praying in the Spirit.

3

THE HOLY SPIRIT: FORMULATING THE MARKS OF THE SPIRIT

IN THE LAST CHAPTER, I made two moves in making an initial sketch of kerygmatic hermeneutics. First, I made explicit a reader's accountability to the Spirit in a Spirit-led scriptural interpretation that reads over-against self and community in a disciplined way. Such a disciplined reading is less likely to be a validation of personal preferences; this makes possible a critical discernment. Second, I placed scriptural interpretation firmly in the context of a community of faith that is trained to discern the Spirit and his working.

In this chapter, I explore *how* the Spirit and his working may be critically discerned in such a Spirit-led interpretation of Scripture. I review a broad picture of the Spirit and all his work with a view to formulating the marks of the Spirit that give a signature to all his working. These marks are also qualities that the Spirit shares with those to whom he gives life everlasting in Jesus Christ. I then locate kerygmatic hermeneutics within this broad picture to understand what the Spirit does with Scripture. This research thus locates kerygmatic hermeneutics within the Spirit's transformative work in making an embodied witness to Jesus Christ. The marks then help us to discern critically when a performance of Scripture is taking place in the Spirit, as he forms the one holy catholic and apostolic church.

Section 3.1 introduces a broad picture of the Spirit and his work—connecting with the Trinity, creation, Jesus Christ, the church, and transformation—in a theology of the Holy Spirit. Here, I read the baptism of the Holy Spirit as an ongoing transformation process in the Spirit. In section 3.2, I draw from this broad picture and formulate the marks of the Spirit: intoxication, life, participation, and revelation of truth. Section 3.3 locates kerygmatic hermeneutics—performing the Scripture in the Spirit—within the Spirit's revelatory and transformative work in this broad picture. Section 3.4 concludes by discussing how the marks of the Spirit will underpin kerygmatic criticism to fully address the discernment challenge that is central in performing Scripture in the Spirit.

3.1 The Holy Spirit and His Work

In this section, I paint a broad picture of the Spirit and his work with a view to discerning the marks of the Spirit and locating kerygmatic hermeneutics within his working.

In painting this broad picture, I survey relevant literature in pneumatology. Pneumatology is probably one of the most challenging areas of study in systematic theology. First, the presence of the Spirit cannot be visibly identified nor his words and works readily determined.[1] Naturally, there are concerns about how one can discern the presence and activity of the Spirit or even make an attribution to him.

---

1. Related to the elusive nature of the Spirit, Pinnock raises the gender issue concerning the Spirit—Is Spirit He, She or It? Pinnock argues that "Spirit is not gender-specific quite the way Father and Son are" (Pinnock, *Flame of Love*, 15). Pinnock observes that Spirit takes on several symbols like *ruah* which is usually but not always grammatically feminine in Hebrew. However, Pinnock argues that personhood of the Spirit is relatively undeveloped in the Old Testament and so the feminine case takes on less significance. In the New Testament when Spirit's personhood becomes clear, *pneuma* is grammatically neuter in Greek, as is *Spirit* in English. These grammatical cases allow the use of *it* for Spirit. The use of *he* for the Spirit is rare according to Pinnock, and this is attributed mainly to the evangelist John who uses *Paraclete* which is masculine (see John 14:26; 15:26; 16:13–14). He concludes that the bible does not conclusively settle the gender use of Spirit and the matter remains open. I would propose the following theological arguments for the use of *He* for the Spirit. First, I proffer that building the case for *She* or *It* or *He* on the basis of grammatical gender is inconclusive. Barr says, "the phenomenon of grammatical gender is logically haphazard in relation to the real distinctions between objects or to the distinctions thought to exist between them. Grammatical gender, then, is a prime example of a linguistic structure that cannot be taken to reflect a thought pattern" (Barr, *Semantics*, 40). Second, *ruah*, *wisdom* and *breath* or *wind* or *fire* respectively are the effects of the words or works of the Spirit, quite distinguished from the Person (John 3:8). Third, there is probably a need not to separate out the Spirit from Father and Son since the Godhead is One in relation to creation and humankind. That is, the Spirit stands in mutuality with the Father and Son; it will appear inordinate for Spirit to take on a gender different from that of the Father and Son respectively.

Second, the Spirit is also somewhat neglected in ecclesial writings. Pinnock, for instance, observes an apparent lesser prominence given to the Spirit, in both ecclesiastical reflections and creeds that are common to both the West and the East. References to the Spirit are brief and perfunctory and can seem to be an afterthought to those of the Father and the Son.[2] As a result, the literature relevant for the purpose of locating and discerning kerygmatic hermeneutics within the Spirit's working is relatively sparse compared to other categories of theology.

Notwithstanding, many scholars have made significant contributions. Some make deep inroads as they concentrate on specific issues, for example, Trinitarianism, baptism of the Holy Spirit, and ecumenism.[3] On the other hand, there are scholars like Yves Congar and Pinnock who have worked on a comprehensive theology of the Spirit.[4] I now paint the Spirit in relation to the Trinity, creation, Jesus Christ, the church, and transformation.

3.1.1 Spirit and Trinity

While God's actions towards creation are indivisible, one differentiates the Persons of the Trinity by their actions among themselves.[5] So what is the distinctive character of the Spirit in this triadic community? This leads us into the mystery of God's diversity in unity and unity in diversity.

In this mystery of God's diversity, the Spirit himself is distinctively mysterious because he is other-referential in the triadic relationship. The Spirit does not speak of himself; he reveals Christ. He is in a sense hidden behind Christ. That the doctrine of the Spirit is often subsumed into

---

2. Pinnock, *Flame of Love*, 10. Also see Rogers, *After the Spirit*, 19–29, and Castelo, *Pneumatology*, 2–13, for a discussion on why Christology has dwarfed the development of pneumatology, especially in the modern West.

3. In particular there has been an extended debate on the baptism of the Holy Spirit enjoined by James Dunn, Roger Stronstad, and Robert Menzies (see, e.g., Dunn, *Re-examination*; Dunn, *Baptism*; Dunn, "Response on Luke-Acts," 3–27; Stronstad, *Theology of St. Luke*; and Menzies, "Luke and the Spirit," 115–38). Scholars who engage in Spirit and ecumenism include Kärkkäinen, *Pneumatology*, and diverse scholars who contributed to Michael Welker's edited collection on pneumatology set in an ecumenical perspective (Welker, "Interdisciplinary Perspectives," 221–32).

4. See Congar, *I Believe*, and Pinnock, *Flame of Love*.

5. See Fee, *God's Empowering Presence*, 829–42, for data that supports the personhood of the Spirit, and Jenson, "Holy Spirit," 101–82. There are not only one, or two, but three distinct Persons in the triadic Godhead communion.

Christology has been a problem with many accounts of the life of the Trinity.[6]

Within the mystery of God's diversity, the Spirit is also the unifying bond of love in the triadic community. Therefore, a neglect of the Spirit causes deficiencies in our understanding of the relationships within God's triune life, since God speaks as One to humankind in creation.

i *The Spirit is other-referential*

Pinnock observes that quite contrary to Greek philosophical thought that defines a person as self-referential, the Spirit, like the Son, is other-referential and does not speak of himself. Pinnock observes that the personhood in Trinitarian communion

> yields a different understanding of 'person' than is common in Western culture, where *person* is equated with the individual. But *person* when seen in the context of the Trinity signifies relationality. The divine Persons exists in relationship with others and are constituted by those relations.[7]

---

6. I discuss this problem of accounting duly for the presence and works of the Son and the Spirit in triune relationality with specific examples in section 3.1.3 "Spirit and Jesus Christ." On this, Eugene Rogers pointedly raises the question: "What does the Spirit do that the Son does not do?" (Rogers, *After the Spirit*, 19–32).

7. Pinnock, *Flame of Love*, 30. Stephen Holmes gives a good account pointing to the understanding in early church traditions that the Logos and the Spirit stand alongside the Father in triadic relationality (Holmes, *Holy Trinity*, 41). However, Pinnock's reading of Augustine's Trinitarianism needs to be qualified in the light of new accounts of his Trinitarian theology that emerge in the last 30 years. These new accounts show up the maturation of many of Augustine's thoughts. For example, while Augustine had insisted on the irreducibility of the persons, Ayres argues that in the decade 410 and 420, he can be seen as moving towards "a sophisticated account of the divine communion as resulting from the eternal intra-divine acts of the divine three" (Ayres, *Augustine and the Trinity*, 3) Moreover, in his mature reading of texts like John 5:19 and Acts 4:32, "Augustine develops an account of the Spirit as the one who—as the Father's eternal gift—eternally brings into unity Father, Son and Spirit" (Ayres, *Augustine and the Trinity*, 6). Yet, Augustine maintained consistent insistence on the inseparability, irreducibility, and unity of the divine three throughout his career. Separately, Welker argues that there are no biblical references to the Spirit that support the cognitive self-referentiality, characteristic of divine life in the Aristotelian philosophical perspective. There is also no hint of the Spirit's return "to itself out of its other" in Hegel's sense (Welker, *Pneumatology and Pentecostalism*, 224). Therefore, the Spirit's workings point the way of the Father and the Son. Similarly, while Jesus Christ, the Word enfleshed, would speak of God the Father to humankind, it is the Spirit who speaks of Jesus Christ in turn. However, it is not to my purpose here to delve very deeply into the

Pinnock means the Spirit is constituted by his relations to the other Persons in the triadic community.[8] To focus on the work of the Spirit does not mean, therefore, a turning away from the Father and the Son—because it is focusing on One whose defining characteristic is in fact to relate to the Father and the Son.

ii *The Spirit fosters love in unifying communion*

The Spirit fosters a unity that is a unity of love, not a unity that erases distinction; it is a unity that is consistent with, and that requires and preserves, the distinction between persons.

Pinnock builds on the idea that the Spirit's distinctive identity is given by the Spirit's relation to the Father and the Son, and the further idea that Spirit's distinctive role is to unite the persons in love. Pinnock draws on a long tradition that sees the Spirit as the 'bond of love' between the Father and the Son—an idea that goes back to Augustine. Pinnock thus proffers that the Spirit fosters love and unifies community.[9] As love is expressed in its circulation in the loving communion, it necessarily underscores the diversity of Persons in unity.[10] Pinnock highlights the

---

technicalities of trinitarian theology.

8. See Rom 8:15–16; Gal 4:6; John 14: 25–26; 15:26–27; 16:13–15. While the Spirit refers to the third Person of the Trinitarian communion, Pinnock names the Spirit as the essence of God as well. He argues that "Spirit is the nature common to all the Persons . . . Spirit is the life common to all and a Person with his own face and the center of distinctive actions" (Pinnock, *Flame of Love*, 32). That is, the essence of the Spirit is other-referential in communion.

9. Pinnock, *Flame of Love*, 29–35. Pinnock appears to take a position of social trinitarianism, meaning that there are three Persons in God who are subjects of their own divine experiences—a society of persons united by a common divinity. This 'person' takes a different understanding from that in the Western mind and signifies relationality. While Pinnock argues that Trinitarian insights into the life of God are derived from revelation from history (economic Trinity—God in history), he acknowledges that God's nature and inner life are internally complex and mysterious. One may speak of this kind of unity that the three Persons share in the economy by the Greek word "*perichoresis*," which originally meant something like "giving place to one another in turn," and which came to mean "being what you are in and through another"—the Latin equivalent being "circumincession," with English translations of "coinherence" or "interpenetration" (Higton, *Christian Doctrine*, 100–101). Again, it is not my intention to get into any technical debate about how this fits the dynamics of trinitarian theology.

10. See Levering, "'Love' and 'Gift'?" 126–42. He concludes precisely so in responding to Hans Urs von Balthasar's challenge that the name "love" is also closely associated with the Father and the Son in biblical texts and may not be distinctive of the Spirit.

need to recognize the dialectics between diversity and unity in the Trinity in order to avoid leaning too much towards its unity in speaking of three modes in one Person instead of three Persons.[11]

Pinnock discusses God's character as love in two dimensions. In one dimension, love refers to the inner life of the triadic community, as the Father loves the Son and the Spirit; and this same love is between all three mutually. At another dimension, God loves humankind and demonstrates this in creation and in giving his Son to save sinners. Pinnock argues from John that God's love for humankind flows from the love in the triadic community (John 15:9). Moreover, this self-emptying love is seen in the sending of Jesus Christ through the Spirit to draw creatures back into this love of the triadic community. The whole economy is the opening up of this loving community for creatures.

3.1.2 Spirit and Creation

This section discusses the mysterious and multicontextual presence of the Spirit and the forms his work takes in creation so we may learn to discern his life-giving and co-creating work. The Scriptures give us many descriptions of the Spirit's mysterious and multicontextual presence: e.g., wind, breath, fire, life, love, wisdom, beauty, power, etc. Some of these are

---

Levering therefore evaluates whether Augustine's naming of the Spirit as "love" and "gift" is overreaching since this is not a reading that contemporary historical-critical exegetes share. He concludes that the difference between Augustine and the contemporary biblical scholars arises mainly from differences in the doctrine of Scripture. For Augustine, Scripture is inspired so we may know the unity and distinctiveness of the Father, Son, and the Holy Spirit and to come to love God more and more. And, the Holy Spirit is given as the greatest gift, love, in Trinitarian communion, who in turn actively distributes charismata gifts to humankind.

11. Some great theologians who take a position leaning more towards the unity of the Trinity include Karl Barth, Karl Rahner, and Hans Küng. On the other hand, social Trinitarians include Richard of St. Victor, Heribert Muhlen, Wolfhart Pannenberg, Jürgen Moltmann, Colin Gunton, Ted Peters, Cornelius Plantinga, Walter Kasper, Joseph Bracken, and William Hill (Pinnock, *Flame of Love,* 32–35). In an attempt to resolve the controversy, Kilby argues against the use of *perichoresis* to name what is not understood, to make three Persons one, and to formulate the social doctrine (Kilby, "Problems with Social Doctrines of the Trinity," 432–35). She proposes an alternative perspective for one to renounce the very idea that the doctrine is to give insights into the inner life of God. Instead, what is needed is a rule or set of rules for how to read biblical stories or speak about characters in these accounts or how to think and talk about Christian experiences. See also Lash's account in *Believing Three Ways* in section 2.3 above.

metaphors and analogies. While the Spirit's working is seen in the wind, breath, and fire but he is not wind, breath, and fire. He is wisdom personified but he is not acknowledged in all discoveries. This mysterious and multicontextual presence of the Spirit in creation speaks of his life-giving and co-creating work.

We can discern three main aspects of the Spirit's life-giving and co-creating work:

1. The Spirit is active in giving life to all creatures. He is the giver of life whose breath all humans breathe.[12]

2. The Spirit enables creatures to exercise their natural capacities. He reveals truth and knowledge in theology, the sciences, and diverse disciplines.[13] He gives wisdom and beauty as he co-creates with humankind in his economy.[14]

3. The Spirit draws creatures to their fulfilment in Christ. Pinnock's thesis is that the goal of creation is the new creation in Christ; that is, our becoming those who, through the Spirit, are able to participate in the Trinitarian communion to become Christlike.[15] Towards this end, the Spirit is that mysterious power that gives life and brings to perfection this new creation in Christ, the *telos*.

I describe each aspect of this work without getting into the technical questions about their relations.

Summarizing, the Spirit's life-giving and co-creating activity encompasses all three aspects but that the same Spirit is involved in all of them. Therefore, recognizing the mysterious Spirit and his life-giving and co-creating work allows us to use such language as "catching believers

---

12. The Spirit blows on everything and gives life (Gen 1:2; 2:7; Job 12:10; 33:4; Ezek 37:1–6; John 6:63). On the contrary, a human being dies when one's breath stops, and the spirit returns to the Father. On this, Pinnock says beautifully, "Spirit is the ecstasy that implements God's abundance and triggers the overflow of divine self-giving. Power of creation, the Spirit is aptly named 'Lord and giver of life' in the Nicene Creed" (Pinnock, *Flame of Love*, 50).

13. Pinnock argues that the Spirit is active in the world, in historical developments until now and is moving it to consummation. He therefore argues that pneumatology is fundamental to Christology, ecclesiology, salvation, and eschatology. The Spirit is the power in the Trinitarian communion who caused the Word to be born and take on flesh, empowered Jesus for ministry, raised Christ from the dead and directs the cosmos to its redemptive goal (Pinnock, *Flame of Love*, 50).

14. See, e.g., Green, "Beautifying the Beautiful World," 103–19.

15. Pinnock, *Flame of Love*, 74.

up in conformity with Christ before the Father," "caught up in the flow of love, wisdom and beauty" and "flowing in the Spirit." On both biblical and theological bases, the Spirit is seen to be involved in this life-giving and co-creating activity, not just in humankind but the cosmos at large.

3.1.3 Spirit and Jesus Christ

The Spirit shaped Christ's life in the world and abides in whomever will be an embodied witness to Christ. The Spirit's intoxicating, life-giving, and co-creating work, catching humankind up in conformity to Christ before the Father, is a drama of sin, salvation, and sanctification. It is about humans being freed from sin and united to Christ's sinlessness; it is about a journey in holiness.

First, the Spirit formed Christ's incarnate life in the world. Pinnock traces how Jesus was a gift of the Spirit in the annunciation. He paints a picture of Spirit interactions in Jesus's baptism and his dependence on the Spirit in life and ministry. Moreover, I engage here Eugene Rogers who gives a more comprehensive account of Jesus Christ, the Word enfleshed who is One with the Spirit in communion. Rogers argues that it is precisely in the events of the annunciation, baptism, transfiguration, and resurrection when the Son and Spirit interacted together that it clearly shows that they are distinct Persons of the Trinity.[16] In going to his death and the Father, Jesus waits in humility and forbearance for the Spirit to gift him with life to his mortal body (Rom 8:11) as well as life to his churchly body (at Pentecost) after his ascension. In so doing, the Messiah receives the gift of the redeemed, including gentiles.

Second, the way that the Spirit forms a new creation is by forming Christ's incarnate life in the world, and then by uniting us to that life. Pinnock argues for a more balanced sense of *both* Logos *and* Spirit in this one mission. Traditionally, theologians think in terms of Logos Christology. That is, Jesus Christ is being interpreted as divine Word becoming flesh, after the Fourth Gospel. Pinnock proposes taking an alternative paradigm where one views the incarnation of Christ as being

16. See Rogers, *After the Spirit*, 200–201. Of interest in the instance of ascension and Pentecost, Rogers observes how the Son defers to the Spirit in order to receive a gift. Rogers proffers that the ascension and Pentecost belong together. Unlike the annunciation, baptism, transfiguration and the resurrection, the Pentecost is missing the Son and the ascension the Spirit respectively in Son-Spirit interaction (Rogers, *After the Spirit*, 201).

a part of the Spirit's mission in creation and life-giving, instead of simply seeing the Spirit as a function of Jesus Christ's work. That is, the Spirit co-creates with Jesus Christ, Word enfleshed, in the Spirit's life-giving work. This is not to negate one in favor of the other but to restore the balance in a both-and paradigm. God sends both his Son and the Spirit in two sendings, but they are sent as part of the one activity of God in the world.[17] Therefore, in one sense, there is one mission.

I concur with Pinnock's *both-and* perspective that gives the appropriate recognition to the Spirit's creation and life-giving work first in Jesus Christ and then in the new creation in Christ.[18] In this research, I propose that a kerygmatic reader, flowing in the Spirit, is caught up to participate in divinity and to grow into the fullness of humanity. It suffices that "Jesus was *without sin*" and that "sin is not an essential feature of fully human life (even if it is endemic in humanity as it stands)" for my proposition on a kerygmatic reader to stand.[19] The Spirit gives life

---

17. Pinnock, *Flame of Love*, 80. On this, Pinnock follows Irenaeus who depicts the Word and Spirit as God's two hands. He observes, "[t]he Son is sent in the power of the Spirit, and the Spirit is poured out by the risen Lord. The missions are intertwined and equal; one is not major and the other minor. It is not right to be Christocentric if being Christocentric means subordinating the Spirit to the Son. The two are partners in the work of redemption" (Pinnock, *Flame of Love*, 82).

18. Pinnock appears to assume kenotic Christology in his use of metaphors like "surrendered the independent use of his divine attributes" and "self-emptying." To Pinnock, it becomes clear that the eternal Son assumed a human nature when the Spirit rested on that nature in the annunciation. Jesus flowed in the Spirit in grace and power. In becoming dependent, the Son surrendered the independent use of his divine attributes in incarnation. The Word became flesh and exercised power through the Spirit, not on its own. The Son's self-emptying comes naturally to God. Creation was a kind of self-emptying when God made room for creatures. Self-emptying is characteristic of God, who is self-giving love itself. Spirit is important for understanding the kenosis. Spirit enabled Jesus to live within the limits of human nature during his life. The Son decided not to make use of divine attributes independently but experience what it would mean to be truly human. Therefore he depended on the Spirit for power to live his life and pursue his mission (Pinnock, *Flame of Love*, 88). Instead, classical Christology, following the Councils of Nicaea and Constantinople, embraces Jesus of Nazareth as fully divine while fully human, being the second person of the Trinity. For the purpose of my research on the new creation in Christ, both kenotic Christology and classical Christology offer compatible views that Jesus of Nazareth was fully human. See Mike Higton on "Christology," "Incarnation," and "Hypostatic Union" in McFarland et al., *Cambridge Dictionary*, 99–101, 235–37, 230 respectively. For "Kenotic Theology" see Law in McFarland et al., *Cambridge Dictionary*, 261–62; Stephen Evans in Evans, *Exploring Kenotic Christology*, 1–24; and Sarah Coakley, "Kenotic Christology," 246–64.

19. See Higton on "Incarnation" in McFarland et al., *Cambridge Dictionary*, 236;

everlasting to the new creation in Christ in order to raise humanity to the level of the Son in relation with the Father. Jesus of Nazareth who was wholly human is an exemplar for the new creation in Christ in the journey into the life of God.

Third, the Spirit's uniting the new creation to the life of the incarnate Christ includes uniting humans to the cross of Christ and crucifying the old Adam for a dying to self. That is, the Spirit's life-giving work also includes a work of putting to death. I will discuss more of the Spirit's work of putting to death in section 3.1.5 on the Spirit and Transformation.

3.1.4 Spirit and Church

The Spirit plays a primordial and central role in the Church in her living out the proclamation of Christ and witness to the world.[20] The Spirit's presence and mission at every assembly contributes to the church's authority, witness, growth, and sustainability. The church, born, sanctified, and unified by the Spirit, propagates Christ's mission of making disciples and manifests the kingdom of God in the power of the Spirit's anointing. That is, the Spirit gathers the Body of Christ, sanctifies it (uniting its members more deeply with Christ), and sends it out in embodied witness.

This work of the Spirit is at least in part mediated through the activities of the church. The training of disciples who are the new creation in Christ is an ongoing transformative work, orchestrated by the Spirit but mediated by the church.[21] Ward argues that mediation (as in the intermediary action) of the church (between her members and God) is animated by the work of the Spirit. Therefore, the participation of members

---

and my discussion on the kerygmatic reader in chapter 5.

20. Stanley Hauerwas and William H. Willimon argue succinctly to accord the Spirit's his first and central role in the church—that it is the Spirit that makes the church and not the church that gives the Spirit a role to play. They explain, "Through the Spirit the church becomes for the world Christ's body, the way the world is given continuing, bodily assurance that Jesus Christ is Lord" (Hauerwas and Willimon, *Holy Spirit*, 39). However, discerning what is not only human but also of God in an embodied witness is one of the key challenges in our review thus far. Pinnock raises a caution over *not* discerning the Spirit's presence and mission—this would subordinate the Spirit to the church, just like the Spirit has been subordinated to Christ (Pinnock, *Flame of Love*, 115).

21. See, e.g., Moschella, *Ethnography*; Osmer, *Practical Theology*; Ward, *Participation and Mediation*; Ward, *Perspectives*.

in church activities, while it exists as church culture, is also a place of transforming glory.[22]

The Spirit's transformative work in this embodied witness to Christ is mysterious just as the Spirit is mystery.[23] This raises questions of discernment—to see when and where the Spirit is at work even while the Spirit works through the activity of the church. That is, it is not enough to use the same ethnographic techniques that can map any human community, to trace the ways in which Christian communities form identity and behavior. There is a further, strictly theological, process of discernment needed *before* that formative work can be identified with the Spirit's work.

In this research, I want to engage in a theologically-driven discernment of the Spirit's work. I also want to discern the Spirit's work in the concrete, visible practices of the church. This fittingly addresses a concern that ecclesiology and ethnography, as an independent and growing area of interest in systematic theology, can sometimes take off on its socio-anthropological enquiry into concrete practices without appropriate discernment of the mysterious Spirit who is the church's life source.[24] Yet, when ethnography is construed theologically, it helps in corporate reflection and self-evaluation of the Spirit-led transformative work, the Spirit's making of a communion of saints. Therefore, I speak to this present challenge in ecclesiology and ethnography in formulating a theology that can speak critically of discerning the Spirit's transformative work in a church's concrete practices.

This need for a critical discernment of the Spirit and his transformative work in a church community resonates with that from our earlier

22. Ward, *Participation and Mediation*, 108.

23. As is the nature of wind, breath, dove, and fire, the Spirit cannot be constrained within physical buildings, structures, and processes.

24. Ecclesiology asks the question—what kind of society is the church? The traditional response has been a dogmatic one. In recent years, there have been various attempts to document ethnographically church practices as phenomena. One then can question whether there is an empirical relation between what is being practiced in a church and the theology that informs the church. Webster observes that "ethnography of such a society will be irregular, even aberrant, and utterly enigmatic if we restrict the matter of ethnography to purely natural motion. The church is a society that moves itself as it is moved by God. Without talk of this divine movement, of the electing, calling, gathering, and sanctifying works of God, an ethnography of the church does not attain its object, misperceiving the motion to which its attention is to be directed, and so inhibited in understanding the creaturely movements of the communion of saints" (Webster, "In the Society of God," 220–21).

discourse on *performing Scripture in the Spirit*. Here, I am interested in what it means to *perform Scripture in the Spirit* (an attending to the concrete practices of reading in the wider practical setting in the life of the church) *and* asking how to discern whether and how the Spirit is working in and through these practices. As much as this *performing Scripture in the Spirit* is embedded within the Spirit's transforming work in a church community, this broad paint stroke tells me how much I need to push to make ordinary the extraordinary and to discern the extraordinary in the ordinary in practical theology.

I next discuss the work of the Spirit in releasing life-giving charisms in church witness and in missions and in unifying the Church. Again, the extant literature relevant for where I want to go with understanding where and how *performing Scripture in the Spirit* fits with this broad picture of the Spirit's work does not go far enough to answer my question concerning a critical discernment of the Spirit's work in these areas.

i The Spirit releases life-giving charisms in church witness and in missions

Pinnock argues that the Spirit works actively in the church in giving gifts. His gifts release life and supernatural powers to bring to completion God's new creation in Christ.[25] Pinnock takes the sense that the Spirit's gifts (*charismata*) means grace that enable the gracious working of God in mission through the church.[26] While the context today is different from that in the days of the apostles, the church's witness and mission, and the spiritual nature of the battle for creation's redemption, remain relevant. Therefore, he argues that the church needs to be open not only to ask for the Spirit's gifts, whether in service or hospitality, or performing signs and miracles, healings and deliverances, but more importantly, to exercise them regularly in her witness.[27]

---

25. Pinnock, *Flame of Love*, 130. Also, Carson, *Showing the Spirit*.

26. See Mark 16:17–20; 1 Cor 1:5–7; 12:7; 14:1; 2 Cor 10:3–6 and Heb 2:3–4. Pinnock does not discriminate between the charisms that flow from liturgical actions and those that flow free of institutional structures (Pinnock, *Flame of Love*, 131). I take the same sense in this research.

27. Pinnock describes the problem commonly observed in many churches: "The problem becomes visible when we think of gifts as falling along a spectrum from *A* to *Z*. Let *A* to *P* refer to gifts we are comfortable with (such as teaching and administration) and *R* to *Z* represent gifts we are hesitant about (like prophecy and healing).

Pinnock believes that new believers, baptised in the Spirit, have every potential to be energized in their faith journey in an ongoing transformation that equips them as fellow witnesses for God.[28] I state its corollary: Denying the Spirit's gifts their place in church and missions, whether local or overseas, personal or corporate, weakens the impact of the Spirit's life-giving and co-creating work in the world. Poor church witness and mission outcomes may in turn feed back into reduced motivation and efforts.[29] The vocation of the church, which is so central to her being, can consequently be relegated to neglect and disfavour only because the Spirit has been so relegated.[30] I have been urging the importance of spiritual gifts, including signs and wonders. But what I have said thus far shows that these gifts matter precisely because they contribute to the overall life-giving work of the Spirit, in forming the church as an embodied witness to Christ in the world.

ii *The Spirit unifies the church*

The Spirit is the *agape* love in unifying communion. He builds up the church by means of the diversity of people he draws into her. I draw from Paul's teaching on the church being the body of Christ, and all believers being baptized into the one body by one Spirit (1 Cor 12:12–3). That is, the Spirit is that love that brings unity of faith by means of the diversity of

---

Whereas the early Christians were open to the full spectrum of gifts, often we are not. Our communities hardly recognize certain gifts as real possibilities. The result is, because we are not open to them, that these charisms are not operative. Limited expectation results in an experiential deficit. Gifts R to Z are impeded from operating in communities that do not acknowledge them as real options. We need to allow the gifts to be rekindled among us as we raise the level of our expectation and allow God to decide what should happen" (Pinnock, *Flame of Love*, 139).

28. I will be defining and discussing the baptism of the Spirit in the next section 3.1.5 Spirit and Transformation.

29. Pinnock observes sharply that mission is not a program. It is not even human effort responding to a commandment or obedience to the Great Commission. Instead, the disciples witnessed spontaneously and freely of God's mighty works after they were filled by the Spirit (Acts 2:1–12; Matt 10:20; 1 Cor 2:4). It is the Spirit that drives mission in a church; and it is not the church that drives mission. Just as Jesus waited for the Spirit's leading in his ministry—Where to go? What to do? When to act?—so the church ought to ask these questions of the Spirit (Pinnock, *Flame of Love*, 142).

30. Jesus's teaching on the parable of the disciples as salt in the world is instructive (Matt 5:13; Mark 9:50; Luke 14:34) for such an instance when the mission and vocation of the church is lost.

race, language, culture, socio-economic, and political categories in a faith community, reflecting the Trinitarian communion.

Again, discerning the unifying work of the Spirit could be a challenge. While he is not schismatic or fractional, it does not mean that there will be an absence of disagreements and errors. Yet, if the Spirit were indeed Lord over the church community and her institutional structures, disagreements may be resolved and errors corrected without bringing dishonor to God and hurt to the body of Christ, even as this *agape* love is being perfected (John 17:22-24). This leaves open the question *how* learning, unlearning and relearning, and a conviction of sin and correction of errors may be done *in the Spirit*.

I now pursue the Spirit's transformative work in the ongoing process of becoming, knowing, and proclaiming Christ.

3.1.5 Spirit and Transformation

The Spirit transforms humans as he catches people up as living proclamations, an embodied witness to Jesus Christ. Spirit baptism is central to this transformative work although its meaning remains controversial today. I do not intend to delve deeply into this controversy. I will simply outline the main views in their broad terms and suggest how my approach differs.

There are at least three popular views on "baptism".[31] The first view is a sacramental view that brings together water and Spirit baptism. That is, water baptism is the occasion for the reception of the Spirit.[32] However, the sacramental view makes it difficult to do justice to texts in which water baptism and Spirit baptism are presented as distinct events.[33] Moreover, 'spirit baptism' is linked in Scripture to the acquisition and display of *charismata*. The absence of charismata amongst those baptized

---

31. "Spirit baptism" is less often used than "baptism" in the Bible.

32. See, e.g., Castelo, *Pneumatology*, 98–110. This model is drawn from Jesus's baptism in River Jordan by John the Baptist. This baptism is a public confession of repentance to fulfil all righteousness (Matt 3:15). Yet the Spirit descended on Jesus in a form of a dove as recorded in the Synoptic Gospels (Matt 3:16; Mark 1:10; Luke 3:22). But it is significant that in the same baptism account, John testified to Jesus as the One who will subsequently baptize in the Holy Spirit (John 1:32–33). This model is adopted by the Roman Catholic and Eastern Orthodox Church.

33. See, e.g., Peter and John at Samaria (Acts 8:14–17) and Peter at Cornelius's household (Acts 10:44–48).

in water then raises a question about whether Spirit baptism has taken place, or, rather, what kind of Spirit baptism has taken place?

The second view is an evangelical view. This upholds that Spirit baptism occurs at conversion-initiation and may be accompanied by ecstatic experiences of the charism of the Spirit at the same time or later on in their faith journey. However, Spirit and water baptisms are distinct phenomena, with water baptism tending to be an event subsequent to Spirit baptism.[34] The only challenge to this view would then be how Jesus's impartation of the Spirit subsequent to his disciples' conversion-initiation in John 20 would be reconciled or if this even needs to be reconciled.

The third view is a Pentecostal view. This subscribes to Spirit baptism as a subsequent event after the conversion-initiation experience (just like the disciples' experiences in John 20 and Acts 2 accounts). This ecstatic experience is often associated with empowerment for mission and service.[35]

For the purposes of this research, the question of the relation between Spirit baptism and water baptism is not important. What matters is having a full, rich picture of the Spirit's work in believers—that it involves putting to death the old Adam, and bringing believers to new life, and granting *charismata* as part of that new life. What matters is that all this goes on in a believer's life, and that they are open to it going on, and pray earnestly for it to go on, and that if this is not all happening, it starts happening.[36] This remains true whatever one's technical theology of the relation between water baptism and the receipt of the Spirit.

---

34. See, e.g., Pinnock, *Flame of Love*; Dunn, *Re-examination*; Dunn, "Response on Luke-Acts," 3–27; Dunn, *Baptism*. These subscribe to an evangelical view and argue against the second blessing or Pentecostal view. They also argue that Spirit baptism and water baptism are distinct events. This view then becomes the middle of the road view between a sacramental view and a Pentecostal view. Dunn believes that Spirit baptism is conjoined to conversion—initiation and one cannot be a Christian unless he or she has the Spirit of Christ (Dunn, *Re-examination*, 5). Therefore, he has been a major opponent to a Pentecostal view in an extended debate.

35. This doctrine of subsequence, together with tongue-speaking as initial evidence of Spirit baptism, become the distinctive for the classical Pentecostal movement and underpins the theological development of Pentecostalism in the early twentieth century. See Stronstad, *Theology of St. Luke*, Stronstad, "Pentecostal Experience and Hermeneutics," 14–30, and Menzies, *Luke and the Spirit*, in conversation with Dunn, *Re-examination*.

36. A characterization of this spirituality is a life of immediate experience of the Holy Spirit. See, e.g., Cartledge, "Charismatic Spirituality," 215; and Kärkkäinen, "Pentecostal Identity," 14–31.

Here, I propose an alternative perspective that acknowledges "Spirit baptism" more by its *outcome* than the event that one describes it to be. After all, the Scriptures hardly use the terminology of "Spirit baptism" apart from the reference that Jesus himself will baptize with the Spirit (and perhaps not with water?) (Matt 3:11; Mark 1:8; Luke 3:16; John 1:26, 33) and with fire. The *outcome* of this Spirit phenomenon, with further clarifications from the Matthew and Luke accounts, is that the threshing will thoroughly separate the wheat from its chaff.

Spirit baptism, as a Spirit phenomenon, entails an *outcome* of separating from a part of oneself. This involves a painful process. The analogy here is that the wheat is being gathered into the barn, but the chaff will be burnt with unquenchable fire. Wheat berry and chaff are integral parts of the wheat plant. The chaff is the dry husk that protects the wheat berry. It cannot be readily separated except by beating and pounding the wheat plant (threshing) until the husk comes apart from the berry. Traditionally, threshing can be backbreaking. Only after threshing can farmers separate the chaff from the berry by winnowing.

Therefore, agreeing to be baptized with the Holy Spirit means agreeing to subject oneself to a painful process of separating the dross from the pure, the bad from the good, falsehood from truth and wrong from right. Rowan Williams, in his interaction with Saint John of the Cross (1542–91), says, "Thus the movement of self or soul is always a stripping, a simplification. And because this means an abandonment of the familiar and secure, it is an immensely costly process."[37] Therefore, while the common understanding is that Spirit experience tends to be ecstatic, an experience commonly associated with Pentecostalism, my formulation of Spirit baptism may plausibly include an inherent negative experience in order to attain its desired positive outcome in transformation.[38]

37. Williams says, "St. John of the Cross is normally associated with an almost inhumanly negative and comfortless view of the spiritual life; and it is true that he sets out the human cost of faith with more pitiless candour than almost any comparable writer (even Luther). Yet it is a movement towards fulfilment, not emptiness, towards beauty and life, not annihilation. The night—to use his favourite image—grows darker before it can grow lighter (*Carmel* I. ii; Peers, vol. 1, 19–21)" (Williams, *Wound of Knowledge*, 167–68).

38. I distinguish this wheat berry-chaff analogy in transformation, which is a judgment for life, from the sheep-goat analogy in the final judgment when the Son of Man comes in his glory (Matt 25:32–33; Ezek 34:17, 20). In this last judgment scenario, God will judge all humankind, not only between those that are in Christ and those that are not in Christ, but he will also judge one against another among those that are Christ's. This reading of baptism of the Holy Spirit as a judgment for life is consistent

In Spirit baptism, the Spirit awakens the believer's desire for the *One* who transforms, the *goal* of transformation, and the *process* of transformation. My approach of framing Spirit baptism by its *outcome*, instead of being concerned with a relation between Spirit baptism and water baptism, can in fact embrace the three main views.[39] In yielding to the Spirit's transformative work, a believer acknowledges the work of grace and commits to a lifetime of following Jesus. Therefore, there is a milestone in one's faith journey where the believer yields access to the Spirit to indwell and perform this threshing in one's life. This milestone can conjoin with one's conversion-initiation or water baptism. It can also be a separate Spirit experience often accompanied by *charismata* and empowerment.[40] While a Pentecostal view sees vocation and mission as a goal of Spirit baptism, my approach sees the church's vocation and mission as the *performance* that engenders the ultimate *outcome* of transformation. While conversion-initiation gives the believer, born of God with his seed, every potentiality of the *outcome* of transformation, one needs to proactively engage the Spirit as Helper, so s/he does not practice sin (1 John 3:9). This proactive engagement is an extended process sustained by one being filled and flowing with the Spirit. Set against this bigger picture of the Spirit's transformative work, the three main views of Spirit baptism in fact add clarity to both form and substance of the transformative process.

The next section draws the marks of the Spirit from this broad picture of the Spirit and his working. These marks bear the signature of the Spirit's working, from which I will formulate a kerygmatic criticism in chapter 5.

---

with that in Congar, *I Believe*. He proffers, "Together with E. Schweizer and M.-A. Chevallier, I think that what we have here is a judgement by the breath of the Messiah or the Son of man; these elements are often closely associated. I am also in agreement with M.-A. Chevallier's interpretation that there is a connection between baptism with water and the gift of the Spirit" (Congar, *I Believe*, 2:191).

39. Pinnock is also not concerned about the relation between Spirit baptism and water baptism. To him, it is not a question of *when* but *whether* one has encountered the Spirit in experience (Pinnock, *Flame of Love*, 170).

40. This is consistent with John Polkinghorne's view. That is, there need not be a specific time ordering of these Spirit experiences if indeed the Spirit is context-sensitive and encounter-sensitive. He argues that the Spirit is not a power that operates the same way in every person and every context (1 Cor 12; Heb 2:4) (Polkinghorne, *Faith*, 71ff, 97).

3.2 Discerning the Marks of the Spirit

In this section, I look to the broad picture of the Spirit and his working on the earthly side of heaven to formulate his marks.[41] His marks flow from this picture of the Spirit's identity and work. All marks characterize the Spirit's present working in his economy. I identify four marks for this research: intoxication, life, participation, and revelation of truth. These characteristics may be described by nouns or verbal nouns that signify the Spirit's presence and working.

3.2.1 Intoxication: Bond of love in communion

Intoxication is the experience of being captivated, of having our desire awoken, of being "caught up" in a reality that carries us along. The emphasis in this experience is that the Spirit's work is not simply something that is done to us, but something that happens in and through us. It is an awakening, a redirecting, and a drawing into new relationships with God and with one another.

The Spirit is both the mystery, the real presence of God, as well as the bond of love that is a participation or sharing in that mystery. This bond of love mediates the communion within the Trinity as well as a human participation in divinity and the glory of God. Williams reflects on the openness of this *agape* love that admits participation by those outside the triadic community—the Spirit is "God's infinite capacity for including new members in his life" for the "formation over time of billions of diverse Son-like, Father-directed lives".[42] Williams explains that the Spirit draws a disciple to stand where Christ stands, before the Father to participate in the *agape* love that flows in the triadic community. The focus here is the way in which the specific relationships between Father, Son, and Spirit are played out in the economy. We do not come to share the general quality of the Trinity's relationality; but we come to stand

---

41. Ben Quash says, "The Spirit is the 'operative condition' for the life of transformation in holiness, as the wind is the operative condition for the movement of leaves, let us say, or the rise and fall of breakers on the shore. The Spirit may be known by a sort of abduction from what our direct experience presents to us: in this respect 'earthly things' can help us to understand 'heavenly things'" (Quash, *Found Theology*, 254–55).

42. See Higton, *Theology of Rowan Williams*, 56, 58 respectively. This Spirit is God's "infinite capacity for 'new' activity, new and yet constant, faithful to His purpose" (Williams, "Spirit," 613–26; 615).

in a specific place within the Triune God's economic opening up of the divine relations. We do not think about this by thinking about the general nature of personhood and of relations between persons, but by thinking about the specific ways in which the Spirit, the Son, and the Father relate in the economy.

The Spirit is love; he is intrinsically desirable. The Spirit, who is love, is also grace. He takes the shape of beauty. The Spirit adds beauty, reality, perceptibility to creation.[43] Karl Barth says this of the beauty of God,

> If we can and must say that God is beautiful, to say this is to say how He enlightens and convinces and persuades us. It is to describe not merely the naked fact of His revelation or its power, but the shape and form in which it is a fact and is power. It is to say that God has this superior force, this power of attraction, which speaks for itself, which wins and conquers, in the fact that He is beautiful, divinely beautiful, beautiful in His own way, in a way that is His alone, beautiful as the unattainable primal beauty, yet really beautiful. He does not have it, therefore, merely as a fact or a power. Or rather, He has it as a fact and a power in such a way that He acts as the One who gives pleasure, creates desire, and rewards with enjoyment. And He does it because He is pleasant, desirable, full of enjoyment, because first and last He alone is that which is pleasant, desirable and full of enjoyment. God loves us as the One who is worthy of love as God. That is what we mean when we say that God is beautiful.[44]

In fact, the Spirit's beauty is the glory of God.[45] The Spirit's intoxicating love draws a believer repeatedly to the presence of God even if it is reading the same Scripture, praying the same Lord's Prayer, reciting the same creed, and singing the same hymn. The analogy is of a pair of lovers sharing the same song, dining at the same restaurant, or watching the

---

43. Rogers, *After the Spirit*, 179.

44. Barth, *Church Dogmatics*, IV/4, Vol. II/1, 650–51.

45. Karl Barth, with his Christocentric focus, concedes this of the Spirit, "It is as well to realize at this point that the glory of God is not only the glory of the Father and the Son but the glory of the whole divine Trinity, and therefore the glory of the Holy Spirit as well. But the Holy Spirit is not only the unity [*das Verbindende*] of the Father and the Son in the eternal life of the Godhead. He is also, in God's activity in the world, the divine *reality* [*Gotteswirklichkeit*] by which the creature has its heart opened to God and is made able and willing to receive Him. He is, then, the unity [*Einheit*] between the creature and God, the bond [*das Verbindende*] between eternity and time . . . It is in this way that [the creature] participates [*nimmt Teil*] in His glory and therefore in the glory of God" (Barth, IV/4, Vol. II/1, 669–70, italics added).

sunset day after day. This believer transcends the concrete practices that mediate the Spirit indwelling and infilling self to be a lover of God and humankind.[46]

Being filled with the Spirit is an intoxicating and pleasurable foretaste that leaves one with little room for any other preoccupation.[47] This is worth stressing—because it is downplayed in some contexts—that the characteristic form of this is, from my perspective, an overwhelming and deeply affective experience. It suffices here that the Spirit has awakened a believer's desire in repentance, salvation, and Spirit baptism. S/he is awakened by being given this foretaste of love, as a promise of the glory that God has for him/her or by being shown something of that beauty in God himself. The Spirit then directs this believer in Spirit-spirit communications in what I would call flowing in the Spirit. This leads us to the next mark—life.

3.2.2 Life: Mediating new life and co-creating

The Spirit's work in catching humans up, flowing in the Spirit, is life-giving and co-creating. The Spirit gives life everlasting to this new creation in Christ. Beyond being filled with the Spirit, rivers of living waters flow from these who believe in Jesus Christ (John 7:38) to give life in turn to others who hear and see and come to believe in their witness by faith (2 Cor 3:1–3). That is, flowing in the nature of the life-giving Spirit, a believer's action is also life-giving. Fundamentally, flowing in the Spirit is a means by which others are caught up by the Spirit in relation to Christ because it witnesses to Christ. Such a believer becomes part of the attractive visibility of Christ in the world. But this fundamental life-giving is accompanied and supported, secondarily, by the life-giving of signs and wonders. Similarly, one could also say that the Spirit worked to form and direct Christ's incarnate life, which was accompanied by Christ's signs and wonders.

---

46. In chapter 5, I will be formulating the concrete communal habits that can mediate the Spirit's indwelling, infilling and outflowing—what I call kerygmatic devotion.

47. Scripture juxtaposes wine with the Spirit (Luke 1:15; Eph 5:18). Wine intoxicates while dulling one's consciousness. S/he who is filled with the Spirit looks intoxicated. The Spirit gives a similar intoxicating sensation yet without causing one to lose his/her consciousness. On the contrary, this filling with the Spirit raises one's consciousness to a heightened state to transcend the spiritual realm, often described by participant observers as ecstatic experiences.

These believers co-create with the Spirit in performing signs and miracles, healings and deliverances at their own hands. We see the Spirit working in and through these believers' actions—including in and through their creativity, their originality, their spontaneity. These are genuinely their actions, genuinely their creativity and so on—but they can also be the means by which the Spirit is working. Moreover, when the Spirit gives gifts of healings, deliverances, and miracles, those gifts are genuinely given: the healings, deliverances, and miracles are Spirit-given, but they happen through the people to whom the gifts are given. We find exemplars of disciples who participate in the life-giving and co-creating work of the Spirit in Stephen and the apostles like Peter, James, John, and Paul.

3.2.3 Participation: Ongoing knowing, becoming and proclaiming

This third mark of the Spirit turns away from the external effects of flowing in the Spirit to its internal effects. While a believer's witness to Christ gives life to those who hear and believe, and co-creates in miracles and healings (the external effects), this witness reflexively impacts oneself in the interiority in a deep surrendering to the activity of God. Participation is this sharing in God's nature—a union of humans with the Life who can burn away all our sins.

Participation is an *ongoing* transformation that works towards a deeper and deeper surrendering over time. This believer may be observed to be historically becoming in his/her transformation. By flowing in the Spirit, knowing and proclaiming Jesus's words *continuously*, one forms character and becomes one who is *logos* enfleshed.[48] Therefore, the Spirit's work, catching humans up in conformity to Christ before the Father, is about growth in sanctification, Christlikeness, and holiness. It is about an ongoing becoming, knowing, and proclaiming of Christ. It is about participation.

In relation to becoming one who is *logos* enfleshed, I note the language used in Eastern Orthodoxy. Williams describes this as 'the deification of man in grace'—not meaning that a person loses his or her finite,

---

48. I will speak more on *knowing* in the next mark on revelation of truth. Concerning *logos* enfleshed, Luther says, "For the Word becomes flesh precisely so that the flesh may become word. In other words: God becomes man so that man may become God" (*Weimarer Ausgabe* 1, 28, 25–32; cited in Kärkkäinen, *One With God*, 47).

mortal creatureliness in this process, but that a person can long for "the identification of his *will* with God's: what he effects is what God effects, his acts are, as it were, God's, while still remaining his." Williams speaks of a longing for a kind of union with God, in which "the self is *surrendered* at a radical level to the activity of God, so that it can no longer be thought of as acting from a center separated from God."[49] This journey of discipleship with the Son, to the Father, and in the Spirit, goes beyond following the exemplar of Jesus, *Word* enfleshed. This is because following Jesus's example is still a process in which a believer remains in charge—s/he acts and patterns his/her action after Christ. But in participation, the deepest springs of his/her action are transformed, so that God's Christlike action flows through him/her as an embodied witness.

In this transforming into *logos* enfleshed, obedience to the Spirit in faithful living is not a knowledge to be grasped or a mechanistic relationship that overtakes oneself.[50] This obedience to the Spirit flows through one's proclamation of Christ in faithful living (because the Spirit works to proclaim Christ). In John 3:8, the Apostle John uses a metaphor of wind for the Spirit—elusive, unrestrained yet real. We have early examples of disciples who proclaimed the gospel of Jesus Christ in the flow of the Spirit (like wind), only for their proclamation (κήρυγμα) to be validated by signs and miracles, healings and deliverances (see examples of Stephen in Acts 6:5–10; Philip in Acts 8:4–8; Paul in 2 Cor 3:17; 4:13 and Rom 15:17–19). In fact, Paul teaches that the Spirit comes in the proclamation of the Word (1 Thess 1:5). That is, as disciples proclaimed Jesus Christ by faith, the Spirit came to give them the words to speak for the

---

49. Higton interacts with Williams, in Williams, "Vladimir Nikolaievich Lossky" and Williams, *Teresa of Avila* (Higton, *Theology of Rowan Williams*, 54–55). Higton paints Christian life as a journey into divinity, a journey into the conformity of Christ, and a journey of discipleship with the Son, to the Father, even as one is being caught up by the Spirit (Higton, *Theology of Rowan Williams*, 54–59).

50. Higton explains the shape of this transformation into Christlikeness, "It is rather a journey into a life in which I am more and more mastered by the reality I am exploring. It is perhaps, a journey into the kind of knowledge one has when one learns to play or sing a piece of music—where it becomes possible to say, 'You are the music while the music lasts.' The reality of the music takes one over, not in violent overthrow or colonization, but in and through one's own action, one's own dedication to it. This is the kind of knowledge where the relationship between knowing subject and known object is not one of distant but accurate inspection; rather it is the kind of knowledge one has when 'What is *happening* in the subject . . . is what the object is doing, the way in which it is making itself present to the subject'" (Higton, *Theology of Rowan Williams*, 54–55).

occasion (Acts 4:13–14; 27–31) just like Jesus would speak only as the Father directed (John 12:49). I therefore argue that faithful proclamation of Christ swept the early disciples into the flow of the Spirit not fearing what others will say and do, and not knowing where he will lead.[51] That is, the proclamation of Christ can sweep a disciple up on a journey of faith and grace in the flow of the Spirit, to be formed and transformed into *logos* enfleshed.

Surely, the Spirit's transformative work for human participation in divinity is a work of grace entirely initiated by God and made concrete in the Word enfleshed of the Johannine gospel. Kallistos Ware clarifies, "The concept of *theosis* will not be correctly understood unless in this context a careful differentiation is made between the levels of nature and grace . . . Through deification, then, we become god *by grace* or *by status (kata charin, kata thesin)*, but not god *by nature (kata physin, kat'ousian)*. We are all of us to be sons of God by grace, but Christ alone is Son of God by nature."[52]

Set against such amazing grace, Pinnock highlights the great cost of non-discipleship.[53] Yet, the deep transformation—the deep surrender to God as described by Williams—is nevertheless one that is enabled by means of specific dispositions, disciplines, and practices. It is not that these simply *produce* sanctification, but that they are themselves a result of the Spirit's work of grace in disciples. First, human efforts are inspired

---

51. David Kelsey makes clear that the Spirit is absolutely uncontrollable and unpredictable as wind . . . "utterly ad hoc, unpredictable, unmanipulable, uncontrollable, occasion-specific." Therefore, surrendering to be baptized and flow in the Spirit is unnerving unless one can find rest in its trustworthiness and faithfulness (Kelsey, *Eccentric Existence*, 618). The corollary is this: A loss of faith could stop one from flowing in the Spirit. This may happen when delight, desire, and devotion give way to indifference, doubt and fear. As in any relationship, there are vulnerabilities that may break the flow of the Spirit: quenching the Spirit (1 Thess 5:19), grieving the Spirit (Eph 4:30), blaspheming the Spirit (Matt 12:31), tempting the Spirit (Acts 5:9) or outraging the Spirit (Heb 10:29). Moreover, the neglect of keeping the body as a dwelling fit for the Spirit can similarly threaten the relationship (1 Cor 3:16–17; 6:19–20). This discussion suggests that stopping the flow of the Spirit would be a cost of neglect and non-discipleship.

52. Ware, "Salvation and Theosis," 176.

53. Pinnock implores the church, "Refusing to be a disciple of Christ and refusing to grow into his likeness is a great loss as well as a wasted opportunity to become what God made us to be. To refuse to be renewed is to refuse abundant life in this age and in the age to come. To refuse to be conformed to Christ's likeness is to forfeit the goal for which we were made. It wounds God's heart and grieves the Spirit, who longs to see us changed (Eph 4:30)" (Pinnock, *Flame of Love*, 177).

by God; they are not independent actions. Second, where human efforts do yield transformation, these still require God's continued gift of grace to continue with practices. Third, these human efforts prepare for and, as it were, long for further work of the Spirit; they subject human desires, hopes, and beliefs that the Spirit is at work to effect testing and sanctification. The Spirit's work of grace is witnessed to especially in the negative experiences in discipleship.[54] In this research, I will discuss dispositions, disciplines, and practices in kerygmatic hermeneutics that mediate the Spirit's transformative work.

3.2.4 Revelation of truth: Conviction of sin and correction of error

The fourth mark—a revelation of truth—also speaks to the ongoing nature of the Spirit's work, as he draws believers deeper and deeper into relationship to the Son and to the Father. On the one hand, there is the ongoing correction of error—the rooting out of sin in us, the putting to death of the old Adam, the rescuing of us from ways in which we still go astray. On the other, there is an ongoing discovery of more of what God has for us—more of the life that God wants us to enjoy and to share, more of what it means to relate to the world, to one another, and to God in the Spirit. There is a revelation of truth in God.

The Spirit is the Spirit of truth. He guides believers into all the truth that is Christ (John 16:13–15) who glorifies the Father. Therefore, the Spirit reveals truth that points to the Person of the Father. Revelation is neither human transformation alone nor a set of propositions on a variety of topics. It is our introduction to a Person.[55] Jesus said, "Whoever

---

54. Just like there is a cost to non-discipleship, there is also a cost to discipleship. See Matt 8:18–22; 16:24–26; Luke 9:57–62; 14:25–33 for examples of the cost of discipleship. Paul testifies to the groaning that comes with bearing the cross while one awaits the redemption of the body (Rom 8:23). In experiences of the dark night of the soul after Saint John of the Cross, God is distant and perhaps withdrawn and not to be found. However, disciples are not to flee wilderness experiences as God uses these to work deeply in transformation.

55. Pinnock says that such revelation is "dynamic, historical and personal, and being faithful means being faithful to God himself in his self-disclosure . . . Theology is a secondary language that lives off the power of the story and explicates its meaning to God's people on the move . . . Revelation is the act of self-disclosure revealing ultimate truth. It cannot be surpassed, but our understanding of its relevance can always be surpassed" (Pinnock, *Flame of Love*, 226–27). Therefore, to the extent that

has seen me has seen the Father" (John 14:9). Revelation is addressed not only to the intellect but also to the whole person. There is truth implicit and explicit in it, but they point to the personal center of God. This general nature of revelation (by which humans are drawn by God into relationship with him in loving fellowship) then provides the context within which believers make sense of an ongoing correction and discovery.

On one hand, the full reality of God has already been given to us in Christ. On the other hand, the Spirit leads us to discover more of what that gift means for us and for our world. Such is an unfailingly abundant gift that we will never exhaust. Pinnock argues that there is a timeliness or immediacy to the Spirit's revelation of *significance* of the Word in the present.[56] In Ben Quash's framing, the Spirit is always going ahead in creative modes in revealing truth, adopting a waiting-to-be-"found" approach.[57] There is then a continuous activity of "finding" God, mediated by the Spirit. It is in encountering the new and unexpected in the world (whether these be new situations, new possibilities, and new meanings) that we are driven back to see what was given to us in Christ with new eyes. The Spirit works through this process to draw us deeper into the truth . . . and to draw us forward into more of the life that God has for us. This is the positive side of this fourth mark of a revelation of truth.

There is a negative side of this revelation. It brings a conviction of sin and correction of error that grow sanctification, Christlikeness, and holiness. A disciple experiences ongoing learning of what the Spirit is

---

our understanding of the significance of the revealed truth is mistaken and is being corrected by the Spirit, believers and the church alike can learn afresh to interpret the revealed truth in the Spirit.

56. Pinnock notes that it takes the spiritual formation of the whole person to discern what God is doing in the unfolding of history before one's eyes. Such spirituality goes beyond biblical knowledge (Pinnock, *Flame of Love*, 215–16). He casts revelation and doctrinal development in a dialectics that does not limit God's continuous self-revelation while preserving the integrity of revelation. Pinnock observes, "Revelation comes to us through what has happened in history, and especially in Jesus Christ, in whom God comes into view. Jesus Christ himself is the self-revelation and image of the invisible God (John 1:18: Col 1:15)" (Pinnock, *Flame of Love*, 226–27).

57. See Quash, *Found Theology*, 5–7. Quash discusses an abduction approach after Ochs. See Ochs, *Another Reformation*. Ochs writes that "abduction is always of the creature as well as of God, and the creature is always fallible . . . Abductions must be tested" (Ochs, *Another Reformation*, 194). Quash argues that like induction, abduction is a synthetic and not analytic form of reasoning. It addresses the challenge of what appear to be anomalies in the observed behavior by generating an alternative hypothesis that will be tested subsequently (Quash, *Found Theology*, 204–5).

saying, through experiences and Scripture, which exposes sin and idolatry in humans in the present. Perhaps there is an un-learning of what is now revealed to be a wrong understanding of the truth. There may also be re-learning of the same truth already revealed of Christ yet now with a different significance for a new situation. Similarly, a church community learns from her mistakes as the Spirit guides her to apprehend the truth with new eyes seen through her present context. This church community is characteristically a learning community—one that is open to the otherness of the Spirit, and to one another, in a confession of sin and error.

In this research, I am moving beyond Quash's idea of "finding" God in new experiences in the world. I move into a somewhat different category of humans co-creating "newness" in the revelation of truth in the Spirit.[58] I am talking about the idea of human participation in new moves of the Spirit, where some new movement in the Church is understood as the Spirit leading people deeper into the truth. Acts 10 is an exemplar of how the apostles and the church participated in and "found" a new theology for gentiles (in the presenting case of Cornelius and his household), under the guidance of the Spirit, to be baptized into the faith. I reiterate that the apostles in Acts 10 did not simply encounter some new work of God in the world that opened their eyes to more of Christ's truth; they participated, through what are rightly their own actions, in the creation of this new work of God in the world. This fourth mark of the Spirit calls the church to attend to, and participate in, the Spirit's present work in the revelation of truth.

In the next section, I will locate kerygmatic hermeneutics within this broad picture of the Spirit and his working. This broad picture serves to give a fuller understanding of the significance of kerygmatic hermeneutics to the Spirit's work in his economy.

---

58. Quash focuses on the way in which, as it were, the ordinary run of *new* experiences in the world can be the occasion for the Spirit's work. Here, the Spirit reveals fresh significance of what has been revealed in God—of *givenness*—for the present as new experiences unfold. Quash's project did not take him far enough for the purpose of this research to make operational how *humans* may *participate* in and *discern* the Spirit's revelation in the present through experiences and Scripture. Notwithstanding, Quash appreciates the importance of discernment—he says, "Many of the found things in the world, many of its particularities, are sinful or sin-affected. My argument in this book for taking the 'found' seriously has not been that every sinful act or effect we may encounter is God-given; it has been that all God-givenness comes to us in the form of history" (Quash, *Found Theology*, 288).

3.3 Locating Kerygmatic Hermeneutics

"Kerygmatic hermeneutics" is the name I use for an account of scriptural interpretation in the Spirit that makes for an embodied witness to Jesus Christ. This well locates kerygmatic hermeneutics within the broad picture that I painted earlier on the Spirit's working

- in the Trinity as a bond of intoxicating love that flows from the triadic communion to draw kerygmatic readers in community to participate in the economic opening up of the divine relations;

- in awakening kerygmatic readers' desire for the *Other* who transforms, the *goal* of transformation and the *process* of transformation in Spirit baptism;

- in creation (and new creation) giving life everlasting to kerygmatic readers who grow in fulfilment in Christ. As is the nature of life, these beget new life and co-create with the Spirit;

- in the forming of Christ's incarnate life in the world, and then by uniting kerygmatic readers to that sinless life, and to his cross in an *ongoing* transformation that works towards a deeper and deeper surrendering to God; and

- in unifying the church, the Body of Christ, releasing life-giving charisms and sending her out as an embodied witness to Christ. This work is partly mediated through the activities of the church, which raises questions of discernment.

Against this broad picture, I then locate *how* the Spirit works with Scripture in the revelation of truth in a learning church community that is open to the otherness of the Spirit, and to one another. This aptly locates kerygmatic hermeneutics within the Spirit's revelatory and transformative work. This work leads the church positively into a revelation of truth in the new and unexpected in the world for faithful living and witness. It also leads this community through negative experiences of correction of sin and error that grow sanctification, Christlikeness, and holiness.

Again, this discourse leaves open the questions on *how* kerygmatic readers in community may participate in the Spirit's transformation—what dispositions, habits, and practices may enable this deep surrender to God and, *how* readers may critically discern the Spirit and his revelatory work with Scripture and in the world. My formulation of the marks of the Spirit from a broad picture of the Spirit and his working—intoxication, life, participation, and revelation of truth—helps to push my arguments to address these research questions.

3.4 Conclusion

Formulating a theology of kerygmatic hermeneutics is challenged by concerns about how one may discern the presence and activity of the Spirit in scriptural interpretation or even make an attribution to him. In this chapter, I have made two moves. I moved to formulate four marks of the Spirit that bear signature to the Spirit and his working in humans: intoxication, life, participation, and revelation of truth. I also moved to locate kerygmatic hermeneutics, a Spirit-led interpretation of scriptural truth, in this broad picture of the Spirit and his working.

These four marks are also qualities that the Spirit shares with those to whom he gives life everlasting in Jesus Christ. Therefore, when we talk about the Person and work of the Spirit in kerygmatic hermeneutics, we speak of his work in the abstract being made concrete in the forming and transformation of humans into *logos* enfleshed, flowing in *agape* love, who is the Spirit.

In the next chapter, I formulate an underlying theology that will inform on a practice of kerygmatic interpretation—a practice that helps form an embodied witness to Jesus Christ. In chapter 5, I develop kerygmatic criticism that allows for a theologically-driven discernment in a testing and evaluation of this practice. Readers in community can make an attribution to him by discerning the marks of the Spirit in kerygmatic criticism. I propose such a practice of kerygmatic interpretation in chapter 6.

4

KERYGMATIC HERMENEUTICS: A THEOLOGY

"When the Helper comes, whom I will send to you from the Father, that is the Spirit of truth, who proceeds from the Father, He will bear witness of Me and you will bear witness also, because you have been with Me from the beginning." (John 15:26–27 NAS)

"And He, when He comes, will convict the world concerning sin, and righteousness, and judgment." (John 16:8 NAS)

"But when He, the Spirit of truth, comes, He will guide you into all the truth." (John 16:13 NAS)

IN THIS RESEARCH, I adopt a constructive theological approach to formulate an underlying theology for an account of a Spirit-led interpretation of Scripture that forms an embodied witness to Jesus Christ. *Kerygmatic hermeneutics* is the name I give to this account. In the last two chapters, I have argued that kerygmatic interpretation is self-critical, with reference to the *otherness* of Scripture and the Spirit's convicting work respectively. My claim is that kerygmatic hermeneutics is capable of yielding an objective reading of Scripture (one that reads over-against readers) even when this practice is located within a community of faith.

In this chapter, I formulate *kerygmatic theology*, a theology of *how* the Spirit makes use of Scripture's otherness or over-againstness to form an embodied witness to Jesus Christ. To do this, the Spirit also enables humans to apprehend scriptural truth—truth concerning God and his ways with the world—by interpreting Scripture in the Spirit. Such Spirit-led interpretation of Scripture takes three forms—illumination, inspiration, and co-creation—that order the shape and fullness of this deep truth concerning God and his ways with the world.

Kerygmatic hermeneutics is concerned with *what the Spirit does with Scripture* in the revelation of truth that catches people up as living proclamations of Jesus Christ. What the Spirit does with Scripture *in a reader* brings an animated participation in a revelation and apprehension of that truth in a concrete act in the present that goes beyond the text. Kerygmatic hermeneutics thus brings a performative proclamation of scriptural truth to the world. This proclamation brings humans into an encounter with God because the interpretive performance of that truth has a concreteness and fullness to its form. In this sense, kerygmatic hermeneutics could address the question: *How may the world hear and see God?*[1] Therefore, I argue that kerygmatic hermeneutics can yield a critical reading of Scripture even when it is located within a community of faith.

I structure this chapter as follows: Section 4.1 sets out the preamble. I formulate a theology of kerygmatic hermeneutics in section 4.2. In section 4.3, I sketch an epistemology of kerygmatic hermeneutics. I conclude in section 4.4.

4.1 Preamble

I make three claims for kerygmatic hermeneutics. First, a Spirit-led process is the proper context for an interpretation of Scripture that forms an embodied witness to Jesus Christ. Second, kerygmatic hermeneutics

1. Apart from a proclamation of the gospel of Jesus Christ in a specific revelation of God, there is also a general revelation of God in creation, because of which humanity is without excuse (See Rom 1:16–32). The Spirit plays an unmediated role in this general revelation of God—for he is the love of God, the beauty, the glory of God, the creativity in created causes, the breath, and the wisdom, the Teacher of truth, the consuming fire and the power of God. However, for the purpose of this research, I shall emphasize more how the Spirit works with Scripture in the revelation of God. Kerygmatic hermeneutics—in the forming of an embodied witness of Jesus Christ—is *one* of the ways the world may hear and see God.

is this account of an interpretation of scriptural truth in the Spirit that brings humans—the kerygmatic reader(s), kerygmatic community and those witnessed to in the world—into an encounter with God in the present. Third, kerygmatic hermeneutics is *one* way in which the world may hear and see God.

These three claims flow naturally from this research's focus on hermeneutics as an interpretation of scriptural *truth* that goes *beyond* an interpretation of some scriptural *texts*. This interpretation is an apprehension of God and his ways with the world so we may know how to act, what to say in many situations. The Spirit enables us to discover God and his ways with the world. In fact, he leads us into a discovery of this truth in the concreteness and particularity of the moment so he may form us as embodied witnesses to Jesus Christ. Therefore, I will explore what *truth* means here. This sets the stage for an exploration of the underlying theology of kerygmatic hermeneutics in the next section.

I use *truth* to mean *general claims that may be embodied in a person*.[2] Specifically, *scriptural truth* would then refer to *the set of general claims that are associated with the whole content of Scriptures being abstracted to the highest level, that is, in God's relating in Trinitarian communion and with humankind*. However, this truth does not remain abstract and propositional. This truth is integral to the acts of God in the world in the present. It was embodied in Jesus Christ for our apprehension. In a similar sense, the Spirit leads us to embody this truth so the world and we may apprehend God. This means an interpretation of scriptural truth is incomplete until it is performed in the particularity of every situation.

Kerygmatic hermeneutics speaks about the lived-out interpretation of the Word in the Spirit. This account of how interpretation works is therefore distinguished from those kinds of interpretation that look to extract meaning from individual texts, or more general meanings from collections of texts, but which regard the application of those meanings in the present as a separate and subsequent move.[3] This account of scriptural interpretation takes off from my exposition of Lash and his claim

---

2. John personifies truth in Jesus Christ (e.g., John 8:31–32; 14:16–17) and the Wisdom literature (including Job, Psalms, Proverbs, Ecclesiastes, and Song of Songs) locates truth in God and its correlate in his people.

3. I use "meaning" as a general category that captures all kinds of yields of an interpretative process—the meaning the original author intended, the meaning likely to have been understood by the original audience, the meanings gleaned by later generations of readers, the meanings understood in the present, etc.

about *performance* in section 2.3—that an interpretation is incomplete until it is performed.[4]

In kerygmatic hermeneutics, with the Spirit working with Scripture, a reader navigates in a *to-ing* and *fro-ing* between *general* claims of God and the patterns of his actions in the world and the embodiment of these general claims in the concrete *particularity* of contemporary living. This to-ing and fro-ing yields an apprehending of God and his ways that shapes an embodied witness to the world. A kerygmatic reader abstracts from scriptural texts and the history of interpretation general claims about God and his ways.[5] Here, I am addressing the challenge that various textual meanings—whether meaning the original author intended, the meaning likely to have been understood by the original audience, the meanings gleaned by later generations of readers, the meanings understood in the present—are always context-specific. On the other hand, God and his

---

4. Kerygmatic hermeneutics may also be distinguished from an account like a reading of a saga, which narrates a historical event and the experience of a community, which has existential implications for the present time of the reader (see von Rad, *Genesis*, on saga). Von Rad speaks as a theologian of the church on the interpretation of Gen 22 (the great temptation). He says, "There are many levels of meanings, and whoever thinks he has discovered virgin soil must discover at once that there are many more layers below that. Such a mature narrator as this one has no intention of paraphrasing exactly the meaning of such an event and stating it for the reader. On the contrary, a story like this is open to interpretation and to whatever thoughts the reader is inspired. The narrator does not intend to hinder him; he is reporting an event, not giving doctrine. Thus, there is only one limitation for the expositor, but it is absolutely valid: the narrative must not be interpreted as the representation of a general unhistorical religious truth" (von Rad, *Genesis*, 243). In one sense, a reading of scriptural truth in kerygmatic hermeneutics that opens up Scripture to speak to the reader in the present time is not inconsistent with the reading of sagas in von Rad (and of legends in Gunkel). However, kerygmatic hermeneutics goes beyond this to embrace integrally (and in fact demand) a performance of that interpretation in the present.

5. I draw on Kathryn Tanner in her claim on how a human community of faith may reflect the structure of God's own self-giving relations in the Trinitarian communion (Tanner, *Humanity and the Trinity*, 81–82). Tanner observes that all of God's acts of giving retains a distinctive shape; and this shape can be summarized in general principles that may be appropriately applied in the particularity of human living. These general principles may then guide the structure of human relations that allows humankind to be incorporated into the triune life of God through Jesus Christ. Here, Tanner is addressing the challenge of *directly* modelling human relations on Trinitarian gift-giving nature. This approach would ignore the differences between social relations and Trinitarian ones; thus, this formulation of human relationships would not be realistic. Tanner therefore argues for a way of navigating between Trinitarian relations and human relations by instead abstracting general claims from Trinitarian relations and then applying these general claims to the particularity of human relations.

ways with the world—God's truth—is constant. General claims matter in this hermeneutical process, not because a reader is turning Scripture into a philosophical system and trying to understand the abstract principles that sit at the foundation of this system, from which the rest of Scripture can be derived. Rather, it is because the reader is trying to catch the sense of the utterly constant picture of God and his pattern of relating with the world, which is embodied in all these particular people and events spoken of in Scripture, so that s/he may embody that same truth in his/her own life.

A kerygmatic reader is trying to *understand* and, more than that, to *embody* this truth. Putting this another way, to embody this truth is to be united to God or to be imprinted with God's character and to act in every situation with the mind of Christ. That is, God is using Scripture, by the Spirit, to imprint his character upon his people. Therefore, a reader has not *performed* kerygmatic hermeneutics if s/he merely *states* what this truth of God is. This is necessary but is not sufficient. S/he needs to embody this truth in his/her particular circumstances; and this embodiment will be context-specific and particular.

There needs to be an interesting tension in what kerygmatic hermeneutics is saying, between insisting that an interpretation yields something *general* (the unchanging, constant truth of God) and saying that it yields something *particular* (the embodiment of God's truth in specific circumstances). These two ends relate dynamically in a to-ing and fro-ing manner—it is *not* a two-step sequential process that a reader grasps the general truth, and then applies it in a particular setting—because a reader only grasps this truth more fully *by* embodying it in a particular setting.[6] Moreover, this dynamism yields a hermeneutical spiral that forms an embodied witness in an ongoing performative interpretation.

Such an interpretation of scriptural truth in the Spirit brings humans—the kerygmatic reader and community, and those witnessed to—into an encounter with God to apprehend him and his truth in the present. Through such an encounter with God, kerygmatic hermeneutics

---

6. This dynamism distinguishes kerygmatic hermeneutics from some modes of scriptural interpretation that break the process down into a two-step sequence, say, into exegesis and homiletics. Here, different individuals may carry out parts of a scriptural interpretation. This allows for scholars and preachers to specialize in their respective abilities, skills, and knowledge. For example, pastors, preachers, and Bible study leaders could lean on the works of scholars and draw out significance of the texts for their listeners in their particular contexts.

can draw a human reception or rejection of God. This is one way how the world may hear and see God.

In the next section, I move to formulate an underlying theology of kerygmatic hermeneutics.

4.2 A Theology of Kerygmatic Hermeneutics

Kerygmatic hermeneutics is an account of reading Scripture in the Spirit that forms an embodied witness to Jesus Christ. In this account, the Spirit makes use of Scripture's otherness to form kerygmatic readers. The Spirit also works in readers of Scripture—to open their eyes to apprehend scriptural truth, enliven them and their agency as an embodied witness to Christ. This involves an ongoing process of shaping, molding, and perfecting humans into the likeness of Christ.

In formulating kerygmatic theology, I model these dynamics in a three-way interaction of the Spirit, Scripture, and readers. The Spirit needs Scripture to work with; and Scriptures need the Spirit to open the eyes of readers and communities to apprehend scriptural truth, else they remain like any other classical texts. As well, kerygmatic readers need Scripture to read *over-against* them in an ongoing process of teaching, reproof, correction, and training in righteousness. These readers also need to learn to walk in the Spirit to embody this scriptural truth. This formulation accounts for the progressive transformation of kerygmatic readers in community.

In section 4.2.1, I focus on *how the interpretation of Scripture works as God's instrument* for forming communities of faith into proclamations of Christ. Scripture's otherness enables it to be such an instrument. The Spirit makes use of Scripture's otherness to form the church.

The Spirit *was* at work in giving Scripture its over-againstness. He *is* presently at work in enabling readers to register that over-againstness. The Spirit also opens up a text to a multiplicity of admissible readings that gives the church an apprehension of God's present working in the world without losing that otherness. In this process, a reader apprehends more and more the deep picture of God and his ways with the world as revealed in Scripture as s/he is led to particular readings in particular contexts. This deep picture is one; the particular readings are many. Such an apprehension happens *in the Spirit*.

In section 4.2.2, I focus on *how the Spirit works in a reader* of Scripture. The Spirit is active in a reader, opening his/her eyes to see. In this process, the Spirit both opens his/her eyes (enables him/her to discern and to receive from Scripture) and enlivens him/her (makes him/her active) in interpreting Scripture.

The Spirit enables him/her to see what is in the text and in the world. The Spirit animates the very agency by which s/he makes connections between the text and his/her context. The Spirit is active in readers animating their agency as new creation in Christ. The Spirit catches readers up so they may be divinized and grow into his likeness. The Spirit also animates this reader's agency as a life-giving embodied witness to Christ. There is also a corporate dimension to all such animation. He animates the church together. In all of his working, the Spirit animates a reader and community to apprehend the deep picture of God and his ways with the world, and to enliven him/her to interpret this scriptural truth together.

In section 4.2.3, I focus on the type of reading that emerges from kerygmatic hermeneutics. This type of reading yields three orders of—or three ways of ordering—interpretation of the same deep picture of God and his ways with the world. Kerygmatic hermeneutics recognizes that the Spirit has revealed, and readers can apprehend *more and more* this picture of God and his ways with the world. Secondly, the Spirit may also reveal through Scripture and readers can learn to apprehend *a different or new shape* to this same deep picture *in the present*. Thirdly, the Spirit enlivens and empowers readers to embody this scriptural truth so they may apprehend reflexively *the fullness* of this same picture of God and his ways with the world.

This ordering of interpretation in kerygmatic hermeneutics is predicated on how readers relate with the Spirit in Scripture reading. It is predicated on the extent to which kerygmatic readers depend utterly on the Spirit in their agency to interpret Scripture. Therefore, the power and efficacy of kerygmatic hermeneutics lie in the intimacy of that relationship that effects the power and efficacy of the Spirit's agency. I now turn our focus to *how* the Spirit makes use of Scripture's otherness to form these embodied witnesses to Christ.

4.2.1 The Spirit uses Scripture's otherness

The fact that Scripture is "other"—in other words, the fact that Scripture does not simply say what we would like it to say but is instead capable of challenging and critiquing our belief and practice—enables it to have authority.

God gives Scripture authority. Webster argues that the reception of Scripture is ordered by its divine origin and inspired nature, and by God's use of it to communicate Godself.[7] Christians obey it because we seek to obey God; so we accept its authority. Christians acknowledge this authority by attending to Scripture's otherness; we read it looking for this otherness, this capacity to challenge us. Moreover, we do this because we understand the critique and challenge (and encouragement and affirmation) that Scripture gives in its otherness to be God's means of forming us into embodied witnesses to Jesus Christ. Therefore, we accept Scripture's otherness or over-againstness as authoritative.

In this research, one of my key claims is that reading Scripture in the Spirit, including in the freedom with which the Spirit leads us to read and embody the text in new situations, does not weaken this commitment to attend to Scripture's otherness, and to obey what God is saying to us by means of that otherness. It does not mean that Scripture says whatever we want it to mean in every new situation, in which case there is no commitment to Scripture's otherness. On the contrary, the Spirit drives us to attend to and discover more of Scripture's otherness, its objective message, in order that we may know God and his ways for us in each new situation. The Spirit catches humans up in intoxication, leads us to yearn to hear more from God, to be shaped more by God, to go deeper into conformity to God's Word. Moreover, he does so precisely by leading us to read Scripture afresh in every particular circumstance in the present. Therefore, reading Scripture in the Spirit may be evidenced by self-criticism; it will involve, amongst other marks, a conviction of sin and correction of error in those of us who are in fact growing in spiritual maturity by reading Scripture in its otherness.

---

7. Webster argues that the reception of Scripture, or how one reads Scripture, is ordered by the divine origin, inspired nature and use by the church towards the end of God's self-communication. Webster concludes that the reception of Scripture and the hermeneutical process are therefore sub-servient to God's self-communication in the Word enfleshed. This ordered relation has critical significance as isolation of scriptural texts from the reception in a community of faith as a revelatory act of grace would result in a disordered ontology of Scriptures. He cites examples of such disorders—the rise of historical criticism in isolation from a community of faith since reformation and the primary reference to uses of biblical texts by readers—as problematic (Webster, *Holy Scripture*, 5). Webster argues that "[f]ormed in this way, the texts acquire certain properties. They are *perfect,* that is, wholly sufficient, having no lack or excess, entirely suitable for the ministry to which they are commissioned" (Webster, "*Illumination,*" 336).

In kerygmatic hermeneutics, this growing in spiritual maturity is described as the forming and transforming of a kerygmatic reader/community. Scripture unveils the mystery of God in Jesus Christ, the *Word* enfleshed, who embodied the *Logos*. The Spirit, in turn, works with Scripture to form and transform readers as *logos* enfleshed—the embodied witness to Jesus Christ—by conforming them to the mind of Christ in their own specific contexts.[8]

Kerygmatic reading relates to a fresh reading that speaks to a reader's present context without losing Scripture's otherness and its associated authoritative demands on him/her.[9] This is because meanings of a text are contextually situated; a history of its interpretations reflects a pluralism of contexts. Reading the same text in multiple contexts helps readers to apprehend *more and more* how the same deep picture of God and his truth may be revealed in particular events and circumstances. In committing to attend to Scripture's otherness, a kerygmatic reading is authoritative for this community of faith, as the apostles' reading was for the early church.

Kerygmatic hermeneutics acknowledges the need for Scripture to retain its authority and timelessness for believers. It re-frames the hermeneutical problem as one where an interpretation of a scriptural text is contextually determined—in an interplay with its author, reader, and tradition—at various historical moments with different contexts.[10] Schnei-

---

8. In this account, conforming kerygmatic readers, *logos* enfleshed, to the mind of Christ is a progressive reality in a hermeneutical spiral.

9. Luke T. Johnson discusses three dimensions of the authority of the New Testament Scripture in the early church. First, the New Testament Scripture is *author*, initiator or that which forms the identity of the early Christian church. Second, the New Testament Scripture is *authorizer* for its own interpretation, acting as exemplar and warrant that allows for its texts to be re-read in the light of changing contexts without losing its authority as normative. Third, the New Testament Scripture has a diverse range of *auctoritates* or opinions that gives a pluralism of practice without sacrificing the core identity of a community of faith (Johnson, *Decision Making*, 40–44). Kerygmatic reading is more directly concerned with what Johnson is saying about the second and third dimensions of Scripture's authority. That is, following New Testament Scripture, which is *authorizer* for a possible re-reading of Scripture in the light of changing contexts, a valid kerygmatic reading may add to the diverse range of *auctoritates* in a history of interpretation of a scriptural text. Johnson points out that the various hermeneutical uses of midrash, typology, and allegory in the history of Christian hermeneutics can find their exemplars in the New Testament itself (Johnson, *Decision Making*, 41).

10. This takes on the same sense as Sandra M. Schneiders (see Schneiders, "Gospels," 97–118). Here, Schneiders clarifies, "The New Testament text is the unchanging

ders gives an insightful interpretation of what scriptural authority means in the light of post-modern hermeneutical pluralism and indeterminacy. She argues from Gadamer that reading a text well requires one to understand when it is predicated on a *question* it is addressing. Therefore, "the normativity of the text has more to do with the *questions* the Christian must engage and the *co-ordinates of appropriate responses* that the text offers . . . than with apodictic prescriptions that would lock Christian experience into the past."[11] What kerygmatic hermeneutics brings to this hermeneutical problem then is that kerygmatic readers in community can perform Scripture in the Spirit in this hermeneutical act.

The Spirit is the driving force in this kind of reading; and the experience of the work of the Spirit here is more intense, captivating, and powerful—being accompanied by signs and wonders—than in most other accounts. The Spirit works with Scripture in every context to help believers read Scripture in its otherness that retains its authority. Kerygmatic readers, *logos* enfleshed and flowing in the Spirit, discern the *truth in question* in the presenting context. The Spirit directs readers to the appropriate scriptural texts that address the same *truth* claim in their historical contexts.[12] Readers discern the co-ordinates of appropriate responses

---

'art object.' However, performed text, as 'work of art,' changes and develops. The narrative content, structures, and dynamics of the text continue to norm every valid reading and thus maintain an organic continuity in the effective history of interpretation" (Schneiders, "Gospels," 111–12).

11. A kerygmatic reading may be distinguished from Schneider's to the extent that the former goes beyond interpreting a text for its meaning: (1) to interpreting scriptural truth, and (2) by demanding a performance of that scriptural truth. Nonetheless, Schneiders's argument—that the normativity of a scriptural text has to do with the *question* that it addresses and the *co-ordinates of appropriate responses* that it offers—is helpful for our account (Schneiders, "Gospels," 111–12). In a kerygmatic interpretation, the Spirit guides a reader to pare down a scriptural reading in its original context to the scriptural truth that addressed the question raised in that context. This scriptural truth, set against what the scriptural text did *not* say in its original context, yields the coordinates of what may be a range of appropriate responses of how Scripture may continue to norm readers' attitudes and behaviors through times and spaces.

12. Historical criticism and a history of interpretation can inform kerygmatic interpretation by helping readers to recognize the changing attitudes of readers through the centuries that span this gap, and how these changing attitudes might have shaped a reading of the scriptural text in its historical context through the ages. For example, the questions of the role of woman and slavery pose complex hermeneutical challenges in different times and cultures; it is not the intention here to explore these questions. I would say, however, that history could inform readers how changing legal rights and access to education through the ages would have shaped scriptural interpretation. The Bible did *not* endorse women not going to university, but this was not an issue then.

that correspond to this truth in question as enacted by particular people in those particular contexts. This reading of a history of interpretation of those texts deepens and widens a reader's apprehension of God and his truth so the reader may creatively embody and perform this truth in his/her circumstance to bring people into an encounter with God in the present. The Spirit, by helping believers in every context read Scripture in its otherness, preserves Scripture's authority for all times and places.

The authority of a kerygmatic hermeneutical reading is authoritative for this community of faith but not necessarily for another community that is confronted with significantly different socio-economic-political and religious context. A kerygmatic community attends to the way the Spirit is bringing them up against the otherness of Scripture, in order to form them more fully into an embodied witness to Jesus. Such a reading is always specific to the particular situation in which they find themselves. This particular guidance is authoritative because it is God's word to the community in this time and place, and they are duty bound to obey it. The text of Scripture, and its otherness, are God's instrument in acting upon the community in this way.[13] In this sense, a kerygmatic hermeneutical process is similar to the Midrash in that it allows for polyphonic voices, even dissenting ones, to re-interpret Scriptures and formulate a narrative of faith.[14] Yet, the Spirit himself will always bring a coherence

---

That is, this was probably not the question that the scriptural text(s) were addressing.

13. Johnson proffers, "Just as midrash is a category that enables us to understand the process of the text's creation, so is it a category that enables us to move in the direction of a properly ecclesial hermeneutic. The Christian church can again learn something from Judaism and regard the New Testament canon as analogous to the Talmud—the authoritative collection of midrashic activity completed around the fifth or sixth century C.E. As the Talmud was a crystallization of a long history of interpretation of Torah mediated by new experiences, which became authoritative for the Jewish tradition not as the replacement of Torah but as the inescapable prism through which Torah would be read and understood, so can the New Testament writings be regarded as crystallizations of reflection on Torah in the light of the experience of Jesus the crucified Messiah and risen Lord. The New Testament writings remain authoritative and normative for the Christian tradition not as the replacement of Torah, but as the indispensable prism through which Torah is to be read and understood" (Johnson, *Decision Making*, 38–39).

14. Johnson explains, "In the study of Talmud, one never listens to only one voice or authority. One never follows the views of Rabbi Judah through every tractate or of Rabbi Eliezer on every topic. Nor does the study of Talmud yield a single abstractable answer that need not be reinterpreted in the light of changing circumstances. Indeed, the whole point of midrash is to hear the various voices in all their conflicts and disagreements, for it is precisely in those elements of plurality and even disharmony that

of scriptural truth if the process is indeed Spirit-led. This is because God is drawing believers to embody the *one truth of God* despite kerygmatic hermeneutical readings coming in forms appropriate to the multiple situations in which readers find themselves.

God unifies the church, the body of Christ, by means of Scripture. The coherence of Spiritual truth gives boundary markers for hermeneutical moves, determining what is permissible and what is not for communities for all times and places.[15] The rule of faith (or rule of truth) can function as a set of boundary markers in kerygmatic hermeneutics—a *minimalist* set of scriptural truths—for what may constitute a valid (and invalid) reading.[16] Specifically, the rule of faith can hold in tension the minimalist set of scriptural truths in apostolic preaching (to the world), apostolic teaching (in the church), and refutation of heresy (by the church) in a kerygmatic interpretation. In this sense, kerygmatic hermeneutics

---

the texts open themselves to new meaning, so that they are allowed to speak to the disharmonies and disjunctions of contemporary life" (Johnson, *Decision Making*, 39).

15. Williams says of the discipline of Scripture, "Its unifying themes are established according to what is understood as unifying the community. This is *not* to reduce its unity to something decided upon by the community to suit whatever happen to be its priorities ... Scripture, with all its discord and polyphony, is the canonical text of a community in which there are limits to pluralism. The history of Scripture, internal and contextual, for all its stresses and cross-currents, is being read as the production of the meaning of a corporate symbolic life that has some unity and integrity" (Williams, *On Christian Theology*, 56). Williams argues that a canonical reading, in a history of Scripture, can provide boundary markers for hermeneutical moves. For example, Williams points to the limits and thus unity in the authoritative point of judgment of Christian communities. William observes, "We simply do not *know* of historic Christian communities that do not introduce people into their structures by a ritual of identification with the death and resurrection of Jesus" (Williams, *On Christian Theology*, 56).

16. Everett Ferguson studies the rule of faith (canon of truth) that emerged from apostolic teachings and practices in the early Jesus communities (Ferguson, *Rule of Faith*). He then analyzes the various functions of the rule of faith—preaching and teaching, instructions of new converts, refutation of heresy, and interpretation of Scripture. Ferguson says, "The rule of faith provided a framework for the interpretation of Scripture ... Authors allowed multiple interpretations provided they did not transgress the boundaries set by the rule of faith. Origen thus defended his theological speculations on the grounds that they were not going against the teachings clearly and generally believed by Christians ... Augustine used the rule of faith as an interpretive device in *On Christian Doctrine*. His uses of the rule in exegesis ... as an orthodox boundary line within which there is exegetical flexibility" (Ferguson, *Rule of Faith*, 76–78).

attends to this otherness and integrity of scriptural truth and *unifies* community identity in every fresh reading of the Scripture.

Within these boundary markers, Scripture has great capacity to be read in multiple different ways without that destroying its otherness. Precisely this under-determinateness of Scripture opens up to embrace the diversity of race, language, culture, socio-economic, and political categories in a faith community, and allows Scripture to speak to the world in the present. Kerygmatic hermeneutics attends to this under-determinateness of Scripture that can address the multiplicity of contingency in contemporary living in every community of faith. Scripture's openness to a multiplicity of meanings does not mean that textual meanings in a history of interpretations can be readily set aside. On the contrary, kerygmatic reading attends carefully to each valid reading, with reflection, study, meditation, and contemplation. This is because each valid interpretation, while being contextual-specific, points to and reveals the scriptural truth in God and its coherence. That is, each valid interpretation helps to set or affirm the boundary markers for all other possible valid interpretations, within which a fresh valid reading may emerge for every new situation. Therefore, kerygmatic hermeneutics does not discard but instead attends carefully to the history of interpretation in keeping Scripture open to a fresh reading.

To attend carefully to a history of interpretation, a kerygmatic reader seeks to discern what aspects of Scriptural truth have been found in the history of interpretation. In fact, seeing the recurring finding of the *same* scriptural truth in God and *how* this has been played out concretely in *different* situations helps deepen and enrich a reader's apprehension of God and his creative ways in the world. S/he learns to discern a pattern of God's ways in the world. That is, a kerygmatic reader learns this deep picture of God's wisdom and creativity to embody his truth in different circumstances. Moreover, kerygmatic reading seeks to discern what new things about scriptural truth in God that a specific context reveals which other readings did not. In these instances, the fresh reading may have to be set aside for a re-reading by other spiritual persons and leaders in the community, especially those with prophetic and apostolic ministries. That is, kerygmatic hermeneutics attends carefully to a history of interpretation of scriptural texts, whether to affirm, refute, enrich or extend such readings.

In other words, kerygmatic hermeneutics does not undermine the otherness of Scripture by making it say what we want it to say because it attends carefully to the coherence of scriptural truth, which set boundary markers beyond which a fresh reading is not admissible. Therefore, kerygmatic hermeneutics attends to God bringing *unity* to the body of Christ by means of Scripture, precisely because of the diversity of sociocultural, economic, and political categories at work in a community as well as the multiplicity of changing circumstances and challenges to faithful living in the world.

Summarizing, the Spirit makes use of Scripture's otherness to form kerygmatic readers as embodied witnesses, conformed to the mind of Christ, and to unify the church because of her diversity. Kerygmatic hermeneutics attends to and upholds the authority of God to stand overagainst the church by means of Scripture. In the next section, I discuss how the Spirit works in a reader.

4.2.2 The Spirit enables a reader to read Scripture

This section focuses on *how* the Spirit works in readers of Scripture. In animating readers' agency to read Scripture, he both opens their eyes (to enable them to apprehend from Scripture) and enlivens them (to make them active in interpreting Scripture in the present).

The Spirit is active in animating readers' *agency*. The *modus operandi* of the Spirit is to work in and through created agencies. The Spirit works in and through kerygmatic readers, the church and Scriptures. These mediate the revelatory work of the Spirit. The Spirit *opens up* a kerygmatic reader to a creative re-reading of Scripture. Jesus's disciples did not recognize the resurrected Jesus until their *eyes and minds* were *opened* to apprehend what is happening in their context. They also did not manage to appropriate Scripture to make sense of Jesus, his death, and resurrection until *the Scriptures were opened* to apprehend what is in the text.[17] The Spirit thus opens readers' eyes to see what is in their context and what is in the text. He animates the *agency* by which readers make connections between their context and the text. The Spirit animates the very agency by which readers apprehend from Scripture the deep truth of God and his ways with the world—which agency I refer to as discernment in the Spirit.

---

17. In Luke 24 the evangelist uses διηνοίχθησαν (v. 31), διήνοιγεν (v. 32) and διήνοιξεν (v. 45) in succession to emphasize how the disciples' eyes, Scriptures, and minds respectively have to be opened for spiritual hermeneutical appropriation.

The Spirit is active in *readers* animating them and their agency as new creations in Christ, forming and transforming them into the likeness of Christ. The life-giving Spirit intoxicates them—fills, overflows and catches them up in the Spirit. The Spirit enlivens readers as new creations and progressively transforms them into *logos* enfleshed. Tanner argues that creation's agency—the power and efficacy of created (human) beings—is fully a created (human) effect only because God has designed it for such power and efficacy. By such design, created (human) effect may be perfected only when creation relates with this God in full dependence.[18] Following Tanner's principle of direct proportion, kerygmatic readers can freely choose and apply themselves to grow in spiritual maturity and holiness into the fullness of humanity with genuine power and efficacy by acknowledging and embracing the free working of the Spirit in themselves. That is, the Spirit is active in readers animating them and their agency to the extent that readers desire themselves to be thus caught up in the Spirit.

Similarly, the Spirit is active in animating readers' agency as life-giving *embodied witness* to Christ. A kerygmatic community mediates the life-giving work of the Spirit through her active witness. The evangelist John, flowing in the Spirit, mediates the Spirit's witness to Jesus Christ. The prologue of John's gospel tells us that "this" Jesus who had recently lived, died and resurrected, was "that" Word who pre-existed with God at the time of creation in the Genesis narrative. In proclaiming the gospel of Christ, John performed signs and miracles, and gave new life to those who heard his gospel and received Jesus Christ by faith. The efficacy of John's life-giving embodied witness grows with his participation in divine agency.

---

18. See Tanner, *God and Creation*. Tanner argues, following Karl Barth and Thomas Aquinas, "A created cause can be said to bring about a certain created effect by its own power, or a created agency can be talked about as freely intending the object of its rational volition, only if God is said to found that causality or agency directly and *in toto*—in power, exercise, manner of activity and effect . . . If power and efficacy are perfections, the principle of direct proportion requires that creatures be said to gain those qualities, not in the degree God's agency is restricted, but in the degree God's creative agency is extended to them. Talk of the creature's power and efficacy is compatible with talk about God's universal and immediate agency if the theologian follows a rule according to which divinity is said to exercise its power in founding rather than suppressing created being, and created being is said to maintain and fulfil itself, not independently of such agency, but in essential dependence upon it" (Tanner, *God and Creation*, 85–86).

Finally, there is a corporate dimension to this animation. The Spirit is active in animating the church *together*; this unifies the church in intoxicating love because of all her diversity. This kerygmatic community mediates the Spirit's *unifying* work in the church.[19] When the Spirit is mediated by believers who are filled in the Spirit (in spiritual intoxication), he brings about a spiritual state of unifying relationships that transcends human tensions in daily living—between fellow believers, husbands and wives, children and parents, and slaves and masters.[20] In such a spiritual state, (mutual and self) teaching, learning and correction flow from believers who have God's word within them. Believers teach and correct one another in community *with* singing in psalms, hymns and spiritual songs, and *with* thankfulness of hearts.[21] That is, holding such tension

---

19. In Eph 4–6, Paul emphasizes the utmost importance of believers co-laboring with the Spirit to preserve the unity of the Spirit in such a community, which principle lays the foundation for all familial and master-slave relationships set in the context of a spiritual battle in this world. This principle—to be filled *by* (instrumental use) or *with* the Spirit—an antithesis juxtaposed against being drunk with wine, points to a similar state of intoxication (which I deem as a spiritual state). However, we note the difference that the former is edifying while the latter is dissipative (viz. Eph 5:15–21). Andrew T. Lincoln highlights the author's imperative to be filled *by* or *with* the Spirit (see Lincoln, "Ephesians"). Lincoln notes Philo's reflections on drunkenness as illuminating. Lincoln cites, "Not only does he identify drunkenness with spiritual folly (cf. *De Ebr.* 11, 95, 125–26, 154), but he also sees a comparison between it and being possessed by God: 'Now when grace fills the soul, that soul thereby rejoices and smiles and dances, for it is possessed and inspired, so that to many of the unenlightened it may seem to be drunken, crazy, and beside itself.' (*De Ebr.* 146–48)" (Lincoln, citing Philo, *Word Biblical Commentary,* 344). Rudolf Schnackenburg points to the author's interest in congregational worship and communion *in* the Spirit when believers experience this fullness of the Spirit (Schnackenburg, *Ephesians,* 237).

20. See, e.g., T. K. Abbott, *Critical and Exegetical Commentary*. Abbott argues from Eph 5:19–21, "Ellicott says: 'the first three [clauses] name three duties, more or less specially in regard to *God*, the last a comprehensive moral duty in regard to *man*,' suggested by the thought of the humble and loving spirit which is the principle of εὐχαριστέω . . . There is therefore no break between vv.21 and 22. Further, the whole following section, which is not a mere digression, depends on the thought expressed in this clause of which it is a development" (Abbott, *Critical and Exegetical Commentary,* 164).

21. On Col 3:14–17, Abbott argues for the genitive, as in εὐαγγελίαν Χριστοῦ, to be read in the subjective following most commentaries—"the word delivered by Christ" referring to the teaching of Christ (instead of the objective) which fully indwell the believers. Therefore, I propose that this one who is *logos* enfleshed, flowing in the Spirit, teaches (positively) and admonishes (negatively) one to another in mutual instruction in this spiritual state. Schnackenburg suggests that such "singing 'to one another' . . . underlines the communal character" of this spiritual state (Schnackenburg, *Ephesians,*

between teaching, learning and correction (a negative experience) with singing with thanksgiving to one another (a positive experience) is the *unifying* work of the Spirit in a kerygmatic community.

In the next section, I formulate kerygmatic hermeneutics as a critical account of how the Spirit is active in readers of Scripture in three ways of ordering *how* this picture of God and his ways with the world may be apprehended. This account depicts *how* readers may relate with the Spirit in these different ways in each instance of scriptural interpretation.

4.2.3 Kerygmatic hermeneutics is ordered three ways

Since the Spirit works in and through readers to interpret Scripture, kerygmatic hermeneutics is predicated on readers' mode of relating with the Spirit. I therefore order kerygmatic hermeneutics three ways to reflect three modes of how readers of Scripture may relate with the Spirit—in illumination, inspiration, and co-creation. This ordering of scriptural interpretation is related to what the Spirit wants to be saying and doing in the present insofar as he is able to work in and through readers of Scripture. That is, this ordering is related as much to the power and efficacy of the Spirit's active work in the world as to the power and efficacy of readers' active relating with the Spirit to do God's work in the world.

In the first order of interpretation—*illumination*—readers ask, "What is your will for *me* in *my* present context? What should I say and do?"[22] The Spirit reveals scriptural truth and readers apprehend *more and*

---

237). See also Moo, *Colossians and to Philemon*, 288–90. Moo suggests the best option is to read "teaching and admonishing one another" and "singing with thankfulness in your hearts to God" as two modes in which the word of Christ can establish its central place in a community. This suggests that the two modes are instrumental to this imperative to have *logos* enfleshed in this community (see Paul's earlier teaching in Col 1:28). Moo has three observations from this one verse that throws light on worship among earliest Christians: "First, the 'message about Christ,' or, more broadly, we could say, 'the word of God,' was central to the experience of worship" (Moo, *Colossians and to Philemon*, 290). Second, various forms of music were integral to the experience. And, third, teaching and admonishing, while undoubtedly often the responsibility of particular gifted individuals within the congregation (such as Paul [Col 1:28] or Epaphras [Col 2:7]) or elders (1 Tim 3:2; 5:17; see also 1 Cor 12:28; 2 Tim 2:2), were also engaged in by every member of the congregation. I proffer that such grace that is extended to *every* member can only take place in this spiritual state of a community flowing in the Spirit who unifies one and all in the body of Christ.

22. The formation of kerygmatic readers and communities is characteristically dynamic and inter-dependent. Individual readers continue to learn and practice

more this picture of God and his ways with the world. Readers apprehend what this truth means for them in their different contexts. In the second order of interpretation—*inspiration*—readers ask, "What are *You* doing in the world in the present? What should I say and do that I may work alongside *You*?" The Spirit reveals scriptural truth as God works in his economy in the present. Readers may apprehend *a different or new shape* to this same deep picture *in the present*. In the third order of interpretation—*co-creation*—readers say, "Let's do this together in the light of what *You* want to be doing in the world in the present." The Spirit enlivens and empowers readers' agency to embody this scriptural truth so readers may apprehend reflexively *the fullness* of this same picture of God and his ways with the world. In this mode of co-creation, readers may appear audacious in invoking the name of God in what they say and do, and how they live, only because these readers' desiring and willing have become consonant with the desires and will of God. These three orders of scriptural interpretation reflect readers' ongoing journeys in the Spirit that spans apprehending God for themselves and apprehending themselves for God. The power and efficacy of readers' interpreting of Scripture in each of these orders also speak of the power and efficacy of Scripture's otherness that stands over-against readers.

In the first order of interpretation, the Spirit *illumines* Scripture to speak to *a reader* in a fresh reading of what has already been revealed of scriptural truth in its givenness. Givenness is what has been given to the church in the history of interpretation of Scripture, in tradition, etc. even though this is still an incomplete and imperfect picture of God and his ways. Nonetheless, through the Spirit's illumination of the same text in different contexts, a reader gains a more and more thorough apprehension of what this same picture would mean for him/her in different situations of life.

---

discernment as they perform their kerygmatic reading—as they relate with the world outside the church community. While the account in this chapter may appear to emphasize an individual reader's discernment in a kerygmatic interpretation, I will make a move in chapter 5 to relate how this individual learning and practice of discernment in kerygmatic reading may be refined to reveal self-deceptive and self-serving tendencies through ecclesial and communal testing in kerygmatic interpretation. I further detail examples of communal practices in chapter 6. Here, a reader's participation in ecclesial discernment reflexively sharpens the shape of his/her kerygmatic interpretation in the world. For example, a kerygmatic interpretation of contemporary issues like the role of woman or same-sex marriage will shape a reader's lived-out witness to Jesus Christ in the world.

For example, in a reading of what *agape* love is in 1 Corinthians 13, the Spirit could be illuminating the text to speak to a reader on how s/he is to be patient in guiding a slow-performing staff at work. In another instance, the Spirit could be speaking to him/her from the same text about bearing with his/her boss who was too quick to blame him/her for a lost contract. Here, the Spirit opens a reader's eyes to see what is in the world, opens up a text in its givenness, connects the text and his/her context, and so illumines the text to speak afresh to a reader—what s/he is to say and what s/he is to do—in the particularity of his/her context. This reader learns to apprehend more and more this picture of God and his ways with the world—what this means for readers in each different context.

In the second order of interpretation, the Spirit *inspires* a reader to read a text *prophetically to a community* in the light of what is found of God's working in the present. The text, in its historical account, remains authoritative in reading over-against the church. Such a prophetic re-reading of the text helps this community to apprehend God's present work in a way that gives a *different or new shape* to this deep picture of God and his ways with the world.

For example, Peter, speaking as an oracle of God after Pentecost, re-read Psalm 16:8–11 in his sermon to the people of Judea in Jerusalem. He opened the Scriptures to show that David had spoken prophetically of the resurrection of the Holy One (Acts 2:22–36).[23] Peter then proclaimed—to open the eyes of these Jews—that this Jesus of Nazarene, whom they had crucified, had resurrected and is alive; many witnesses had attested to this fact. He then connected that text with his context in a prophetic re-reading—that Holy One whom David prophesied of is now re-read prophetically, in the light of what is found of God's working in the present, as the Christ. A reading like *"this* Jesus is *that* Christ" significantly *changed the shape* of this picture of God for Jews and gentiles alike, so much so that many Jews could not apprehend its new shape. In

23. Luke follows the traditional ascription in the Hebrew and Greek texts of Ps 16 to David in Acts 2:25. Bruce argues for a messianic interpretation of Ps 16—that David prefigured himself as the Messiah who would come from his line, "and in whose name he spoke those words by the Spirit of prophecy" (Bruce, *Acts*, 65). How Luke understands the original sense of Ps 16, however, is not without dispute. Nonetheless, the main idea in this example is to illustrate *how* the Peter re-read the Hebrew Scripture—how he made his argument using Scripture "that the risen one is the Lord (2:25-31; 34–35), an argument from the testimony of eyewitnesses and the Spirit's present confirmation that Jesus has risen (2:32–33), with the resulting conclusion that Jesus is the Lord (2:36)" (Keener, *Acts*. See also Barrett, *Acts,* vol. 2).

this example, readers are apprehending the same truth of God, except now it has taken shape in Christ Jesus. The Spirit thus inducts readers in community to partner him in his present work in God's economy—to attend to what it *wants to be* saying and doing as a corporate body, only in the light of what God *is* saying and doing in the present.[24]

There are other examples of this second order interpretation in the New Testament. First, James re-read Amos 9:11–12 prophetically in the light of God's present working in Simeon Peter's story (Acts 15:15–18).[25] Speaking as an oracle of God himself, James pronounced the prophets to agree with Peter's story, not otherwise.[26] Then, in the fourth gospel, John

---

24. Contrast this with a first order of interpretation. Here, the Spirit draws a reader to attend to what s/he *wants to be* saying and doing, in the light of who God is and what God had said and done. The Spirit reveals scriptural truth in an inspiration, catching readers up in participation in an act of grace. However, this second order of interpretation also demands a kerygmatic reader to sustain a participation in divinity in flowing in the Spirit. Even though this is an act of grace, a reader can prepare to be found ready for God to work through him/her by allowing the Spirit to transform his/her disposition and disciplining himself/herself to practice flowing in the Spirit through daily kerygmatic devotion. Therefore, it is not surprising why many Christians today, including kerygmatic readers, may feel that they cannot, in all honesty, replicate Peter's hermeneutics. However, this example of a second order interpretation in an inspiration remains valid precisely because it remains an act of grace for God to choose whomever he pleases to reveal his work in the economy.

25. James read Amos 9:11–12 from the LXX. The variations between the Masoretic Text and the Greek text have made this reading difficult. For example, J. B. Lightfoot cites alterations in the LXX, reading "restore" for "possess" (as in "possess the remnant of Edom"), and "Adam" for "Edom," together with both additions and omissions (Lightfoot, *Acts*, I, 197–98). He notes, "The Hebrew says in effect that the tabernacle of David was and held sway over all the nations; the Greek, that all the nations should seek it, seek the Lord (see Alford)" (Lightfoot, *Acts*, 1:197–98; Alford, *New Testament*). While Peter and James were possibly familiar with the history of interpretation of the Hebrew Scripture, including the midrash, they independently gave a fresh interpretation in the Spirit here. Besides complications that arise from differences between the Hebrew Scripture and LXX, Barrett also cites interpretive issues in Acts 15:16—on whether Luke (or James) may have interpreted the prophecy of the restoration of the fallen tent of David to refer to the Messiah (with his resurrection), or, the restoration in the sense of the conversion of Israel. Such divergence of readings could imply, for decision making in the current context, that the way is now open for the gentiles to become the people of God, or, the conversion of the gentiles must defer to the mission for the conversion of the Jews (Barrett, *Acts*, 2:725–26).

26. Again, notwithstanding the various textual and interpretive challenges, the main idea that I try to illustrate with this example is this: James made his argument using Scripture, in the light of the testimonies of Paul, Barnabas, and Peter. That is, James used the apostles' testimonies to the presenting situation to interpret Scripture. This gives us the twin principle for what constitutes a valid reading in kerygmatic

opened the eyes of his readers to re-read prophetically that the Word is the One through whom all things (in the Genesis creation account) was made (see John's prologue in John 1:1–18). He also opened their eyes to make the connection that this Jesus Christ, whom John the Baptist testified of, is that Word who has now come in the flesh.[27] In both accounts, the apostles re-read scriptural texts prophetically even though the original authors or redactors would probably not have intended those texts to speak thus.[28]

The New Testament also gives us the authority to say that such prophetic re-readings are subject to prophets and apostles in the church. In Ephesians 3:1–10, Paul finds God's working in his present time as an unveiling of the mystery of this Christ Jesus, which had been hidden for ages. Moreover, he finds that God is using the church to reveal this truth in Christ Jesus to the world and the rulers and authorities in the heavenly places in the power of the Spirit. The Acts of the Apostles point to a coherence of this found scriptural truth across prophetic proclamations in the early church, by Peter, James, John, and Paul.

Finding truth in God's unfolding story in creation is subject to discernment by apostles and prophets. I note the Pauline formulation of ἐν πνεύματι, χάρις and δύναμις that accompany his proclamation of this revelation.[29] Here, unlike that for the first order interpretation, biblical

---

hermeneutics: a discernment of the realist claim(s) and the cogency of the contextual rightness in the light of what the Spirit is saying and doing in the world.

27. Beasley-Murray observes that in the beginning, which pre-existed the creation, God expresses himself through the Word; we see the Word's activity in creation, revelation, and redemption. The finality of this revelation of the glory of the Father, full of grace and truth, comes in the flesh in the Logos-Son (Beasley-Murray, "John," 16). Peder Borgen reads John 1:1–18 as a homily for the beginning of the creation account in Genesis (Borgen, "Logos," 115–30; Borgen, "Targumic Character," 288–95).

28. I note that these two examples are different in terms of the exegetical challenges they pose. The Acts 15 account is much more problematic. However, I am using these two accounts to illustrate what a prophetic re-reading might look like in the Spirit's inspiration.

29. In Eph 3:5, Paul acknowledges that the *mystery* of Christ has been revealed to his holy apostles and prophets in the Spirit (ἐν πνεύματι). These apostles and prophets, who are and who proclaim God's *logos*, are the foundation of God's house, Christ Jesus himself being the cornerstone (Eph 2:20). Kerygmatic hermeneutics acknowledges that these offices are Christ's grace (χάρις) (Eph 4:11–14). This χάρις is given to all the churches of the saints, where the spirits (πνεύμα) of prophets are subject or submitted to prophets, so judgment and discernment may be learnt by all that the church be encouraged (1 Cor 14:29–33). That is, Paul teaches that such discernment and learning (with correction) are done in a community of faith: prophets (and apostles) are also

scholarship plays a helpful but not as critical a role as reading the Scripture in the light of what God is doing and saying.[30] Such a reading *in the Spirit* requires one to transcend created causes and effects, including tradition and the history of scriptural interpretation. This second order interpretation, subject to discernment by apostles and prophets, is authoritative *for the church* in that they should hear, accept, and follow it.

In a third order interpretation, the Spirit enlivens and empowers readers' agency to embody truth in co-creation. Co-creation is a life-giving act of grace in the Spirit. This embodied witness to Christ often involves a performance of signs and miracles, healings and deliverances, and doing of all good. This creative proclamation of scriptural truth in the particularity of life—in the particularity of *how* a reader lives out a proclamation of the gospel of Jesus Christ, exercises gifts of healings and deliverances, performs signs and wonders, and doing all good—have two yields. First, this performed interpretation yields to readers an apprehension of a *fuller* picture of God and his ways with the world revealed in Scripture.[31] Compared to propositional truth, an embodiment of the same can effect an apprehension more efficaciously through discernment, intuition, reason, and senses altogether. This brings readers reflexively into a participation with the Other. Second, such an embodiment of scriptural truth also brings the world into an encounter with God. This embodiment, *logos* enfleshed, gives a *fuller* picture of God's unchanging truth that goes beyond mere proposition; this truth can be heard, seen, touched, and experienced.

Jesus Christ is the exemplar of a kerygmatic reader who flows in the Spirit in a third order interpretation in co-creation.[32] In proclaiming that the kingdom of God is at hand, Jesus performed various signs and miracles that manifested the glory of the Father. His disciples and some of those who saw and experienced them believed him while others rejected

---

historically becoming.

30. See section 4.2.1 above on how biblical scholarship is helpful in this account of how readers read Scripture in its otherness that retains its authority.

31. The church, the *body* of Christ, is the *fullness* of Christ. Christ fills and fulfils all members of this body in all ways (Eph 1:22–23).

32. This account of performative interpretation goes much further than what Lash speaks of in *Performing the Scriptures*. There, Lash speaks of a lived-out interpretation of Scripture in the liturgical life *of the church*. Here, kerygmatic hermeneutics goes further to speak of *how* a reader, as embodiment of scriptural truth, not only proclaims truth but interrupts the lives of other humans to bring them into an encounter with God.

him.³³ In each of Jesus's interpretive performance, the world was brought into a paradigmatic encounter with God. In every interruption into these people's lives, Jesus called for a response from all who experienced the glory of God. This *logos* enfleshed brings a breaking in of the divine, so people may catch a glimpse of the divine. This third order of scriptural interpretation in the Spirit is life-giving.

Though there are distinctive characteristics to the three ways of speaking of a Spirit-led scriptural interpretation, one may also see something of a spectrum across illumination, inspiration, and co-creation. That is, the Spirit reveals scriptural truth in ways that need not be mutually exclusive. Every instance of an illumination of Scripture for what a reader wants to do in the present contains an element of inspiration of what the Spirit wants to be doing and is doing in the world. Every instance of inspiration that reveals prophetically what God is doing in the world contains an element of illumination for what this reader will want to do that allows him/her to participate in God's project to varying extents. As well, every instance of an illumination and inspiration may also contain an element of co-creation that is life-giving when this reader enacts what the Spirit is revealing of Scripture for the present. These three ways of speaking of such Spirit-led revelation of scriptural truth map to a spectrum that orders the shape of *how* this reader is being caught up *more and more* to participate in divinity. While a reader may be more concerned with what s/he wants to do in his/her situation in an illumination, s/he would be more concerned to speak of what God wants to do in the world in an inspiration. In co-creation, a reader is caught up in intoxication in the flow of the Spirit to enact the Spirit's life-giving work.

Second, there is also a spectrum in the sense of *how* the Spirit enables a different scriptural reading in each new instance. The Spirit works with words already given and with meanings already grasped, even if he does new things with those materials, since every instance in which readers read Scripture is new. This divine agency can open up the text to admit figural reading without causing the text to lose its authority.³⁴ This

---

33. See, e.g., Jesus's turning water into wine in John 2:1–11; Jesus's encounter with Nicodemus in John 3, the Samarian woman at the well and the Samaritans, and the royal official in John 4; Jesus's healing of the sick man at Bethesda in John 5; Jesus's feeding of the five thousand in Galilee and walking on water in John 6; Jesus's healing of the man born blind in John 9; and Jesus's raising Lazarus from the dead in John 11.

34. On figural reading, see, e.g., Dawson, *Christian Figural Reading and the Fashioning of Identity*; Hays, *Echoes of Scripture in the Gospels*; Radner, *Time and the Word. Figural Reading of Christian Scriptures*. Radner recovers a creative, traditional

divine agency gives the otherness to such scriptural reading in the Spirit. It gives a coherence or integrity to the reading of this picture of God and his ways with the world.

Richard Hays cites the priority of the Spirit's hermeneutical agency and its coherent outcome.[35] Specifically, the Scripture and reader mediate the revelatory work of the Spirit, a self-gift of God. On the other hand, it is

---

(patristic) practice in figural interpretation of Scripture in lieu of historical criticism. "'Figural' . . . refers to the 'everything' of God's act in creation, as it is 'all' given in the Scriptures. And 'figural reading' of the Bible is that reading that receives this divinely-given 'allness'—who is the Christ." It takes the comprehensive meaning of a "spiritual" sense held by the Fathers, as contrasted with what is "historical" or "literal" (Radner, *Time and the Word*, 7). Figural reading is not really a "method"; it is "about the nature of a world that God has made in relation to which a certain divine text rises up, hovers over, and orders. There is a creative reading of 'figures' of Scripture differently—whether typology, allegory, tropology, and anagogy—drawing "from one set of referents or beings to another, across times and spaces." This reading seeks "to open up the created world to those visible windows onto God's eternal being that are grasped otherwise in the Scriptures" (Radner, *Time and the Word*, 80). Hays, in reading the Gospel of John figuratively, concludes, "John's figural hermeneutic allows him to articulate his extraordinary (and polemical) claim that all of Israel's Scripture actually bears witness to Jesus: 'If you believed Moses, you would believe me, for he wrote about me' (John 5:46). Thus, even more comprehensively than the other Gospels, John understands the Old Testament as a vast matrix of symbols prefiguring Jesus. All this works hermeneutically because, at the beginning and the end of the day, Jesus is the *Logos*, the Word present before creation. All creation breathes with *his* life . . . For John the Evangelist, therefore, all of Israel's Scripture is a figural web woven with latent prefigurations of the One without whom not one thing came into . . . being" (Hays, *Echoes of Scripture*, 344). In kerygmatic hermeneutics, kerygmatic readers who now can look backwards to Jesus Christ, the Word enfleshed, are therefore read as *logos* enfleshed, an embodied witness to Jesus Christ.

35. Hays comments on the question of whether it is the Spirit who illumines scriptural text or whether it is Scripture that measures and constrains one's experience of the Spirit, "Paul's unflinching answer, to the dismay of his more cautious kinsmen then and now, is to opt for the hermeneutical priority of Spirit-experience. This choice leads him, to be sure, not to a rejection of Scripture but to a charismatic rereading, whose persuasive power will rest precariously on his ability to demonstrate a congruence between the scriptural text and the community summoned and shaped by his proclamation" (Hays, *Echoes of Scripture*, 108). Similarly, Fowl argues for the hermeneutical significance of the Spirit. He observes, "Experience of the Spirit provides the lenses through which Scripture is read rather than vice-versa. This is perhaps the most significant point the New Testament has to make about the hermeneutical significance of the Spirit; and it runs against the grain of modern interpretive presumptions" (Fowl, "How the Spirit Reads," 358). While Hays does allude to reading Scripture backwards, "in the light of the resurrection *under the guidance of the Spirit*" (italics mine), he does not go far enough to clarify *how* this reading under the guidance of the Spirit works or *what* it looks like (Hays, *Reading Backwards*, 86).

also undeniable that the key concerns raised earlier on the indeterminacy or discernment of the Spirit has continued to lead many to obliterate or restrain the access of the Spirit to believers' lives with perhaps a subconscious subjection of the Spirit to reason and objectivity. This proposition that the Spirit and his works are indeterminate and hence such engagement is to be avoided can possibly be self-fulfilling if the Spirit were consciously boxed out of the life of believers and the community of faith. Therefore, Paul's prohibition—do not quench the Spirit—speaks of the freedom and contingency in created agency and created causes that may be observed in the narratives of those being transformed by the Spirit.

In the next section, I further discuss Spirit epistemology and readers' power and efficacy in the apprehension and reception of scriptural truth in these three orders of interpretation.

4.3 An Epistemology of Kerygmatic Hermeneutics

Jesus therefore answered them, and said, "My teaching is not Mine, but His who sent Me. If any man is willing to do His will, he shall know of the teaching, whether it is of God, or whether I speak from Myself. He who speaks from himself seeks his own glory; but He who is seeking the glory of the One who sent Him, He is true, and there is no unrighteousness in Him."
(John 7:16–18 NAS)

How may any reader (or the world) know whether claims to speak for God were true? Kerygmatic hermeneutics takes its epistemology for that knowing from Jesus's teaching.[36] Jesus teaches that to know whether his

---

36. In John 7:14–18, Jesus taught from the Hebrew Scripture even though he was not schooled in any rabbinic teachings. By this standard, he would be deemed as uneducated in Hebrew Scripture. See Beasley-Murray, *John*, 108; Brown, *Community*, 316; Thompson, *John*, 171. Notwithstanding, Jesus teaches how readers may interpret Scripture, as well as discern if such a teaching is from God. Jesus did not appeal to rabbinic authorities. Instead, Jesus said he was merely teaching what he heard from his Father God. Therefore, He appealed to the authority of his Father God in his re-reading of Scriptures. He claimed a relationship with God by which he apprehended God in Scripture reading. Jesus laid out two criteria for discerning if such a claim to a re-reading were true. First, its truthfulness is evident to those who *desire to do God's will*. That is, these will share the same desire with Jesus. These will have the same mind and do the same things to please the Father; these will know that what Jesus taught is true because these would also teach what they hear from the Father, and the otherness

claims to speak from his Father (and not himself) were in fact true we could observe if Jesus had sought to glorify his Father and not himself.[37] I argue that we can know whether claims to speak for God were true by applying this same principle of otherness as a test in discernment against self-deception and self-serving tendencies—we can observe if these readers seek to glorify God and not themselves. As these readers flow in the Spirit, they are, like the Spirit, non-self-referential; they bear witness to Christ.[38]

How may readers of Scripture *know* scriptural truth in God? In this epistemology, kerygmatic readers know what Scripture is saying about God because they know the Spirit personally—this Spirit who first inspired the original authors or redactors and who continues to open the eyes of readers to apprehend the same deep picture of God and his ways with the world. Therefore, readers can appeal to the authority of the Spirit because readers are apprehending what the Spirit is revealing to them from Scripture about God and what he is saying and doing in the world. Readers apprehend what the Spirit is saying and doing, and what he wants them saying and doing with reference to scriptural texts. Here, the Spirit is free to use some, or all, hermeneutical principles like Scripture, tradition, experience, reason, and every human efficacy, in an act of grace. This epistemology of kerygmatic hermeneutics is therefore concerned with revelation and apprehension, and reception and performative interpretation in the Spirit.

Kerygmatic hermeneutics is about *knowing* what to say, how to act and live in the Spirit. There are different understandings of what is involved in responsibly searching for truth as one does these. Some epistemological approaches may be concerned with the revelation and

---

of God means that what they hear from their Father would be what Jesus would have heard from his Father. These readers can discern if Jesus's scriptural interpretations were true. Second, the reader (as in Jesus) seeks only to glorify the One who sends him/her. That is, there is an objectivity to the intended outcome of the re-reading of Scripture.

37. Moreover, these hearers who could discern such claims would be those who were personally willing to do God's will. In a later teaching on how his disciples could *know* his Father God, Jesus teaches that they can *know* by observing him and his life because he is the embodied witness to his Father. Moreover, disciples *know* by the evidence of works that can validate his words that are his Father's words (John 14:8–11).

38. Recall my discussion on the work of the Spirit in section 3.1—The Spirit reveals Christ (and Christ glorifies his Father). I pick up this thread again in my discussion of kerygmatic criticism in chapter 6.

reception of, for example, a set of fact claims about what took place in history. Kerygmatic hermeneutics, however, is concerned with the revelation, apprehension and reception of what God is doing here and now, and what God is asking God's people to do here and now. It opens up human participation in divinity on this side of heaven for the new creation in Christ.

Kerygmatic hermeneutics is located primarily in the spirit realm and transcends the horizons of the author or redactor, the text, the reader, and the community of faith. That is, what a kerygmatic hermeneutics reader is looking for when reading is guidance on how to live in the Spirit here and now—a discernment of how to act in the specific circumstances in which s/he finds herself. That goes beyond looking for the meaning intended by the author or the redactor, who (of course) knew nothing of the reader's own situation. It goes beyond the reader in the sense that it is not simply asking what the reader, as an autonomous individual, happens to make of the text. It goes beyond the community in that it is not simply asking what sense the community habitually makes of this text. It goes beyond all that because it is seeking what life in the Spirit demands right here, right now. Of course, the Spirit is guiding the reader into that truth in part by means of a text that does have an author and redactors, and which is approached in certain ways by the community of faith. The reader who is seeking the truth of the Spirit for today is also someone who is reading this text in the light of his/her existing experience and knowledge, and so on—but the ultimate focus is on something that goes beyond all of that. Therefore, epistemological categories in kerygmatic hermeneutics relate to *how* humans can know God in his self-revelation in the spiritual realm.[39]

In this section, I propose three epistemological categories in an appropriation of truth in the Spirit: illumination, inspiration, and co-creation. In the last section, I formulate these as three orders of what the Spirit wants to be saying and doing in readers in the present. I now

---

39. See Webster, *Holy Scripture*, and Barth, *Church Dogmatics*. Both argue that the doctrine of revelation has to be informed by the doctrine of the triune God. Webster gives his thesis statement: "*revelation is the self-presentation of the triune God, the free work of sovereign mercy in which God wills, establishes and perfects saving fellowship with himself in which humankind comes to know, love and fear him above all things*" (Webster, *Holy Scripture*, 13). Barth argues, "God, the Revealer, is identical with His act in revelation and also identical with its effect" (Barth, *Church Dogmatics*; Barth, "Revelation," 1:296) For this reason, I have advanced scriptural truth as the general truth claims that are embodied in God himself.

discuss these same three categories of the Spirit's work in revelation as what readers are learning in apprehension, reception, and performance in the Spirit. Therefore, these categories relate to the power and efficacy of readers' active relating with the Spirit to do God's work in the world.

Illumination is a *fresh and timely interpretation* of scriptural truth as the Spirit leads readers to read a text differently in each new situation—to hear what the given word is saying in that situation. In the Spirit's illumination, readers read a text and their particular situation interdependently. They discern their present situation in relation to a particular text. The Spirit opens their eyes to connect the dots, so they learn to read the text in a new way for the present. Readers then say in the Spirit, that *this* event that they now encounter in the present is *that* spoken about in some passage of Scripture. They make a "this" is "that" connection in kerygmatic hermeneutics.

This discernment of a connection between context and text works *with* the ways in which the text has already been read in a history of interpretation—that is, with meanings it would have had for its original audiences, or the meanings it has had for subsequent generations of readers. The Spirit catches readers up with him in a process of creative appropriation of Scripture for what it means for living out the proclamation of Christ here and now. The Spirit allows the same text to give different significance to different readers at the same time, or different significance to the same readers at different times. Through the Spirit's illumination, readers apprehend *more and more* the same picture of God and his ways with the world.

Inspiration is a *fresh* Spirit-breathed *revelation* of scriptural truth being found in a prophetic elucidation of God's ongoing work in creation. Here, the Spirit catches readers up in the Spirit to seat them with Christ in the heavenly places. From this vantage point, readers discern what *new* things God is doing in the present that changes the shape of God and his ways with the world that has till then been revealed in Scripture. The Spirit opens readers' eyes to connect this *new* work with particular text(s). Readers learn to re-read the text(s) in a *new* way that opens them up in *found* theology for the present. In this re-reading, readers speak prophetically, whether in foretelling or forth telling, as oracles of God. Readers also apprehend what God wants them to do to participate in this *new* revelation of scriptural truth, for the bigger purposes in the Kingdom of God.

When God is doing *new* things that change the shape of revealed truth, looking back at a history of interpretation of Scripture to re-read a text may be helpful but it will not be adequate. Something more is needed. In these situations, readers depend even more on the Spirit to inspire afresh scriptural texts in finding new meaning in Scripture for what new things God is doing in the present. These revelations are indeed *new* in relation to what has been revealed of the will and purposes of God in Scripture.

The paradigm of such inspirational reading is the early church's reading of Israel's Scripture in the *new* context created by Christ's work. We also observe other biblical examples when the apostles read against Israel's Scripture prophetically in interpreting anew. Examples include the Pentecost phenomenon when the Spirit and the charisms fell on the early church believers, the role of circumcision as a mark of the people of God after gentiles responded to the gospel of Jesus Christ, and the role of the Spirit in scriptural interpretation after the Spirit was given after Jesus's ascension. Since the Spirit is Lord of creation and the church, hermeneutical questions of what God is doing in writing his story in humankind would also be asked of the church. Does the church have a prophetic voice as in the days of Samuel, Daniel, Isaiah, Jeremiah, Ezekiel, Joel in the Old Testament, and then Jesus, Stephen, Peter, John, and Paul in the New Testament?

Co-creation is the Spirit-empowered lived-out interpretation of scriptural truth that is life-giving. This mode of interpretation of scriptural truth is performed as life; it is incarnate in the readers as embodied truth. This mode of interpretation is life itself and is life-giving to those who receive this truth.

Co-creation is accompanied by signs—pointing to both miracles that are a breaking of natural laws as well as miracles that are not. Readers, in living out this truth, can expect to call into being signs and wonders, healings and deliverances in doing all good in the contingency of the particular. The signs constitute the interpretation itself; they are not merely responses to Scripture. The signs also enhance an objectivity to the interpretation; they confirm that God is working out his work in and through these readers. This mode of interpretation does not simply find a connection between the text and the context but *makes* a connection between the text and the context. It acts to transform the context in such a way that the transformation resonates with Scripture, and Scripture and this action interpret one another. This mode of embodying scriptural

KERYGMATIC HERMENEUTICS: A THEOLOGY   103

truth in the Spirit gives a fullness to this deep picture of God and his ways with the world.

The power and efficacy of this mode of scriptural interpretation—co-creation, just as for illumination and inspiration—is predicated on readers' relationship with the Spirit. However, this dependence on the power and efficacy of the Spirit's life-giving agency is most acute and visible when embodied witnesses to Christ exercise their creative imagination to embody *and* give life to a particular context that resonates with Scripture. Therefore, the ordering of these three modes of interpretation—in the order of illumination, inspiration, and co-creation—reflects the increasing power and efficacy of readers' active relating with the Spirit to do God's work in the world. Kerygmatic readers exercise creativity to embody scriptural truth. This embodiment brings humans into an impactful encounter with God who gives life. For example, Jesus, Word incarnate, in proclaiming the gospel and the kingdom of God, demonstrates creative imagination in performing healing on a man born blind—he spat on the ground to make clay of the spittle before applying clay to the blind man's eyes (John 9). In addition, he instructed the blind man to go to the pool of Siloam and wash.[40] Finally, Jesus proclaims the purpose of his coming to this world: that the blind may see and the seeing may be blind.[41] Jesus could have simply sat down at the synagogue to teach this truth: that one can only see God with spiritual discernment ("eyes") that grows one's faith. However, he did not. He creatively performed an object lesson instead. How many different ways could kerygmatic readers perform the same truth efficaciously in every situation, so the performance resonates with scriptural truth in all its fullness?[42] Since all interpretations properly

40. Beasley-Murray comments that these "actions of Jesus, including the command to wash in Siloam" (narrated in vv1–7) "were signs to aid the blind man's faith" (Beasley-Murray. *John*, 151–56). That is, these signs point to God, whom the blind man should take faith in. In our epistemology, this sign, in a co-creative act of giving physical healing and spiritual salvation to the man born blind, constitutes the interpretation of scriptural truth itself—*this* Jesus is *that* Christ who is to come from God. This sign is not a response to Scripture. In this sense, this sign (Jesus) and what it signified (the Son of Man) are one in embodiment.

41. Thompson shows how the dominant motif of (physical) blindness has acquired a figurative meaning as well. She observes, "As the man gains his sight, he also gains greater insight into Jesus's identity: sight becomes a figure for the insight that perceives the significance of what Jesus has done and who he is . . . And though the light has come into the world for salvation and not for judgment, not all will see or want to see (3:17–21)" (Thompson, *John*, 204).

42. It is in this context of the giving of the Spirit that Jesus says, "Truly, truly, I say

have a performative element, there is something of a spectrum; what I am calling co-creation here brings this performative element to the fore.

In the next section, I further discuss the motivation for a Spirit epistemology that flows from our theology of kerygmatic hermeneutics.

4.3.1 Spirit epistemology

The goal of reading on a specific occasion is, for kerygmatic hermeneutics, discernment of how to live here and now, in response to the text. However, the present moment is always specific; it is never simply a repetition of what has happened in the past. Therefore, no past interpretation of the text can simply be lifted from the past and used in the present. In fact, no accumulation of earlier valid interpretations exhausts that task: they may *inform* how we read and respond to the text here and now, but they do not *determine* it. Something new—something creative that goes beyond the history of interpretation—is therefore needed in order to respond to the text in the present. For kerygmatic hermeneutics, that should not simply be *our* creativity. That is, it should not simply be our independent decision or invention about what we want to do with the text—because we are seeking for what *God* would have us do here and now. We need to think about this creativity as, ideally, a work of the Spirit in us. Therefore, this research proposes a Spirit epistemology in kerygmatic hermeneutics.

The Spirit speaks to a reader through Scripture in the contingency of the particular even in particular interpretations where there is a good deal of continuity with previous ones. Even if the present moment appears to be a repetition of the past, drawing from a history of valid scriptural interpretations may still not speak directly to the context except to add to the ever-growing list of valid interpretations from various readers' contexts. This is because each valid interpretation, including that of the author or redactor in the scriptural text, has been endogenously determined from a somewhat different set of socio-economic, political, and spiritual contexts. Therefore, what evolves as an appropriate response in a given text or context may not be appropriate for what God would want us do here and now, even if the *same* scriptural truth is upheld.[43] In this

---

to you, he who believes in Me, the works that I do, he will do also; and greater works than these he will do; because I go to the Father. Whatever you ask in My name, that will I do, so that Father may be glorified in the Son. If you ask Me anything in My name, I will do it" (John 14:12–14, NAS).

43. One example could be how the ecclesial discourse on slavery has evolved over

instance, a reader needs to make that hermeneutical move in the Spirit from meanings in a text to scriptural truth before re-contextualizing that truth for a new context. This is the work of the Spirit in a reader.

There is a greater hermeneutical challenge when the present moment is *more* than an apparent repetition of the past, when there is an even stronger element of a discontinuity in the order of things.[44] In Acts 10, the work of the Spirit in determining a radically new reading of what God would have his disciples do there and then was central. When Peter went into prayer, God showed him a vision in a trance. Then the Spirit directed Peter to go up to Cornelius's household in Caesarea. Flowing in the Spirit, Peter proclaimed the rhema of Jesus Christ with the Spirit falling on all who listened. These gentiles were baptized in the Spirit, speaking in tongues and praising God. Reading the Spirit, Peter connected "this" gift of the Spirit to the gentiles (Acts 10:44–46) with "that" in the earlier scriptural re-reading of the Pentecost experience for the Jews (Acts 2:1–21).[45] Here, it is again the creative work of the Spirit to illumine a reading of 'this' is 'that'. Beyond illumining Scriptures so that

---

the centuries. This is a complex theological issue and deserves separate and careful reading beyond this research. Nevertheless, I note that we could be making judgments now in the plain sense of the text when we are indebted to previous discussion between the then (of the ancient authors and audience) and the now (of the present readers). Specifically, slavery in the ancient world was socially and institutionally embedded while there is no structural regulation of slavery now.

44. Quash's account of "finding" is about this need to read the Spirit afresh for what new things God is now doing in creation. Quash says, "The baptism of the Gentile centurion, Cornelius, and his household under the guidance of the Holy Spirit in Acts 10 shows how a new theology had to be found then, and yet it is a story that continues to suggest the possibility of discoveries and surprises close at hand now. Such examples of Found Theology at work powerfully heighten our sense that in the age of the pouring out of the Spirit, we must live in the expectation of more findings still to come" (Quash, *Found Theology*, 5).

45. Lightfoot aptly observes, "Moreover, as Cornelius' house was the first fruit of the Gentiles, as the Jewish converts of the day of Pentecost were of the Jews, we find the two events brought into parallelism. The outpouring of the Spirit (with the external token of the gift of tongues) is declared by St. Peter to be the same as that manifested on the day of Pentecost" (Lightfoot, *Acts*, 157). Barrett observes this of Luke in his redaction of the Spirit baptism event in Acts 10:45—"Luke however is thinking primarily of the Gentiles present, who, on the basis of nothing but the proclamation of Jesus, had manifestly been brought within the scope of salvation" (Barrett, *Acts*, 529). Reading both Peter and Luke, I observe that there seems to be this repetitive moving, in a to-ing and fro-ing, between what the Spirit is doing with the Jews first, and then the gentiles. The apostles were reading the miraculous signs of Spirit baptism and using them to validate the Spirit's work of giving life in a new work of salvation.

readers may apprehend more and more the picture of God and his ways in an outpouring of the Spirit in the present, the Spirit *also* inspires Peter to prophesy in unveiling the new shape of scriptural truth with the giving of the Spirit. That is, God has graciously extended his salvation by faith in Christ Jesus to both Jews and gentiles alike in a new order through the baptism of the Spirit. Responding to this scriptural truth at work, Peter ordered these gentile believers to be baptized in water there and then. It took one flowing in the Spirit like Peter to discern a radically new thing that God was doing; he then responded with an apostle's direction for a new practice to embrace a gentile church.

The work of the Spirit is central in both of these instances where a past reading may inform without determining a reading in the present, whether there be a good deal of continuity or discontinuity. Another good hermeneutical example that demonstrates how sometimes these two instances could be at work *at the same time* concerns the practice of circumcision in Israel. Moses commanded this as a sign of the covenant between God and his people (Gen 17:9–4; Lev 12:3). In Acts 15, the council of apostles and elders in Jerusalem met to look into the debate of whether circumcision and the keeping of the Law are necessary for gentiles' salvation, when these responded to the gospel of Jesus Christ.[46] In that one hermeneutical act, the Spirit opened the eyes of the apostles and elders to connect the Spirit's work in the gentile believers from the testimonies of Peter, Paul and Barnabas with that in the Jewish converts at Pentecost—there was the same outpouring of the Holy Spirit.

In the Acts 15 account, there was both a fresh interpretation of scriptural truth in an illumination as well as a fresh revelation of scriptural truth in an inspiration.[47] First, there was a fresh interpretation to

---

46. See, e.g., Barrett, *Acts*; Keener, *Acts*; Lightfoot, *Acts*. Barrett compares this Lukan account with Paul's account in Gal 2:1–14, "The correspondence is not exact for in Acts the Jerusalem travellers to Antioch appear first, the Council follows; in Galatians the order is reversed. Luke's order has the effect—an intended effect?—of representing the disagreement as only temporary, whereas Galatians shows that it was not ended by the Council, and was intense at the time the letter was written" (Barrett, *Acts*, 697). Notwithstanding various interpretive challenges, Barrett's commentary on Acts 15:11 concludes that what Peter was disputing here was the need to obey the law in order to be saved; "whether the Jews kept it for other reasons was a secondary matter" (Barrett, *Acts*, 721). I note that Peter's to-ing and fro-ing between the events of Spirit baptism first among the Jews and then the gentiles had perhaps led him to conclude that God has introduced a new order of salvation through the baptism of the Holy Spirit.

47. Barrett observes that the Acts 15:6–29 account gives a decision-making process that appears to be paradigmatic for the early Christian church. He observes, "This

the practice of circumcision as the sign of the covenant. These re-read the Abrahamic covenant (arising from a relationship between God and his people) in the Spirit rather than by the letter of the law of Moses. Second, the apostles and elders also discerned from a reading of the Spirit and Scripture a prophetic *finding* of a new covenant in Christ Jesus. The second hermeneutical *finding* then questions the practice of circumcision and the observance of the Law as requirements of this new covenant.

This was an interdependent move between the text and context in this account. After listening intently in the Spirit, James triangulated the witness of Peter, the work of the Spirit through signs and wonders performed among these gentile believers at the hands of Paul and Barnabas, and Scripture. The Spirit opened James's eyes to connect what the Spirit was doing in the present with the scriptural text in Amos 9:11–12. He then determined that 'this' enfolding of gentiles into God's covenantal relationship with humans is 'that' enfolding of the nations as a rebuilding of the tabernacle of David in Amos 9:11–12.[48] James then pronounced that these words of the Prophets agree with Peter's witness that God had taken from these gentiles a people for his name. The text informed what was in

---

paragraph . . . is the best example of a pattern that occurs several times in Acts and represents the way in which Luke conceived the progress of Christianity. In this pattern a difficulty is encountered; steps are taken to deal with it; not only is the problem solved but a notable advance takes place as a result" (Barrett, *Act*, 709). In this instance, the Holy Spirit is centrally involved in this decision-making process.

48. Recall our earlier discussion on possible readings of Acts 15:16–17 in section 4.2.3. Among various textual challenges, Barrett discusses whether Luke (or James) may have interpreted the prophecy of the restoration of the fallen tent of David to refer to the Messiah (with his resurrection), or, the restoration in the sense of the conversion of Israel. These two possible readings could respectively imply, for James and the decision making in the current context, that the way is now open for the gentiles to become the people of God, or, the conversion of the gentiles must defer to the mission for the conversion of the Jews (Barrett, *Acts*, 2:725–26). How did James decide? I note James re-read Amos 9:11–12 in the light of the apostles' witness (he was probably aware of the textual challenges from his use of the LXX). Paul, Barnabas, and Peter not only witnessed to what the Spirit was doing in and through believers but were themselves agencies of the Spirit to bring gentiles to faith in Jesus Christ. This argument (that re-reads Scripture in Amos 9:11–12) for the enfolding of the gentile converts was more consonant with what the Spirit was discerned to be doing in and through the apostles. That is, this reading drew its validity from a realist claim that was discerned *and* a cogency that carried contextual rightness in the light of the Spirit's working in the present. This re-reading was again tested and evaluated against competing readings by a *community* of apostles and elders. This argument had also found acceptance by the whole church in Jerusalem. This re-reading was thus authoritative for all to follow in the Jerusalem church.

the present as it then spoke prophetically that "this rebuilt tabernacle of David *is* the church of Christ, the abode of David's son".[49]

The council at Jerusalem *collectively* apprehended the fresh revelation of scriptural truth—the inception of a new covenant in Jesus Christ; the Jews are also to be saved by grace through the Lord Jesus Christ in the same way that the gentiles are. This scriptural interpretation that is made in the flow of the Spirit is *both* an *illumination* and *inspiration* of the Spirit. Moses's law of circumcision did not determine the practice in the present. The Spirit gave a new shape to God's covenant with humankind and what this then means for believers to say and do in the there and then. Here, an inspiration in the Spirit informs on a fresh interpretation of scriptural truth concerning the practice of circumcision.

The Jerusalem council of apostles and elders, full of the Spirit, had adopted a Spirit epistemology that reads the Spirit of truth (Acts 15:28–29; also John 14:16–17; 25–26; 16:12–14). In this Spirit epistemology, knowing God is an act of grace because the Spirit enables and empowers all human efficacy to knowing what God has revealed. In the Acts account, the Spirit opened the eyes of the Jerusalem council (and the church) collectively and shifted the structures by which they interpreted the world and Scripture, and apprehended God and his ways with the world. What emerged from the council's deliberation was a collective decision attributable to the Spirit and worded in a language that is "suitable for a decree".[50] This reading in the Spirit carried authority for the early Christian church.

---

49. Lightfoot notes the authority of James's judgment in Acts 15:19—"ἐγώ κρίνω Authoritative, but not necessarily final. The circumstances do not allow the latter" (Lightfoot, *Acts of the Apostles*, 1:199). Barrett observes that James is "at least acting as a chairman and expressing in his own words the sense of the meeting. If Luke is right in the picture at which he hints James occupies in the assembly a position if not of pre-eminence at least of great prominence." The apostles and elders in the council at Jerusalem subsequently collectively confirmed the decision that the gentile converts must not be pestered; that is, the demands of the full legal observance must not be made although a gentile convert must have a similar appearance to that of a Jewish Christian (Barrett, *Acts*, 2:729). Instead, these will be asked to follow basic and minimal observance for table fellowship to maintain that unity with Jewish Christians. These necessary qualifications are not moral rules (Keener, *Acts*, 2258).

50. Keener observes, "What is remarkable is not the literary form but the content, especially who participates in the decree: this matter seemed good to the Holy Spirit as well as to them. This statement provides a pneumatological climax in Acts: the Spirit was promised to empower witnesses for the Gentile mission (Acts 1:8), guided them to the nations, in a proleptic sense, even at Pentecost (2:5–11), expressed empowerment by providing genuine foreign languages unknown to the speakers (2:4: 10:46; 19:6),

In this section, I have argued for a Spirit epistemology that flows naturally from kerygmatic theology. What is significant is that the early church could discern, and so know, what the work of the Spirit was. That is, the early church appropriated the Spirit's work in revealing God's truth through illumination, inspiration, and co-creation. The question remains: *How* does the church appropriate the Spirit's agency in revealing scriptural truth? I discuss this in the next section.

4.3.2 Apprehension and reception

We ask, what do kerygmatic readers in community need to do to appropriate the Spirit's agency in revealing scriptural truth through illumination, inspiration, and co-creation? The Spirit *illumines* Scripture for readers' apprehension in every new situation, *inspires* readers to speak as oracles of God, and *co-creates* with these as an embodied witness to Jesus Christ.[51] In this section, we consider what readers in community do in the apprehension and reception of scriptural truth that the Spirit reveals in the present.

First, a kerygmatic community learns to *apprehend* the Spirit and his work in the present.[52] Kerygmatic hermeneutics is about this leap from various senses of meanings of a text to the scriptural truth that the

---

initiated the Gentile mission in 8:29 and 10:19, and confirmed it in 10:44–47. Now the same Spirit has led the Jerusalem church to a theology that welcomes Gentiles" (Keener, *Acts,* 2291).

51. I recapitulate the meanings of these terms for easy reference: *Illumination is a fresh interpretation of scriptural truth in givenness as the Spirit leads readers to read a text differently in each new situation—to hear what the given word is saying in that situation.* It is a generative experience in *givenness;* it generates fresh significance for a text that opens up new possibilities for transformation in a reader's structures of consciousness. *Inspiration is a fresh Spirit-breathed revelation of scriptural truth being found in a prophetic elucidation of God's ongoing work in creation.* It animates a new reading of God and the pattern of God's ongoing work in the world. *Co-creation is the Spirit-empowered lived-out interpretation of scriptural truth that is life giving.* This performative interpretation transforms the context, so it resonates with the text in a reading that is life giving.

52. Johnson observes that reading a text is primarily guided by a reading of the Spirit. Johnson says, "What is remarkable, however, is that the text is confirmed by the narrative, not the narrative by the Scripture. As Peter had come to a new understanding of Jesus' words because of the gift of the Spirit, so here the Old Testament is illuminated and interpreted by the narrative of God's activity in the present" (Johnson, *Decision Making,* 84).

text signifies.⁵³ Kerygmatic reading acknowledges hermeneutical challenges in reading a text when meanings of words could have changed.⁵⁴ A reading of scriptural truth in the Spirit—beyond a reading of a text and its meaning enables a reader to overstep the challenges posed by any discontinuities in time, concept, and purpose.⁵⁵

To illustrate the dynamism of an apprehension of the Spirit, I liken illumination, inspiration, and co-creation to three modes of a kerygmatic reader's dancing with the Spirit. This dynamism is central to an epistemology of a Spirit-led interpretation of Scripture. When a reader is caught up in the Spirit's intoxication, there flows a moment-to-moment interaction between a reader and the Spirit. In this interaction, a reader becomes an active partner in the dance; s/he is not merely passively led.⁵⁶ This reader co-creates a dance in the Spirit; s/he wafts rhythmically and creatively. This dance takes a life of its own in a participation in divinity and revelation of truth.

---

53. See Kelsey, *Eccentric Existence*. Kelsey argues that a metaphorical use of "translation" can stretch the concept into unintelligibility, as it obscures the fact that there may be a *conceptual discontinuity* between what a biblical text says and what a theological proposal says. Kerygmatic hermeneutics acknowledges this potentiality. It also argues that reading the Spirit is *not* a "translation" in this hermeneutical sense. It is a moment-to-moment relating with and flowing in the Spirit.

54. For example, Lash gives an illustration of how meanings may change over time when one is held to the same narrative or text. He explains, "If, in thirteenth-century Italy, you wandered around in a coarse brown gown, with a cord round your middle, your 'social location' was clear: your dress said that you were one of the poor. If, in twentieth-century Cambridge, you wonder around in a coarse brown gown, with a cord round your middle, your social location is curious: your dress now says, not that you are one of the poor, but that you are some kind of oddity in the business of 'religion.' Your dress now declares, not your solidarity with the poor, but your amiable eccentricity" (Lash, *Way to Emmaus*, 54).

55. Nicholas Lash and Krister Stendahl each discusses a typical hermeneutical problem in post modernism. Lash raises the interesting question of how martyrdom may be recognized in current day context for which the Spirit's illumination may be needed (Lash, *Way to Emmaus*, 75–92). Similarly, Stendahl, who advocates that a reader navigates from "what the text meant" to "what the text means," writes on a hermeneutical challenge that provoked him while he was a doctoral student in the early 1950s. He describes the challenge that plausibly calls for the Spirit's inspiration for the here and now: Does the Bible allow for the ordination of women in the Church of Sweden? (Stendahl, "Selections from 'Biblical Theology,'" 239–52).

56. Kerygmatic hermeneutics is a non-competitive account of divine and human agency. Here, humans' complete dependence upon the God's action is not shown in their passivity, but in their activity. A kerygmatic reader's action—his/her creativity—can be one of the modes in which s/he is receiving and participating in God's action.

This principle of non-competition of divine and human agencies in kerygmatic hermeneutics resonates with Tanner's project on *Jesus, Humanity and the Trinity*.[57] The sovereignty of God undergirds Spirit epistemology. Human, as free acting agency, is also a way of God's acting in the world.[58] At the human level, a kerygmatic reader may appear as if s/he were being led, sometimes leading, else being locked in-step with the Spirit. In first mode of reader-Spirit relating, *the Spirit leads* a kerygmatic reader in illumination that "this" in the present is "that" in scriptural text. In second mode of reader-Spirit relating, a kerygmatic reader dances *in-step* with the Spirit in a *finding* and gives inspiration as truth is *found*. While the first two modes of reader-Spirit relating concern interpretive speech and text, the third mode involves these and more. It involves an interpretive performing of *logos* that is incarnate in the reader. *A kerygmatic reader* acts as if s/he *leads* the Spirit and co-creates with him to bring the Kingdom of God into the contingency of the particular. Summarizing, while a kerygmatic reader learns to read *and* flow in the Spirit—whether leading the Spirit, being led by him else being locked in-step with him—s/he also learns to apprehend more and more deeply and fully this shape of God and his ways with the world. While we are clear that there is genuinely creative human action that makes something truly new happen, there is not a moment when we can deny that all this is utterly dependent upon God's action. That is, the power and efficacy of creative human action is not inconsistent with humans being utterly dependent upon God's action, and the power and efficacy of the Spirit's

---

57. Tanner observes, "United with Christ, we are ourselves only as we incorporate what is God's very own within ourselves; our acts are perfected only as we act along with and under the direction of God, whose powers become a kind of principle of our own, now compound operation, through the gift of Christ's Spirit" (Tanner, *Humanity and the Trinity*, 9–93).

58. For example, in Acts 3:1–10, the apostles Peter and John healed the lame beggar at the temple. Peter pronounced healing in the name of Jesus Christ and, seizing him by the right hand, raised him up. The lame beggar leapt up when his feet and ankles were strengthened, and he walked. In this instance, Peter and John made a free and creative decision on what to say and what to do. What triggers this act is certainly Peter's free decision and creativity. However, that God wants to heal that lame beggar is also foreseen and willed by God. While this healing is genuinely Peter's decision, the whole process by which Peter decides happens within the providential will of God. At one level, there was a human decision taken that was followed by Spirit-empowered action that healed. Therefore, at the human level, it appears *as if* Peter's act led the Spirit's co-creation with humans. At another level, however, this sequence of events was merely working out God's will.

agency. More significantly, I draw attention here to a reader's power and efficacy in human agency to apprehend God in all his fullness through the creative performance of supernatural signs and miracles. This human agency also mirrors the Spirit's agency to apprehend humans in a participation in divinity through an interpretation of scriptural truth.

Second, kerygmatic readers in community consider questions of authority in a *reception* of a Spirit-led scriptural interpretation. How does a reader receive the Spirit's illumination?[59] I differ from Pinnock on the reception to the Spirit's illumination: this mode of an interpretation in the present is not necessarily of any less authority than that of the ancient authors since the scriptural text itself is also an interpretation of God and his truth by these ancient authors. Instead, I argue that the Spirit who first inspires continues to *lead* readers into an *illumination* of that truth. There is the authority that an interpretation has in the present moment: it may, even though it is genuinely creative and new (rather than simply being the application of a message already grasped) have the force of a divine command in the present moment, such that to reject it would be a form of disobedience.[60] In that sense, one might say that it has the same

---

59. Pinnock explains the difference between inspiration and illumination. Inspiration is the Spirit's work in securing the Scriptures for the church, divine self-revelation being given in a literary attestation. "We use the term *inspiration* to refer to a divine activity that secures in written form the portions of revelation that God wanted to have fixed in writing" (Pinnock, *Flame of Love*, 227–31). Pinnock then uses *illumination* to refer to ongoing interpretation by readers as the Spirit opens up the Word to truth. Note that while my use of *illumination* is consistent with Pinnock's—illumination is meant to enable readers to recognize Scripture's timely meaning—I have a different reading for *inspiration*. Other scholars do not make this distinction. For example, Arrington argues, "[w]hen the modern reader's experience of the Holy Spirit reenacts the apostolic experience of the Spirit, the Spirit serves as the common context in which reader and author can meet to bridge the historical and cultural gulf between them" (Arrington, *Hermeneutics*, 382). In response, Pinnock confesses that as an evangelical, he had not encouraged this development "because of an anxiety about how tradition might take primacy over Scripture" (Pinnock, *Flame of Love*, 231). Pinnock provides some guidelines for an evaluation of development. He observes, "Therefore, it is important always to observe the principle of *apostolicity*. Any insight being claimed as a valid interpretive development must be tested by revelation. All interpretations must be in harmony with scriptural revelation and at least implicit in it. Revelation must not be increased or changed by subsequent illumination" (Pinnock, *Flame of Love*, 231).

60. Consider the example of the Spirit's illumination of scriptural truth in the debate of whether gentile converts are required to observe circumcision and the Law of Moses for their salvation. The decision of the council at Jerusalem carried authority for the church in Jerusalem and the gentile churches planted by Paul and Barnabas and the other disciples.

authority as any other word of God spoken into that moment for this community.[61]

What then is the reception for the Spirit's illumination? Kerygmatic hermeneutics can in principle yield discernments for the present moment that really are telling us what God wants us to be doing right now; they are not simply "opinions." They are more like commands—they are the Word of God spoken to us in this moment. Therefore, we may not want to say that only the meanings the text had in past contexts—especially the context of the original author and the original audience—are authoritative. We may be required to believe, say, or do the same things as they were, and that may be part of our obedience to the Spirit—but that is not, for kerygmatic hermeneutics, the whole story. This is justified by the way that New Testament authors found authoritative meanings in Old Testament passages that they read in ways that clearly went beyond the human author's intended sense. However, the truth unveiled in illumination is authoritative for one community, but it may not be for another community living in a different context. The latter flows in the Spirit to determine the truth for its own and what is authoritatively required of it to do and live out in the Spirit. Therefore, a reception of the Spirit's illumination is likely to be community-specific.

A reception of the Spirit's inspiration—when a reader dances in-step with the Spirit and speaks prophetically as an oracle of God—can carry church-wide authority.[62] This interpretation of scriptural truth

---

61. I note there is a question of privileged interpretation, and the canon is the shorthand for an enormously complex process of ecumenical ecclesial reception. Not all early Christian authors are included in the canon. There are also conciliar decisions, for example, in the fifth and sixteenth centuries that demonstrate the complexity of the ecumenical reception history. While this question would demand a thorough examination, I acknowledge for my discussion that there are these factors whose impact is unpredictable and can affect some believers more than others; this history of interpretation makes a difference to how we may read and respond to the Spirit at the present time.

62. Recall the earlier example on the Spirit's inspiration of scriptural truth: In the new covenant enacted in Jesus Christ, the Jews are saved through faith by the grace of God the same way as the gentile converts are. This fresh interpretation carries church-wide authority for all who subscribe to the apostolic tradition. Inspiration is distinguished from illumination in the context from which one reads. An *illumined* reading gives a fresh interpretation of scriptural truth *from a reader's particular context* to text. This interpretation is authoritative for the reader and his/her community that *together* are held accountable for this. On the other hand, an *inspired* reading gives a fresh interpretation of scriptural truth *from God's context* to text. Of course, when God is doing something new in his ongoing work in creation, this will have systemic and even

in the Spirit's inspiration is authoritative *for others* in that they should hear, accept, and follow it. The Spirit's inspiration of prophetic utterances is authoritative for the church. Some examples of this Spirit-speech (sometimes called *rhema*) had prophesied of the annunciation of Jesus (Luke 2:8–20) and Jesus as the Christ (Luke 2:41–52; John 5:47; 6:63, 68; Mark 9:32).[63] This is because the Spirit is the same God who is at work in creation, redemption.[64] Notwithstanding that there remain interpretive questions that are difficult to negotiate, we know that what the Spirit demands in any given moment in an inspirational interpretation will be consistent with the overarching story of God's ways with the world—even if discerning that continuity might sometimes be difficult.[65] Therefore,

---

permanent implications for many readers. This is consistent with Arrington, though he stops short of identifying who this modern reader is, how one may recognize such a reader and how such an inspiration process may be re-enacted. Arrington qualifies, "If the 'apostolic experience of the Spirit' is used to pre-qualify such a reader who may have the authority to inspire scriptural interpretation, one can quickly conclude that this would disqualify the majority of the Pentecostal-charismatic communities which may have some experience of encountering God through the use of the spiritual gifts without necessarily having to pay a cost for apostleship or discipleship. For certainly, the apostles' positive experiences of spiritual encounters were also accompanied by the sufferings and persecutions in bearing the Cross of Jesus Christ" (Arrington, *Hermeneutics*, 382–83).

63. It is pertinent to note that such Spirit-inspired truth claims are to be evaluated from the perspective of God's continuous work in the cosmos, humankind and his church that points humankind to the future. This is to be distinguished from purported truth claims and prophecies concerning God's will, purpose, and working in individual lives that may be motivated from self-deception or self-serving desires. Recall, we are using inspiration to speak to the shape of scriptural truth, the shape of this picture of God and his ways with the world.

64. This is not to deny that there have been very challenging and complex interpretative questions, e.g., those surrounding the reformation, what is true of God, as well as sexual practice, about which faithful Christians standing on both sides have been disagreeing.

65. To this challenge, the Doctrine Commission of the Church of England advocates at least two criteria for scriptural interpretation: the coherence model of truth as well as the apostolic witness to the gospel of the cross, and the inner witness of the Spirit (England, *We Believe*). Its position on the Spirit and truth echoes a similar tone for the currency of inspiration in the work of the Spirit: "Discussions about the nature of 'inspiration' usually operate on at least two different levels. One level concerns continuity, or internal coherence, between the givenness of a past which includes the founding events of the Christian faith, and lived experience in the past . . . On the other hand at a different level claims about 'Inspiration' are also located firmly in the present . . . in the inner witness of the Holy Spirit" (England, *We Believe*, 132–33). Reference to testing the spirits is invoked in 1 John 4:2–3, 5:1. I will be discussing testing the spirits in both chapters 5 and 6.

a reception of the Spirit's inspiration is authoritative in the otherness of God.

In this section, I have described *how* a kerygmatic reader and community can *know* scriptural truth in the apprehension and reception in the Spirit. In the next section, I conclude this discussion on the theology and epistemology of kerygmatic hermeneutics by taking an overview of its theological categories.

4.4 Conclusion

This underlying theology of kerygmatic hermeneutics yields propositions on *how* the Spirit makes use of Scripture's otherness to form an embodied witness to Jesus Christ. The power and efficacy of the Spirit's agency to do this is primarily related to the power and efficacy of readers' agency to appropriate an apprehension and reception of this scriptural truth—truth concerning God and his ways with the world. Therefore, the power and efficacy of kerygmatic hermeneutics is predicated on readers learning to read Scripture in the Spirit in community.

In this chapter, I formulated an underlying theology of *what the Spirit does with Scripture* in the revelation of truth that catches people up as living proclamations of Jesus Christ. There are three ways of speaking of such Spirit-led revelation of scriptural truth—illumination, inspiration, and co-creation. Each orders in different ways the shape and fullness of the deep truth concerning God and his ways with the world. In the next chapter, I will develop kerygmatic criticism that undergirds this theology of kerygmatic hermeneutics. Kerygmatic criticism explicates the self-criticism made possible by the otherness of Scripture and the Spirit. These give form and shape to an embodied witness to Jesus Christ.

5

KERYGMATIC CRITICISM

"No one who is born of God practices sin, because His seed abides in him; and he cannot sin, because he is born of God." (1 John 3:9 NAS)

"The glory which You have given Me I have given to them, that they may be one, just as We are one; I in them and You in Me, that they may be perfected in unity, so that the world may know that You sent Me, and loved them, even as You have loved Me."
(John 17:22–23 NAS)

THE LAST CHAPTER GIVES an account of *what the Spirit does with Scripture* in the revelation of truth that catches people up as living proclamations of Jesus Christ. This chapter continues the account and focuses on *what the Spirit does with readers in community* in the making of an embodied witness to Jesus Christ. This chapter gives shape to the dynamism and fullness of this account.

Kerygmatic hermeneutics involves two sets of dynamics by which the Spirit forms an embodied witness to Jesus Christ. The first set of dynamics involves the Spirit catching readers up into a participation in divinity, leading them into the depths of their interiority in the forming of *logos* enfleshed. Here, the Spirit uses the otherness of Scripture to bring readers into an encounter with themselves in Christ. In the second set of dynamics, the Spirit sends readers out into the world as the kerygma in a performative interpretation of scriptural truth. This brings the world into an encounter with God. Readers' apprehension of God and his ways in the world—through the Spirit working with Scripture to reveal truth in Christ Jesus—is deepened through the interaction of the two sets of dynamics at work. That is, an interpretation of scriptural truth is incomplete until Christ is proclaimed in the power of the Spirit to bring life; and the proclamation of Christ gives a fuller shape to readers' embodiment of *logos*, God's speech in Christ Jesus. In this sense, both sets of dynamics are integral to kerygmatic hermeneutics.

Kerygmatic criticism—kerygmatic hermeneutics' self-criticism—gives dynamism and fullness to the account. In my formulation of kerygmatic theology, I address these questions: How may readers of Scripture know that their interpretation is truly of God? How may others know that what these readers of Scripture interpret is true of God? I am proposing that the dispositions, habits, practices and outcomes involved in kerygmatic hermeneutics can be tested to see if they bear the marks of the Spirit, and that if they do, that is enough to confirm that the interpretation is truly of God. Moreover, these embodied dispositions, habits, practices, and outcomes of readers in community also lend themselves to socio-scientific empirical evaluation. In this sense, kerygmatic hermeneutics is self-critical because the outworking of the Spirit in embodied witnesses is open to both spiritual discernment in practical theology as well as empirical enquiry in humanities and social scientific disciplines.

Spiritual discernment is the capacity of readers to read the Spirit and to interpret Scripture in the Spirit.[1] It involves discerning the marks of the Spirit, so we can make attributions to the Spirit and identify his working. Discernment is integral to kerygmatic hermeneutics. It is integral to the revelation, reception, and proclamation of scriptural truth for a kerygmatic reader and community. Therefore, discernment is not something extra that is practiced (in a separate project or after the fact) by a theologian who is removed from the community. Discernment is a way of life in the Spirit. A kerygmatic reader grows discernment when s/he grows in the apprehension of God and his ways in the world. S/he grows in the apprehension of God and his ways in the world when the

---

1. I will further discuss spiritual discernment and how a community practices this collectively in chapter 6. Keener argues that "biblical faith" gives a reader access to scriptural truth, which "is perceived and embraced by trust and dependence on the God who reveals it" (Keener, *Spirit Hermeneutics*, 175. See also Keener, "Pentecostal Biblical Hermeneutics/Spirit Hermeneutics," 270–83).

Spirit catches him/her up in a daily devotion to community habits and practices.

It follows that spiritual discernment is integral to the two sets of dynamics by which the Spirit forms an embodied witness to Jesus Christ to the world. This witness takes a concrete shape; it has a particular socio-economic, cultural, and political context in the present. Therefore, this lived-out theological interpretation is contextually located; it necessarily takes a shape and fullness that attends directly to the needs of the moment. While this is necessary, this is not sufficient for a good kerygmatic interpretation. Attending directly to the needs of the moment in the particular is not the end goal of a kerygmatic interpretation. What makes a kerygmatic interpretation good is that it is efficacious in a self-emptying and self-abandonment in the Spirit so that what may be observed and evaluated is not only the reader but also the Spirit who interprets Christ.[2]

---

2. At the risk of over-simplification, a hypothetical example would be the doing of all good in missions and charitable work, like helping with disaster relief or volunteering to care for the homeless and widowed. This is certainly what a Christlike believer is likely to do to meet the needs of the moment, where appropriate. In fact, doing all good—caring for the poor, the widowed, the oppressed and the weak—is expected of a good Christian witness. Good works that are self-giving, sometimes at great personal cost, flow from a Spirit-led hermeneutic of faithful living in the love of Christ and a witness to Christ. This witness is often expressed in the mundanity and ordinariness of life. When this interpretation is done right, those who have been cared for can acknowledge God, and not just the reader, regardless of whether they respond to or reject Christ and his salvific works. That is, a good kerygmatic reading, when accompanied by good works, would make an attribution to Christ, so the world may hear and see God through us. For this reason, many churches organize various ministries of care as a corporate witness. In these instances, non-believing beneficiaries (and the world) can readily make some connection to Christ. However, it could be more challenging for the world to make such an attribution to Christ if individual kerygmatic readers do good, say, in a religiously oppressive or post-Christian environment where an overt witness to Christ may be legally forbidden, unwelcome or inappropriate. Here, testing and evaluating what is a good kerygmatic reading (reader or community) is less straightforward. It could not involve a counting of, for example, how many of the poor people who had been fed had heard the gospel and had started to pursue knowledge of who this God is because of the witness of this reader or community. But it is about asking those questions and addressing what other shapes the answers could have taken given the particular context of the reader or community, and to what extent a reader or community may have interpreted scriptural truth with more or less fullness under the circumstances. These difficult cases suggest that a testing and evaluation of what makes a good kerygmatic reading has to account for that interdependence between scriptural truth in the generalizable and abstract and the contexts of the authors and readers in the particular and concrete. This explains why I did not try to formulate kerygmatic criticism as a list of criteria to be applied in all

The goal is a representation of the Body of Christ that manifests Christ and radiates the Father's glory. This goal gives us a litmus test of the impact of a kerygmatic interpretation—Does this (performative) reading point to Christ and glorify the Father?[3] Does this reading speak objectively in the sense that it stands over-against self and the community?[4]

Spiritual discernment empowers reader to apprehend the objective truth of God. The corollary is also true. This discernment also empowers readers to apprehend when a truth claim about God is invalid, distorted, or misrepresented.[5] The Spirit enables readers to discern *an invalid reading*. Contrary to what a valid reading is, an invalid reading is one that is *not* true of God and his ways in the world, *and*, that is *not* contextually

---

circumstances. In this research, I have instead made moves thus far to paint a picture with a coherent shape of scriptural truth that takes on a fullness that is appropriate and specific to the context of a reader or community.

3. The Spirit's working culminates towards this goal of forming the Body of Christ that manifests Christ and glorifies the Father. That is, this litmus test gives us the attribution to the efficacy of the presence of the Spirit and his activities in the world.

4. Recall my account of the working of the Spirit (that gives us the marks of the Spirit) in chapter 3. To corroborate the testing of these outcomes and impacts that are made visible and vocal in an embodied witness to the world, I have formulated the marks of the Spirit that may further evidence the presence and activity of the Spirit in the transformation process that takes place in the interiority in reader dispositions, community habits, practices of readers in community. These marks help to capture the observable effects of what is the invisible and mysterious in the working of the Spirit—intoxication, life, participation, and revelation of truth. These marks help readers better apprehend this realism—a mystery—which is not readily apparent. While the Spirit may reveal these marks and enable a reader to apprehend them in an act of grace, this does not prejudice the possibility that he may choose to act in ways apparently uncharacteristic of these marks. There remains an otherness of the Spirit that a good kerygmatic reading will embrace.

5. Throughout this research, I have attempted to present a picture of this true claim about God. This takes on a shape of the presence and activity of the Spirit in the world. I argue that a reader can recognize what is non-truth when s/he can readily recognize what is truth in all its fullness in Christ Jesus. Similarly, this reader can recognize what is an invalid reading—one that does *not* carry reason or logic that befits what the Spirit is doing in a particular context—when s/he can recognize what is a valid reading. I further discuss in this chapter's conclusion in section 5.7 how a summary testing and evaluation may be done for difficult readings like the examples discussed here. While it is not my intention to generate a (check) list of critical criteria, a reader may certainly create such a list himself/herself from the discourse from chapter 2 onwards. Here, I argue that a reader would naturally discern (in the Spirit) what may not be a good reading (one which is invalid or distorted) when s/he habituates a good kerygmatic reading.

relevant and sensitive to what the Spirit is doing in the present.[6] In discerning between valid and invalid readings, I evaluate whether a particular reading grasps hold of something of the truth of God in and through discovering how that truth can be embodied in the specific demands of the present moment. Between the polar cases of what are valid and invalid readings, there are the half-truths and the grey. These are distorted or misrepresented truth claims about God which are harder to discern. There could be a distorted reading when a participating reader himself/herself (s/he who performs the scriptural truth) discerned or performed wrongly and so yielded a distorted shape and fullness to the scriptural truth.

There could also be a distorted reading when people looking on a human interpretive act discerned God wrongly, and so apprehended scriptural truth in a way that was partial or distorted. This could happen when people could not recognize the truth even when a reader had performed a valid reading, as was the case for many when the Word became flesh in Jesus Christ. Therefore, these would have a partial or distorted grasp of what God was doing in Jesus. This could also happen when other readers or the world wrongly attribute to God what is merely human in a human interpretive act that is flawed by self-deception and self-serving tendencies. This also yields a partial or distorted grasp of what God was doing in the world. In kerygmatic criticism, discerning readers, who can discriminate between valid, invalid and distorted readings, would discount these distorted readings and set aside the invalid ones. These readers can discern a performative interpretation of Scriptural truth that fully reflects the self-giving God and his ways in the world.

Kerygmatic criticism does not come in the form of a (check)list of criteria although a careful tracking of this account of the Spirit's presence and activity in the world (from chapter 2 onwards) could yield a list of these criteria.[7] The Spirit enables a reader to weigh all the dimensions

---

6. Recall my discussion in section 4.2.1 on how the rule of faith (or canon of truth) can give us the boundary markers for a minimalist set of core scriptural truths. A claim to a kerygmatic interpretation that is inconsistent with the rule of faith (or canon of truth) would be deemed as *not* true of God and his ways in the world. A reader would therefore judge this as an invalid reading; s/he would also discern whether this reading is invalid because it is contextually irrelevant and insensitive to what the Spirit is doing in the present.

7. Examples of such criteria in testing and evaluation can include: (1) the interpretation is not self-referential but manifests Christ (since the Spirit is not self-referential; he manifests Christ); (2) the interpretation fosters love in communion in the Body of

that may characterize the uncharacteristic ways of his working in a particular (performative) reading to address the hermeneutical question(s) at hand.[8] In this sense, kerygmatic criticism is not reducible to a formu-

Christ; (3) the interpretation is life-giving (people experience wholeness, healing, and the salvific work of Christ in the proclamation), etc.

8. Testing and evaluating an interpretation of scriptural truth by, say, acclaimed prophets and servants of God could be complex, especially when these are accompanied by apparent acts of healings, deliverances, etc., in gospel rallies or healing services. There are probably Christians who find themselves on both sides of the debate about whether in fact what they saw was true of God. Similar debates also surround the preaching of TV evangelists. I present a hypothetical event of an acclaimed prophet of God who preached Christ with performances of healings and deliverances in a stadium-like setting. There were camera crews and all the paraphernalia that would create a sense of excitement of a performance. During the time of prayers and ministry, there were people who stood up and walked away from their wheelchairs or crutches and testified to their healings. There were also people, apparently demon-possessed, who were gathered in the arena; these demons, as was supposed, started to manifest, and these people made repeated movements in violent or strange acts throughout the entire time of ministry. The prophet repeatedly called on the name of Jesus Christ to deliver them. It was not clear that people were delivered as it looked like many of these remained in possessed states. Meanwhile, there was much attention on the prophet from the entire stadium as people praised and thanked God for his mighty acts and salvation. Is this a valid interpretation of scriptural truth of a God who loves and makes us whole, gives us life, and sets us free from demonic powers and spiritual oppression? Does this prophet look like Jesus Christ who embodied this truth? I argue that there is more than one hermeneutical questions here, and one may possibly eclipse another. For example, there is first a truth claim that God loves and heals people. Presumably, criticism would call for an evaluation of the medical history and medical follow up of the people who stood up and walked away from their wheelchairs and crutches, to establish if in fact these had been healed. Third party participants and online observers would find difficulty in assessing this critically without adequate evidence. However, those affected (with their loved ones and caregivers) would probably know if in fact they had been healed. Yet, there could still be a question of self-deception. There is a second truth claim that this prophet's interpretive performance gives an appropriate shape and fullness to this Christ who loves and heals people. However, this testing and evaluation would call for a different type of discernment. It calls for a spiritual discernment as to whether this prophet's hermeneutic was "non-self-referential," one that was self-emptying and self-abandoning, that manifested Christ and glorified the Father. Suppose the prophet's hermeneutic was discerned to give a distorted representation of the shape and fullness of Christ's likeness. Suppose his hermeneutic was discerned to seek a glory for the self that eclipsed that of the Father. Even so, I argue that this poor embodied witness to Christ would not preclude the Spirit from choosing to work through blemished vessels (as may be the case for many biblical characters and believers through the centuries, including myself). In this hypothetical example, the first truth claim may be tested and evaluated to be valid, while the second may be deemed invalid. The Spirit can enable readers to address the two hermeneutical questions by discriminating between a valid reading and one that is invalid. The composite reading

laic set of criteria. There is a dynamism in this Spirit-led process that may not fit any systemic weighing across criteria, or reductive categorization. Kerygmatic hermeneutics' self-criticism directs our discernment in testing and evaluation to where other readers may have gotten their interpretation wrong.[9]

As a matter of practical theology, kerygmatic interpretation, as well as being open to the kind of spiritual discernment I described above, is also open to qualitative and quantitative analyses (drawing on methods from the humanities and social sciences). Communal structures, dispositions, habits, and practices in the revelation, reception, and proclamation of scriptural truth are integral elements of kerygmatic interpretation. Therefore, kerygmatic interpretation makes possible these empirical forms of kerygmatic criticism.[10] This also opens an inter-disciplinary discourse between theology, and the humanities and social sciences (e.g., anthropology, ethnography and development theory) *because* the Spirit works in and through embodied witnesses.[11] Therefore, his working takes

---

in this case, however, is a distorted performative interpretation to God and his ways in the world. Christians on both sides of the debate here may actually be justified. More significantly, if Spirit-led believers were testing and evaluating this event collectively in a community, they should be able to agree on this discernment in a communion of love without losing sight that the ones on the opposite side are their Spirit-filled brethren who can read over-against them.

9. In the above hypothetical example of an acclaimed prophet performing healings and deliverances, a distorted reading could arise because this prophet himself (who proclaimed that God loves people and heals and delivers them) could have performed wrongly by seeking glory for himself. This highlights the problem of self-deception or self-serving tendencies. This can happen when the messenger is not conflated with his message (I further discuss this in sections 5.1 and 5.5 on the theological characterization of kerygmatic readers). A distorted reading in the world could also arise because a third-party reader looking on a valid interpretive act could have apprehended God wrongly. That is, this reader could have discerned wrongly that there had been no healing and deliverance, and God did not heal and deliver.

10. Fowl laments the apparent lack of capacity or capability for self-evaluation on a community's life in the Spirit. He writes, "We Christians are generally suspicious about claims about the Spirit; we are not generally a people who either testify well or listen wisely to the testimony of others. We largely favor self-authentication and despise common patterns of discernment. We abhor the notion that our lives ought to be disciplined by a concern for one another. In short, most Christian communities lack the skills and resources to debate what a life marked by the Spirit might look like in the present. Without these communal practices and structures in place, one cannot be hopeful that most Christian churches will be able to do more than pay lip-service to the hermeneutical significance of the Spirit" (Fowl, "How the Spirit Reads," 363).

11. There is a postliberal idea that prevailed at Yale in the 1980s and 1990s that

on visible and concrete forms in the world.¹² Given appropriate categories, and appropriate tools, the effects of the Spirit's working in the world can be publicly identified, discussed, even potentially measured. We make a claim in kerygmatic theology that a kerygmatic reader grows into the fullness of humanity as s/he becomes a spiritual person. However, a reader's humanity and spirituality are not two distinct categories that are in relation.¹³ This inter-disciplinary discourse in practical theology adds empirical support for identifying the Spirit's working by critically teasing out the extraordinary in the ordinariness of a lived-out proclamation of Jesus Christ.¹⁴

theology can take on some characteristics of cultural ethnography. See, e.g., Rogers, *After the Spirit*; Tanner, *Theories of Culture*; Lindbeck, *Nature of Doctrine*. Rogers argues, "The clue to recovery of a robust Spirit-talk runs through and not around the social sciences, precisely for good theological reasons: Christians believe that Christ has become incarnate in a human being, subjected himself, therefore to the human sciences; after his ascension, Christians say that Christ's body is the church—in which Christ subjects himself to sociological analysis. Any theology that rejects the social sciences is anti-incarnational; any theology that thinks they are evil by privation of good and nothing else forgets that by its own teaching what is assumable is redeemable" (Rogers, *After the Spirit*, 55).

12. Moberly raised an example of a difficult reading in the case of Martin Luther King Jr. (Moberly, *Prophecy and Discernment*, 239–42). He raised the question, "Since adultery is something specified by Jeremiah as a mark of a prophet who is not to be heeded (Jer 23:14, 29:21–3), does it follow from this that King (an ordained Christian minister) should not be recognized as of 'prophetic' stature?" (Moberly, *Prophecy and Discernment*, 240). Moberly argues that Martin Luther King has an effective witness to God's love and justice in his sermons and speeches. his proclamation is also matched with an integrity of non-violent actions to oppose racial injustice. Therefore, Moberly argues that King may rightly be recognized as "prophetic" in his proclamations, in continuity with those of biblical prophets.

13. When the Spirit unites one with Christ, s/he is naturally empowered to live a full human life in his/her vocation in all the particularity of human pain and suffering. However, the dynamism does not work the other way—one does not become naturally more spiritual in the pursuit of living out the range of human experiences. Ironically, it is in the yielding in the Spirit, the dying to one's humanity, that one lives to life's fullest. This hermeneutical spiral helps us make an attribution—the Spirit (not humans) brings humans up to their humanity—that is at work in kerygmatic criticism. That is, evidence and observation of a kerygmatic reader doing all good is a necessary but not sufficient argument for a good kerygmatic reading. We look for all four marks of the Spirit to corroborate such a truth claim. Section 5.5 will further discuss the characterization of kerygmatic readers.

14. The case of Martin Luther King Jr. can illustrate how a critical testing and evaluation may be done of a proclamation of truth in the world. In this case, the proclamation is done in the public square, and not within a church community. This opens the testing and evaluation readily to empirical enquiry because of the nature and amount

Kerygmatic criticism is open to the fact that God is never fully knowable apart from God's self-gift and revelation from the *beyond* in the heavenly places. However, the truth of God that is embodied in readers in community provides a lens into a knowing and apprehending of God when humans are caught up in the Spirit. Kerygmatic criticism is also open to the fact that any human discipline, including theology, is epistemologically relative in relation to the *givenness* of what God has revealed. God is truly at work in the world, whether we recognize it or not, and all the intellectual disciplines by which we seek to identify and discuss that work are attempts to do justice to that reality; and we are led to revise these attempts as we are led to discover more and more of his work.[15] And more so, when kerygmatic living throws up 'surprises' in

of evidence that may be found in open sources. Again, there are more than one truth claims here. Is this a valid interpretation of scriptural truth of a God who loves and makes us whole, gives us life, and sets us free from oppression arising from racial discrimination (as in King's context, in the light of a history of slavery in the US)? A testing and evaluation in kerygmatic criticism would call for a discernment if this realist claim is indeed true of God. Readers also discern the validity of this scriptural interpretation in the light of what the Spirit is doing in the US (and in the world) in the history of slavery up till then. The second truth claim is this: Does this prophet look like Jesus Christ who embodied this truth? A third-party assessment, testing and evaluating of King (as a reader) could involve ethnographical studies of King—his speeches and sermons, autobiographical and biographical accounts, video library of his public appearances, commentaries, etc. In all these searches, we are looking for indications of the marks of the Spirit in his personal dispositions, community habits, and practices so that we can make an attribution of this embodiment of truth to the presence and working of the Spirit in his interiority. Recall our argument that a narrative of good works cannot sufficiently support a claim to a life in the Spirit, while a life in the Spirit would probably lead one to doing of all good. To what extent then is King becoming more and more self-emptying and self-abandoning? Is there a confession of sin and correction of error? To what extent is the impact of his Baptist church community (and the wider American churches?) in his non-violent civil rights movement reflecting an embodied witness that manifests Christ's likeness and radiates the Father's glory? I note that King's "renunciation was not expressed in terms of repentance, but rather in terms of a prudential recognition of the need to be more 'spartan' in accordance with his world stature" (Moberly, *Prophecy and Discernment*, 241). To the extent that King appears to be wanting in some dimensions when evaluated against the marks of the Spirit (which means the presence and working of the Spirit may be less apparent in some dimensions than in others), this could give a somewhat distorted representation of the fullness of this scriptural truth in the world. Again, in this case, we may possibly see a mix of valid as well as invalid readings to the various hermeneutical questions at hand. What may be more helpful is to address the hermeneutical question of whether any such distorted reading is getting less distorted as readers learn to interpret better in the otherness of the Spirit, Scripture, and community.

15. Therefore, I am adopting a critically realist stance: realist, in the sense that the

what new things God is doing and revealing in the present—a prophetic *finding* that would call for a fresh reading of Scripture, dogma, tradition or theories. Therefore, kerygmatic criticism embraces an ongoing self-learning, unlearning, and re-learning in the Spirit and makes a humble articulation of this realism.[16] While recognizing that it is epistemologically relative, kerygmatic criticism is yet able to speak into the Spirit's transformative work in a kerygmatic reader and community to evaluate the extent to which a reader and community are caught up to live a life in the Spirit as embodied witnesses to Jesus Christ.

There is a conviction of those of us who propound kerygmatic theology that God is objectively at work. What is the basis of this conviction? We believe it is the same Spirit who originally inspired the Scriptures who works in believers now. It is because of this pneumatological fact that we can expect some relation between what Scriptures meant in their original context and what they mean for us today. We *trust* that it is the same Spirit, but we also seek to *discern* in what way it is the same Spirit and are open to questions about *whether* it is really the same Spirit. That is, when we believe that we have heard what the Spirit is saying to us today through a particular passage, we have good pneumatological reasons for asking the question, 'In what way is the Spirit who speaks now by this text the *same* Spirit as the one who spoke by it in the past?' In response to this

---

object I am talking about (scriptural truth in God) is there independent of all our representations of it; critical realist, in the sense that I think our representations of this reality are properly subject to ongoing critique and development—because all our representations (all our theories, explanations, descriptions) are historically and socially situated, and so partial. So, there is a kind of epistemological relativism here: all our representations are *relative* to our locations. For example, many communities of faith in modernity continue to embrace cessationism (whether strong or moderate cessationism) until the three waves of the Pentecostal-charismatic movements swept across the world. Some communities then critically re-learnt from this divine action, corrected their interpretation of Scripture, which translated to new practices in witness, praise and worship, etc. that are open to the practice of *charismata*. The disciples' account of their fresh reading of the Hebrew Scripture after their eyes were opened to apprehend the resurrected Christ on the road to Emmaus is instructive (Luke 24:13–26, Mark 16:12–14; also John 21:1–4). God is real and exists independently of humanity's epistemology.

16. See, e.g., Searle, *Construction of Social Reality*; Wright, *Christianity and Critical Realism*; Root, *Christopraxis*. Searle asserts, "Realism is the view that there is a way that things are that is logically independent of all human representations. Realism does not say how things are but only that there is a way that they are" (Searle, *Construction of Social Reality*, 155). In this sense, kerygmatic criticism goes further to articulate how things are—that is, who the Spirit is, what and why he does what he does.

question, we need to offer some kind of account of *how* it is discernibly the same Spirit. This is the account sought by kerygmatic criticism.

What is being evaluated of kerygmatic hermeneutics is whether the entire account of *how* the Spirit catches readers up to read Scripture in the Spirit bears the marks of the Spirit. It is because it is the one Spirit who works in the whole church that we can expect some relation between what the Scriptures mean for one group of Christians and what they mean for another. It is because it is the one Spirit who sanctifies that we can expect reading in the Spirit to lead into holiness. It is because it is the one Spirit who bears witness for Jesus Christ as Lord that we can expect reading Scripture in the Spirit to bring people to faith in Christ Jesus through our witnessing. It is because it is the one Spirit who gives signs and wonders that we can expect reading in the Spirit to be accompanied by these works of power that manifest the kingdom of God. It is because it is the one Spirit who leads deeper into Christ that we can expect reading in the Spirit to lead to becoming *logos* enfleshed. It is because it is the one Spirit who flows us into a participation in divinity that we can expect reading in the Spirit to bring us into the fullness of our humanity in Christ Jesus. Moreover, it is because it is the one Spirit who is love that we can expect reading in the Spirit to unite the church as one body of Christ, rising above all diversity and charismata. In all these ways and more, there is the same coherence that flows in the communion of the Trinitarian God.

In section 5.1, therefore, I first present the theological categories that characterize kerygmatic criticism—Christology, Spirit, and Logos. This characterization helps readers discern the truth of the realist claims with regards to God made in kerygmatic hermeneutics. These realist claims with regards to God are open to critical evaluation because the Spirit's working has transformative outworking in concrete and visible expressions both in the church as well as the world.

To help us see how this entire account—of how the Spirit catches readers up to read Scripture in the Spirit for the making of an embodied witness—is self-critical, I present in sections 5.2 through 5.6 respectively the theological categories that underpin the entire transformation process that covers reader dispositions, community habits, practices, outcomes, and impacts. In the conclusion in section 5.7, I summarize this complex process of discerning the marks of the Spirit in readers and communities. Kerygmatic criticism directs discernment in testing and evaluation to where readers (including ourselves) may have gotten the interpretations wrong. Kerygmatic criticism, if done well, directs discernment in testing and evaluation so that a Spirit-led community is able to discriminate across valid, invalid, and distorted hermeneutical readings. It gives a sense as to how well readers are reading over-against others in community. Kerygmatic criticism can also be applied to the public square in a testing and evaluation of truth claims proclaimed in the name of Christ to the world.

I now present the theological categories that underpin the entire transformation process that covers reader dispositions, community habits, practices, outcomes, and impacts.

5.1 Theological Characterization

The key theological categories that characterize kerygmatic hermeneutics are Christology, Spirit, and *Logos*:

Christology—The core idea here is that we can be by grace what Christ is by nature. In Christ, a fully human life is unreservedly united to divinity, and displays that divine life in the world. It is in that sense a divinized human life. He lived this life from the moment of conception onwards, perfectly and completely, without sin. We, by grace, can share in that life: we can be born again as Christ's brothers and sisters. We are both granted this status by God's grace and called to grow into it by growing in love, holiness, and obedience, and turning away from sin.

Spirit—The core idea here is that to participate in this divinized human life by grace is to "flow in the Spirit." When a human is caught up and "flows in the Spirit," s/he bears the marks of the Spirit. S/he also grows in the fullness of humanity just as the Spirit had formed Christ's humanity. "Flowing in the Spirit" is in one sense simply another way of describing how a human grows to be divinized alongside Christ or to become a communication of the life-giving Word.

The Spirit is the one who empowers the speaking of the Word. Focusing on the Spirit, however, helps place particular emphasis on the *process* of growth and discovery. It places particular emphasis on the *context-specific* nature of that growth (the way that the Spirit leads us to respond in particular ways in particular circumstances). It also places particular emphasis on some of the signs of that growth. The Spirit leads us into signs, miracles, and healings. The Spirit empowers us to do all that Jesus did and more.

Logos—The core idea here is that the principle of a divinized human life is the Word *(logos)*, God's speech. It is God's seed (σπέρμα) that comes in the form of articulated speech. We are born again by this Word by being recipients of God's life-giving Word.[17] We in turn can beget life by articulating the same Word—by becoming united to that Word, and so becoming people who communicate it. We become, in fact, communications of the Word. We become the Word's proclamation—*logos* enfleshed—just like Christ was the Word incarnate.[18]

I now characterize this entire transformative process by its underlying theological categories. This characterization is helpful in discerning the realism with regards to God in kerygmatic criticism.

5.1.1 Christology

A christological characterization of a kerygmatic reader places an emphasis on the concrete in human experience of God. A christological account speaks of human dispositions, habits, and practices that constitute the ordinariness of a life of tension set between hope and suffering. This has been modelled by the Christ narrative of annunciation, baptism, passion, powerlessness, resurrection, and ascension.

A kerygmatic reader takes on a christological characterization that reflects, while not being identical to, the union of humanity and divinity in Jesus Christ. The key difference is that Jesus's humanity is perfectly united to divinity.[19] Humankind needs to be born a second time by God's

---

17. See 1 Pet 1:23, or by the similar imagery in the parable of the sower (Matt 13:18–23; Mark 4:1–25; Luke 8:4–15).

18. There is a similar self-sustaining dynamism and neat circularity here as well: We are reborn by receiving the proclaimed Word of God; and we are reborn to become ourselves proclamations of the Word.

19. The christological account in kerygmatic hermeneutics resonates fairly closely with a classic "Alexandrian" account in the henosis (union or unification) theory. See, e.g., O'Collins, *Christology*, 188–205; McGuckin, *Christological Controversy*. That is, the unity of Christ exists on the level of person and the duality on that of his human and divine natures (see Council of Chalcedon). McGuckin explains, "Each and every single act of the incarnate Lord was, for Cyril, an act of God enfleshed within history; and thus an act where deity and humanity were synchronised as one theandric reality. This synchronic interpenetration was the essential mystery that at once allowed the divine majesty to stoop down to the encounter with humanity at a direct and personal level, and the humanity to be caught up in this divine condescension so as to be elevated into a new condition and a realm of utterly new possibilities. The point of the incarnation is thereby demonstrated" (McGuckin, *Christological Controversy*, 200–201).

seed to participate in divinity by grace, that is, the deposit of the Holy Spirit. That is, on the one hand, there is a hypostatic union between humanity and divinity in Christ. On the other hand, there is a union of grace between humanity and divinity in humankind.

Through the Spirit, the divinization of humankind begins with the new creation in Christ. It is significant that a new creation in Christ is being born of God with his seed—the Word that was proclaimed (1 Pet 1:23–25; 2 Cor 5:17). Through the Spirit's work at Jesus's annunciation, Jesus was born fully divine and there is no sin in him (1 John 3:5). Similarly, this seed of God, bearing the σπέρμα or DNA of God, gives humankind the right to become true children of God with a divine character that cannot sin (John 1:12–13; 1 John 3:9).

There is a significant change in nature of a human being when one is born a second time (as Jesus explained to Nicodemus in John 3:1–8). This human being takes on divine nature and begins a journey of life in the Spirit into the life of God.[20] This growing in God's divine nature is a transformation of one's humanity—including one's dispositions, habits, and practices—even as one remains fully human.[21] Therefore, this new creation has both human and divine nature, with the potentiality of a fully human life that flows in divine communion without sinning.

Kerygmatic hermeneutics is an account that shows how one may develop a fully human life. Perfection consists in following Christ, being conformed to the mind of Christ and participating freely in divinity to love God and one's neighbor.[22] A pursuit of perfection, wholeness, and

---

20. Higton explains in McFarland et al., *Cambridge Dictionary*, 108–9—"*Communicatio Idiomatum*"—"The divinisation of the humanity consists in its receipt of all the communicable attributes of deity—all the attributes that are consistent with the flesh's continued creaturely existence. It is asymmetric in that, as John of Damascus says, 'The nature of the flesh is deified, but the nature of the Logos does not become carnal' (*Jac.*, in *PG* 94:1461C)."

21. On incarnation, Higton explains succinctly, "The one qualification that classic incarnational theology has made is that Jesus was without sin. This, however, was not understood as a diminishment of his humanity, but rather as confirmation of the fact that sin is not an essential feature of fully human life (even if it is endemic in all human beings except Jesus after the fall)" (Mike Higton, "Incarnation," 236).

22. An ecumenical understanding of sanctification (Wesley's reference for perfection, or *theosis* as used in Orthodox churches) is consistent with the *unifying* work of the Spirit in the body of Christ. Edgardo Colón-Emeric, in attempting to examine the doctrine of perfection ecumenically, brings Wesley and Aquinas into conversation. He says, "What I propose to show is that when Thomas Aquinas and John Wesley speak of perfection they are talking about the same reality albeit in different theological modes:

holiness leads to the stable state when "sin is not an essential feature of fully human life."[23] Wesley, a practical theologian, teaches perfection as a goal of Christian living for *all* believers and describes the way to attain freedom from sin.[24]

Likewise, in kerygmatic hermeneutics, the intoxicating spiritual journey of divinization can give *all* humans a christological characterization as they grow into the likeness of God.[25] In this hermeneutical spiral—in a circularity of participation and proclamation, of being reborn by receiving the proclaimed Word of God in order to become ourselves proclamations of the Word—readers in community grow in holiness and truth. Therefore, the role of the Spirit in relation to Scripture in forming kerygmatic readers in community may also be understood through the lens of Christology, soteriology, and ecclesiology.

Aquinas as *scientia*; Wesley as 'practical divinity'"... In ecumenical dialogue, "much is already achieved when one clearly admits that different words often refer to the same content and, more important, that behind the same words there can be different concepts and even whole systems of categories" (Colón-Emeric, *Christian Perfection*, 5).

23. See above footnote on incarnation (Higton, "Incarnation," 236).

24. See Colón-Emeric, *Christian Perfection*, 1–67; Olson, *Christian Perfection*, 2. Olson demonstrates a good balance between perfection and ongoing sin and repentance by holding things together richly. Olson identifies an Achilles heel in Wesley's doctrine of sin: internal inconsistencies that deny the very perfection he seeks to advocate. Olsen argues that Wesley affirms humans' continual need for Christ's atonement even after they attain perfection on one hand, while he denies that involuntary transgressions are sin. Moreover, Olsen shows that Wesley's responses to his critics' objections "does not solve the dilemma his dual definition of sin creates for his perfection claims. He simply chooses to conveniently limit his definition of sin to make room for his claim that in perfection all sin is removed, while continuing to affirm these involuntary transgressions expose to God's justice and require daily confession and forgiveness. *This is a real Achilles heel since both claims cannot be consistently maintained at the same time*" (Olson, *Christian Perfection*, 378).

25. John L. Peters documents theological shifts in the doctrine of perfection from the time of Wesley to the twentieth century (see Peters, *Christian Perfection*). He notes uneven attention to Wesley's practical theology: e.g., zealous Methodist preachers had emphasized repentance more than perfection; revivalists' teaching on perfection had skewed more towards instantaneous perfection rather than progressive growth in holiness. Kerygmatic hermeneutics holds in balance readers' participation and proclamation in a hermeneutical spiral.

5.1.2 Spirit

A kerygmatic reader is characterized by a *life* in the Spirit. This life in the Spirit bears the marks of the Spirit. This life in the Spirit is a participation in a divinized human life by grace through flowing in the Spirit. We may discern this energy act of flowing in the Spirit as readers concretely grow in the fullness of their humanity.

What does it mean for one to flow in the Spirit? Primarily, there is a losing of control, say, of what readers do in a day's work or activity. They are open to changing course within a day's routine even though plans have been made for the day.[26] Readers are open to be completely surprised in where they go and what they do. They are continuously vigilant to the Spirit's leading and guiding, as in responding to a dance partner's lead.

Kerygmatic readers, flowing in the Spirit, can be confident that Father God will do abundantly beyond all that they ask or think. They are nonetheless surprised and perhaps even stunned at the outcome and impact of this spiritual experience, which may be objectively observed and evaluated. They are surprised because the speech and work do not flow from their conscious thoughts nor are they planned. They are also stunned because the outcome and impact are beyond human expectations given the context. The Spirit's work of the revelation of truth and grace shows forth the glory of God.

Nonetheless, God also gives readers the freedom to work out their proclamation in creative ways in the particular. There is often a 'floating' sensation when the Spirit co-creates a narrative with readers. There will be moments when the Spirit tacitly and gently pulls them back when they move out of step. Readers learn from the various missteps in life how the Spirit guided and re-directed their paths. This guided freedom to move a couple of steps ahead of the Spirit at times is what makes kerygmatic hermeneutics attractive.

Kerygmatic readers, created with all-natural capabilities, potentialities, and powers, are free to exercise their will and all creative imagination in an interpretation of what life in the Spirit is. Such creaturely freedom by no means limits or challenges the sole sovereignty of God. For even this creaturely willing to flow in the Spirit is what God creatively willed

---

26. One cannot predict what one who is born of the Spirit will say and do, and where s/he will go (John 3:8).

them to do.[27] This divine agency provides for such readers' free willing to speak and act in the particular, influencing and perhaps even obligating the transcendent God to attend to their desires without needing God to abandon his sovereignty at any moment. For such is God's creative intentionality for their created agencies, to which grace the Spirit attends.

I therefore uphold the idea that there is no competition between divine agency and created agency. Speaking of divine agency and grace when the Spirit co-creates with a kerygmatic reader does not demean created agency; and created agency in no way qualifies divine agency.[28]

5.1.3 Logos

Logos (Word) is the principle for kerygmatic living. *Logos* is *God's seed (σπέρμα), divine in nature, which comes in the form of articulated speech.* It is God's speech. As in the creation (Gen 1) and Johannine (John 3) accounts, the Spirit acts on this Word to give life. Therefore, distinct from the Spirit, the Word gives a disciple his/her principle for a divinized human life so that his/her *logos* in turn may also be life-giving when s/he flows in the Spirit.

Kerygmatic readers are characterized as *logos* enfleshed; they proclaim and reveal God's speech in the Spirit.[29] As they articulate God's

---

27. See Barth, *Church Dogmatics*, 285. Barth holds this proposition on God's sovereignty and the created order's freedom to act as a common thread in *Church Dogmatics*, 2:1. Also see Tanner, *God and Creation*, 81–119.

28. Tanner argues that using these rules for talking about God's action and human activity—avoiding composition talk by putting them into competition—"may also be a means of opposing a form of theology known as rationalistic supernaturalism where miracles tend to become the exclusive locus of direct divine influence on the world" (Tanner, *God and Creation*, 103). For example, in Eph 3:16–21, for one who is flowing in the Spirit (knowing the *agape* of Christ, which is beyond knowledge, and participating in the divine, being filled up to all the fullness of Christ), s/he is free to ask or think in the particular of the context, and God is just as free to *work* beyond what is being asked or thought according to (or by virtue of) the power that *works* in him/her. Abbott argues, "ἐνεργ is clearly middle, not passive . . . Onthovius, indeed, defends the latter view, maintaining that ἐνεργεῖται is always passive in the N.T., even Rom. vii. 5; 1 Thess ii. 13; Jas. v. 16" (*Bibliotheca Bremensis, Classis* 4ta, 474). According to Winer, St. Paul uses "the active of personal action, the middle of non-personal. Comp. Col. i. 29" (Abbott, *Exegetical Commentary*, 101–4). In the use of middle voice in personal or non-personal action, "work" then can suggest either one's voluntary action or God's sovereign act or both, in a participation in God and his narrative and work in the kingdom of God.

29. Higton gives at least three senses of the Word's incarnation: "incarnation has

speech, the Spirit comes to give life to the *logos* and to catch them up into perfect union with *logos*. It is in the proclamation that they become *logos* enfleshed. Therefore, kerygmatic readers' vocation is the proclamation of *logos,* the gospel of Jesus Christ. Through kerygmatic readers and their proclamation of this gospel, the world may hear God.

This perfect union with God goes beyond an encounter that the world may have with the divine. Judas (not Iscariot) asked Jesus, "Lord what then has happened that You are going to disclose Yourself to us and not to the world?" (John 14:22, NAS).[30] I argue here that Jesus is possibly referring to another mode of his revelation (*emphanizein*) that

been understood as a matter of the making visible or making tangible of God's life— and so a proclamation or revelation of the nature of God. Jesus has therefore been understood as the true prophet who has not simply been given God's self-revelatory Word to speak, but who has himself been given to the world as the embodiment of that Word, and as the true image or representation of God's being. From a somewhat different direction, the incarnation has been seen as the catching up of a human life into perfect union with God, and so as a matter of the perfection or sanctification of human life. Jesus' life has been understood as God's temple, as the perfect tabernacle in which the God of Israel meets with God's people; he has been seen as the sinless high priest who alone has been made worthy to stand in the presence of God and intercede for his people. Jesus has also been seen as the embodiment of the kingdom of God, and the incarnation as the establishment of that kingdom in history. All people are understood to be called into this kingdom, and the incarnate Jesus is seen both as the perfect model for their citizenship and as the embodiment of their king . . . " (Higton, "Incarnation," 236).

30. The apostle John's account of Jesus's farewell discourse is helpful in understanding what it means to be *logos* enfleshed—in coming into a union with *logos.* See Beasley-Murray, *John*; Thompson, *John.* Thompson highlights that "[t]he word translated 'reveal' (*emphanizein*, 'to lay open to view, make visible' [BDAQ]) is used only here in John 14:21–22" (Thompson, *John*, 315). Beasley-Murray suggests that Judas misunderstood Jesus to mean he will reveal himself to the disciples in another theophany that is more splendorous like that of Moses on Mt. Sinai (cf. Hab 3:3–15; Isa 9, 11; Zech 9) (Beasley-Murray. *John*, 259). On the other hand, Thompson suggests that Judas's question indicates "that the disciples do not yet understand that they will 'see' him because he has risen, but that his resurrection will not imply a return to life as before. Here is a contrast with Lazarus, who resumes his life as before, eating and drinking in public, and becoming an object of public curiosity (12:2, 9). As in the other Gospels, Jesus appears only to his disciples; at least they alone recognize who he is (21:7). The resurrection appearances are not manifestations of Jesus for all to see, any more than all see the glory of Jesus in the flesh. 'Seeing' or recognizing Jesus depends upon his revelation or manifestation of himself to them." Here, Thompson rightly associates Jesus' resurrection appearances to his disciples as testimony to "his living presence, here pictured in terms of Jesus and his Father 'making our home' with the disciples. If Jesus has 'revealed' himself to the disciples, he can do so because he is living and will continue to be living among and with the disciples" (Thompson, *John*, 315).

is restricted to those disciples who love (*agapao*) him and so keep his commandments, and this revelation is not accessible to the world. This mode of revealing the (Father and the) Son through indwelling (*monē*) is to be distinguished from those of Jesus's resurrection appearances to the disciples, the Messiah's public appearing and the Day of the Lord. This indwelling during a disciple's earthly existence is also to be distinguished from the disciples' dwelling in their eternal home.[31] More importantly, this promise to indwell the disciples who love Jesus extends beyond the Easter experience to all disciples post-Easter.[32] Through such indwelling, the Father and Son form "Son-like" disciples as *logos* enfleshed after that of Jesus Christ. This perfect union with God goes beyond an encounter. It engenders a transformation that starts inside out from a disciple's interiority in a participation with divinity.

In this formulation of kerygmatic theology, I first propound how the marks of the Spirit can help us discern the truth of realist claims with regards to God—Christology, Spirit, and *Logos*. We may also observe the effects of this realism in the concrete expressions of kerygmatic hermeneutics. I now outline these concrete and visible expressions in reader dispositions, community habits, practices, outcomes, and impacts that can help us make an attribution to the Spirit and his working. I conclude by laying out a framework that allows an attribution of these concrete and visible expressions to the Spirit. This frames for us a testing and evaluation of the impact of kerygmatic hermeneutics through discernment and socio-scientific empirical enquiry.

5.2 Reader Dispositions

Kerygmatic hermeneutics is primarily driven by a reader's *desire to know God and to do his will*.[33] This desiring and willing is the work of the Spirit,

---

31. The "dwelling" or "home" (*monē*) in John 14:23 and John 14:2–3 is contrasted in location. After Jesus's death, he goes to prepare a "home" in the Father's house, for those who believe in him and the Father, and he will come again to bring them to their prepared homes. In v.23, however, the Father and Son come to the disciples and make their home with them in their earthly beings.

32. While Jesus's promise to reveal himself to his disciples in John 14:18 refers to his Easter appearances, that in John 14:21–23 is open to disciples in the post-Easter era, and in a different mode of indwelling.

33. In kerygmatic hermeneutics, Spirit baptism marks the beginning of the Spirit's transformative work in a believer. In Spirit baptism, the Spirit awakens the believer's desire for the *One* who transforms, the *goal* of transformation and the *process* of

a work of grace. A kerygmatic reader's disposition is marked by intoxication, being caught up in a flow of *agape* love, to desire and will to do what s/he would otherwise not.

There is a transformed desire and willingness to live out God's will, reading Scriptures in the Spirit in a community. This is a desire and willingness to commit to a life in the Spirit and to one another. That is, there is a transformed desire and willingness to commit to community habits and practices. Since the Spirit is *agape* love, this commitment to a community life in the Spirit is ultimately a commitment to flow in love and to love itself—that is lived out in community. Such a commitment is likely to be pleasurable and not burdensome. In other words, there is a pleasurable desire and willingness to live out kerygmatic hermeneutics in communal habits and practices.

How do we discern this intoxication when a reader would desire and will to do what s/he would otherwise not? Besides a transformed desire and willingness to live out scriptural truth in pleasurable or ecstatic experiences, this also includes a desire and willingness to stand against lies, to embrace learning and correction in the spirit of prayer and worship in a community of faith. These negative experiences include confronting one's self-deception and pride. Therefore, intoxication is characterized by the *willingness of a kerygmatic reader or community* to experience not only positive experiences but also to endure negative ones. The latter include a conviction of sin and correction of error in learning and holding oneself accountable not just to the Spirit but, in humility, also to other fallible beings in community.

In this section, I have argued that a participation in divinity could start with the Spirit's awakening of human desire for God. A reader desires God, desires to know this ultimate-*Other* and to please him. This is a work of grace. Yet, this work of grace calls for a human response in willed discipline. S/he exercises volition and commits herself/himself in community habits and practices that teleologically form a kerygmatic reader. I first discuss some of these community habits.

5.3 Community Habits

Kerygmatic devotion is the name I give for an account of a kerygmatic reader's daily spiritual disciplines. These spiritual disciplines are community habits because they are the collective response to the Spirit's

---

transformation (see section 3.1.5 Spirit and Transformation).

awakening of a desire for God. To the extent that the Spirit first awoken this desire in readers, this collective response is also the work of the Spirit; it unifies the community of God's people. These community habits form community identity.

Kerygmatic devotion is spiritual because it is a practice in spirituality; it is concerned with things of the Spirit. This practice takes readers into the flow of the Spirit, who then transforms them into spiritual persons. This practice presumes that readers have been baptized in the Spirit.[34] On the other hand, this practice involves restraint, real effort, diligence, and vigilance. That is, it really is a matter of discipline. Each discipline makes proper sense only when understood as part of the larger orientation of one's whole life towards God. Each involves elements of purgation (being freed from disordered desires) and filling (sustaining a flow in the Spirit). As a spiritual discipline, each discipline involves ultimately going beyond discipline (i.e., beyond diligent effort) into flowing in the Spirit (i.e., taken beyond what even our Spirit-guided efforts can produce, and into activity that relies upon and is open to the inspiration of the Spirit in each particular moment). That is, the pursuit of a regime of daily disciplines is that catalyst that takes a reader and community into the flow of the Spirit to participate in divinity.

These actions are both human actions, as well as the Spirit's work in humans. They are our disciplined and determined action, by which we work on ourselves and change ourselves. More fundamentally, they are the Spirit's work in us because he has awoken our desire for the goal that these actions serve. He has taught us what actions we need to perform to pursue that goal. He prompts us to undertake these actions by making them attractive to us. He strengthens our wills to adhere to them and he guides us in our performance of them. However, there remains an ongoing resistance to the Spirit's transformative work in us in an overcoming of our disordered desires and loves. Though the final victory is assured, the battle is not yet over.

I formulate kerygmatic devotion as a model of reading Scripture for faithful Christian living. This daily regime is practiced by individual readers at their own times and locations. However, a community or smaller groups can also practice this together for teaching and learning.

---

34. This formulation of kerygmatic devotion flows from my reflection on Spirit baptism in section 3.1.5 on Spirit and Transformation: "In my formulation, Spirit baptism marks the beginning of the Spirit's transformative work in a believer. In Spirit baptism, the Spirit awakens the believer's desire for the *One* who transforms, the *goal* of transformation and the *process* of transformation."

I model kerygmatic devotion broadly after the monastic tradition of *lectio divina*.[35] Kerygmatic devotion, as a regime of daily disciplines, comprises five steps of Bible reading, meditation, prayer, contemplation, and proclamation.[36] In this devotion, the Spirit orchestrates readers' participation. He works with Scripture to draw readers along in the flow of *agape* in their obedient living as kerygmatic witnesses to Jesus Christ. Kerygmatic devotion when practiced in a daily regime provides both structure and expression to a kerygmatic reader's occupation and preoccupation with God's *agape* and *logos*.[37] Therefore, kerygmatic devotion is a habituated practice of spirituality.

Kerygmatic devotion features core elements in a practice of spirituality that find close parallels in some versions of *lectio divina*. Nonetheless, kerygmatic devotion has some characterizing emphases. First, kerygmatic devotion sets aside times for and in anticipation of the Spirit's *surprises*. Second, kerygmatic devotion cultivates *a specific practice* of praying in the Spirit, in a form that I am going to explore later. Third, unlike the monastic tradition that practices much silence, kerygmatic devotion is a practice of *vocalization* in the *logos* and the *Spirit*—in reading, praying, and proclaiming—while also being meditative and contemplative.[38] It is

---

35. From traditional monastic accounts of *lectio divina*, I note that different orders and traditions could have different understandings and practices in growing spirituality. Notwithstanding, many writers on the monastic traditions speak of moments—in an ascending series of steps—that grow one's spirituality: *lectio, cogitatio, studium, meditatio, oratio, contemplatio*. See Magrassi, *Praying the Bible*, 19; Delatte, *Commentaire*.

36. These moments of Bible reading, meditation, prayer, contemplation, and proclamation are graduated because they lie in a continuum and are not discrete activities—time is spent praying, listening or flowing in the Spirit in overlapping moments of reading, meditating, praying, contemplating, and proclaiming. The moments are also graduated because some are devoted to grow a reader more in Christlikeness in the objective *logos* while others are devoted to flow him/her more in the subjective *agape* of the Spirit. For clarity, "meditation" in kerygmatic devotion embraces that part of this chain of activities and daily disciplines that grows the Word in a reader through reflection, Bible study, and meditation and more.

37. Jacob explains that Christian *agape* demands a voluntary act on a believer notwithstanding its nature of *caritas*. Jacob proffers, "Various Christian thinkers might characterize *agape* as the fruit of spiritual discipline, the achievement of moral labor, or the unearned gift of the Holy Spirit, but no one would say that the kind of love, of God or neighbor, that Jesus commands and Augustine endorses simply 'happens to us.' Rather, it is a matter of the will, and thus in the etymological sense voluntary, rather than given. How, and by what force, the will may be redirected is a matter of theological dispute, but that it requires redirection in order that we might meet Jesus' commandment is axiomatic for Christian theology" (Jacob, *Theology of Reading*, 32).

38. In our characterization of a kerygmatic reader, s/he first vocalizes God's speech,

important to hear oneself vocalize in the *logos* and the *Spirit* in a daily discipline, and finding that sacred time and space for this vocalization is essential for effectual formation of a kerygmatic reader.[39] Fourth, *praying* is the pivotal moment in kerygmatic devotion that transposes a reader from the earthly realm to have him/her speak from the heavenly realm.[40] Fifth, proclamation, as in preaching and witnessing, is less commonly observed in *lectio divina* practices; this is emphasized in kerygmatic devotion.[41] This proclamation of the gospel of Jesus Christ in the daily activities of life goes out in the power of the Spirit so the world may hear and see God.

Kerygmatic devotion forms a kerygmatic reader's identity because spirituality and spiritual disciplines are identity-forming.[42] Kerygmatic

---

logos. The Spirit comes to give life to the *logos* and to catch him/her up into perfect union with *logos*. It is in participation in the flow of the *Spirit* that s/he becomes *logos* enfleshed. In this sense, kerygmatic devotion sets aside times to practice a vocalization in the *logos* and the *Spirit*. On the other hand, meditation takes a reader in a deep-dive that allows *logos* to take flesh: understanding, studying, analyzing, memorizing, reflecting, and "chewing" it again and again to form the mind of Christ. Vocalization is generally not practiced in meditation and contemplation.

39. This practice is premised on the assurance that the Spirit will teach us what to say for the moment of witness, testing, and persecution; so we can decisively depend on his guidance without any need to script a testimony (see Matt 10:19–20; Luke 12:11–12; 21:12–15). Therefore, such a practice of vocalization in the Spirit trains a reader for such moments. This is not to mitigate the need to ingest and internalize the *logos*. Rather, this practice launches readers into flowing in the spirit of the *logos* after its study and meditation.

40. My formulation of *prayer* in kerygmatic devotion is distinguished from that of *oratio* in *lectio divina*. *Oratio* is often interpreted as a response to God speaking through Bible reading, and meditation. It is a word-filled prayer of human response to God, encompassing an agenda of confession, petition, intercession, thanksgiving, and praise, often using the newly learnt vocabulary from the Scripture as prayer language. Many, especially those who are habituated to speak from the conscious mind, face challenges in experiencing a flowing in the Spirit. It is in dispossessing themselves, including a detachment from their thoughts, that readers may experience literally the infilling and outflowing of the Spirit in prayer, vocalizing spiritual thoughts of God.

41. See, e.g., Heisler, *Spirit-Led Preaching*; Heisler, "Spirit," 197–202.

42. Joanna Collicut argues that spirituality in psychology may be understood as anthropologic or human centered. She aptly cites Thomas Merton (1915–68), "You think you can identify a man by giving his date of birth and his address, his height, his eyes' color, even his fingerprints . . . But if you want to identify me, ask me not where I live, or what I like to eat, or how I comb my hair, but ask me what I think I am living for, in detail, and ask me what I think is keeping me from living fully for the thing I want to live for. Between these two answers you can determine the identity of any person" (Collicut, *Christian Character Formation*, 16). Also see Merton, *Seven Storey*

devotion is then the habit that grows this relationship with God and his church by spending unhurried time together with God in each other's presence.

I next elaborate on these steps of Bible reading and meditation, prayer and contemplation, proclamation and witness.

5.3.1 Bible reading and meditation

The Spirit transforms readers in this vocalized Bible reading and meditation.[43] The Spirit helps us to read Bible and to meditate. A kerygmatic reader is open and sensitive to the *logos* coming alive as the Spirit speaks to him/her through the word. This practice forms the *logos enfleshed*.

This transformation involves being drawn into a relationship with the One who speaks in and through Scripture, and about whom Scripture speaks.[44] This calls for a reading whose object is God's Word, but it is also a reading where God reads the text in and through a kerygmatic reader's reading. It is listening to God (so the *logos* is vocalized just as God speaks) who initiates the love relationship and draws humans to himself.[45] Therefore, Bible reading is the first step that seeks to know the Word, who is not some impersonal scriptural truth. As I proffered earlier, scriptural truth is located in a Person. There is an idea then that Bible reading is coming to a Person, One who seeks us out to speak with us.

Mountain, for his autobiography.

43. *Lectio divina* (divine reading) is similarly transformation-seeking, apart from the differences highlighted earlier. On *lectio divina*, see, e.g., Badley and Badley, "Slow Reading," 29–42; Foster, *Reading with God*.

44. In kerygmatic hermeneutics, the disciplines of Bible reading and meditation, prayer and contemplation, proclamation and witness are *together* significant for the transformation that a consistent and regular relating with the *Other* would bring. That is, kerygmatic hermeneutics, unlike philosophical and theological hermeneutics, is set in tension between orthodoxy and orthopraxis (see Carruthers, *Craft of Thought*. Carruthers argues that orthodoxy (explicating canonical texts) and orthopraxis (experiencing of God through a set of techniques or a way to enlightenment) co-exist in Christianity, where monasticism, as a way of life in God, is one such practice (Carruthers, *Craft of Thought*, 1). Kerygmatic hermeneutics, while is also set in tension between orthodoxy and orthopraxis, goes beyond a monastic practice because it is openly devoted for witness of God and his ways to the world. A kerygmatic contemplative is known by his/her acts in the world. In his/her encountering God in the prayer closet, s/he desires even more to encounter God in the world. This is because it is in the proclaiming and witnessing that s/he is united with Christ in the Spirit, so it is Christ who speaks and acts in the world.

45. Magrassi, *Praying the Bible*, 19.

Therefore, the idea is also that reading is listening to the particular *Other, Jesus Christ.*

Meditation takes reading beyond into Bible study, reflection and meditation proper.[46] In this discipline, the *logos* enters into the reader as s/he enters into the *logos*. This represents a ceaseless process of chewing up the *logos,* perhaps memorizing it, writing it on the tablets of one's heart, only to be brought up again and again for reflection and imagination, and chewing through repeatedly until the *logos* takes form in speech and life, and the reader becomes the *logos* enfleshed.[47] That is, the *logos* inhabits the reader and s/he inhabits the *logos*. Bible study may involve critical biblical studies and theological training at a theological department or seminary. Yet scholarly Bible studies are at the service of spirituality.[48] Meditation is that discipline that transforms what may be fragmented texts into coherent expressions of scriptural truth to be lived out in speech and life in the particular.

This reading contrasts with other forms of Bible reading where reader transformation is either not in consideration or is a mere

---

46. See, e.g., Carruthers, *Craft of Thought,* and Peterson, *Eat this Book.* Peterson argues that meditation is the discipline that keeps memory active in the act of reading as it moves the reader from looking at the *words* of the text to entering the *world* of the text. It is also the primary way of keeping the revelation of God in a coherent reading and guards against the fragmentation of Scripture (Peterson, *Eat this Book,* 98–102).

47. Hays explores what it means for modern day believers to read Scripture figurally. He observes, "First of all, it would mean cultivating a deep knowledge of the Old Testament texts, getting these texts into our blood and bones. It would mean learning texts by heart in the fullest sense . . . But alas, many Christian communities have lost touch with the sort of deep primary knowledge of Scripture—especially Israel's Scripture—that would enable them even to perceive the messages conveyed by the Evangelists' biblical allusions and echoes, let alone to employ Scripture with comparable facility in their own preaching and renarration of the gospel story" (Hays, *Echoes of Scripture,* 357). He suggests that perhaps we could learn the language through worship in liturgical traditions. However, deliberate efforts and hard work would be required for the latecomers to these traditions. In this sense, kerygmatic devotion trains readers to memorize Scripture and more.

48. Following Fodor and Higton, "Scripture, Devotion and Discipleship," 123–40, I suggest that historical-critical Bible studies and kerygmatic hermeneutics are two distinct forms of Bible readings but there are overlaps in these practices. The former, with its critical reading, is helpful though not primordial for one seeking truth in kerygmatic hermeneutics—it raises questions that interrogate and challenge a reader's assumptions and is potentially transformative. Historical-critical readings of a scriptural text are evaluated in their own history of reception. A kerygmatic reading, however, may give quite a different reading to a community at the end of prayer listening to the Spirit. That is, historical-critical Bible studies can contribute to reading Scripture well, but its significance depends on the question that a community is asking in the Spirit.

secondary possibility.⁴⁹ Notwithstanding, kerygmatic devotion attends to both challenges and opportunities that may arise from overlaps of this form of transformative Bible reading and meditation with other practices like critical reading. In its overlaps with critical reading, for instance, a kerygmatic reader attentively abstracts from scriptural texts and the history of interpretation general claims about God and his ways that could deepen and enrich his/her apprehension of God in the world that s/he may be united with him.

5.3.2 Prayer and contemplation

Prayer and contemplation in kerygmatic devotion is a Spirit-led transformation—the Spirit penetrates the cognition, emotion, and volition of humans in a Spirit transformation that catches humans up in a flow of the Spirit.⁵⁰ I next formulate this prayer and contemplation in turn.

Readers can discern the paradigmatic work of the Spirit in their praying in all the multifaceted expressions that may be appropriate to their contexts.⁵¹ Expressions of praying in the Spirit may take various forms. First, it may come as a miraculous gift of speaking in a known language never learnt (as in the days of the apostles at Pentecost). Second,

---

49. For more discussion on the relation between critical reading and *lectio divina*, see Fodor and Higton, "Scripture, Devotion and Discipleship," 123–40. They conclude with some rules of thumb for exploring the roles that Scripture reading play in theology. "Ask, of each practice, what standards of excellence are internal to it—what it means to read well in this specific practice . . . Ask what questions are raised by this practice—what assumptions it makes about the nature of Scripture, what claims about history it involves, what kinds of thing it takes for granted. But also pay attention to the questions it doesn't pose, the assumptions it doesn't involve, even though they matter to other practices of reading. Attend to the overlaps between different practices of reading . . . What challenges and opportunities does it create? Reading practices are not static . . . they have histories, they evolve, and some of the energy for that evolution is generated precisely at the overlaps, the places where one reading rubs against another" (Fodor and Higton, "Scripture, Devotion and Discipleship,"139).

50. Therefore, any perturbations of the psyche are derived and secondary effects of the Spirit's work. On the other hand, psychologists and psychiatrists would probably attribute this phenomenon primarily or even solely to the psyche.

51. Praying in the Spirit can mean different things to different people. Cox uses "primal speech" to highlight the spiritual significance of what others call "ecstatic utterance" or "glossolalia" and what the Pentecostals call "speaking in tongues" (or what is commonly known as "praying in the Spirit"). Cox uses "primal speech" to mean elemental speech that speaks to the deepest core of one's being and consciousness (Cox, *Fire from Heaven*, 81–82).

it may flow in a spiritual language known only to God. Third, it may lapse into a wordless "prayer of the heart," one that goes beyond words. Praying in the Spirit, which may include ecstatic experiences, is paradigmatically non-rational.[52] Yet, they are not involuntary; they are within one's conscious control. A kerygmatic reader retains full consciousness and can decide to cease participation in the spiritual reality at will. That is, these expressions come in uncharacteristically characteristic ways that may be discerned in the Spirit.

Praying in the Spirit is a wider experience within which spiritual discernment and scriptural interpretation in the Spirit take place.[53] It is paradigmatic because the Spirit catches people up in an experience of a spiritual reality that frees one from physical, perceptual, cognitive, and emotional modes of being. Readers would recognize that such thoughts are above their thoughts. Therefore, praying in the Spirit here can be Spirit talk to God, the reader, or other hearers, all in the flow of the Spirit.

There is also a contemplative prayer with which the Spirit transforms readers in the depths of their interiority. Rowan Williams speaks of this dispossessed language "before God," that articulates one's incompleteness (lack of wholeness or holiness) in the practice of theological integrity.[54] This is the language of contemplation.

Contemplation in kerygmatic devotion is the way into the fullness of humanity in Christ.[55] It is in getting themselves dispossessed that read-

---

52. The Doctrine Commission of the Church of England observes, "... where the experience of charismatics and of contemplatives so significantly converges: in that profound though often fleeting or obscure, sense of entering in prayer into a 'conversation' *already in play*, a reciprocal divine conversation between Father and Spirit which can finally be reduced neither to divine monologue nor to human self-transcendence" (England, *We Believe*, 36).

53. I will be discussing a practice of spiritual discernment and scriptural interpretation in the Spirit in the next chapter (see sections 6.2 and 6.3 respectively).

54. Williams articulates succinctly, "Religious practice is only preserved in any integrity by seriousness about prayer; and so, if theology is the untangling of the real grammar of religious practice, its subject matter is, humanly and specifically, people who pray. If theology is itself a critical, even a suspicious discipline, it is for this reason. It seeks to make sense of the practice of dispossessed language 'before God'. It thus lives with the constant possibility of its own relativizing, interruption, silencing; it will not regard its conclusions as having authority independently of their relation to the critical, penitent community it seeks to help to be itself" (Williams, *On Christian Theology*, 13).

55. Contemplation is used to mean different things to different people, including non-Christians and non-religious people. Within the church, both across and within Catholic, Orthodox and Protestant persuasions, there are also different

ers may embody God. Here, a soul is freed not just from itself, but also from its enemies, i.e., the devil and the world. To embody God's disinterested love, the Spirit, readers learn to abandon all other loves, including self-love. It is a journey away from sin and its distortions, and failures that keep one back from God, which one too easily mistakes for what it is to be human. Therefore, it is a journey, not away from one's humanity, but in fulfilment and perfection of humanity.[56]

Contemplation in kerygmatic hermeneutics is also paradigmatic. It is characteristically uncharacteristic; experiences vary across persons and at different points of one's spiritual journey. However, from the various accounts of contemplation in traditional monastic practice, I find that of Saint John of the Cross most informing and illustrative of what it takes to constantly read over-against self in a journeying with the Spirit to transform nature into supernature (in the words of Williams). This reader grows into the fullness of humanity. Saint John of the Cross's account is succinct yet complex.[57] He speaks of the passive night of sense,

---

understandings. Magrassi describes contemplation, which is centered on the object of prayer, the Bible, and not on the inner states of the praying subject as "objective" spirituality (Magrassi, *Praying the Bible*, 117). Contemplation in kerygmatic devotion is *not* limited to or focused on Magrassi's sense of "objective" spirituality. While these may be helpful categories, I am also conscious that theological formulations could limit a wholistic understanding of the Spirit and his work. I am careful that kerygmatic hermeneutics does not become reductionist because the Spirit's working in embodied witnesses cannot be fully described in reduced forms.

56. Williams argues that this going beyond the confines of self to share in God's freedom is in keeping with a human's deepest vocation, and this should not be confused with an attitude that devalues the created order (Williams, *Wound of Knowledge*, 159–79, on Saint John of the Cross). Williams observes, "St John does not seek an 'escape' from creation, but he does regard the purpose of nature as leading towards 'supernature.' The goal of the created order is to point the soul to self-transcendence. Thus the movement of self or soul is always a stripping, a simplification. And because this means an abandonment of the familiar and secure, it is an immensely costly process" (Williams, *Wound of Knowledge*, 164).

57. Saint John of the Cross, *Dark Night*. He explains how this dark night came to be. "Now this is precisely what this Divine ray of contemplation does in the soul. Assailing it with its Divine light, it transcends the natural power of the soul, and herein it darkens it and deprives it of all natural affections and apprehensions which it apprehended aforetime by means of natural light; and thus it leaves it not only dark, but likewise empty, according to its faculties and desires, both spiritual and natural. And, by thus leaving it empty and in darkness, it purges and illumines it with Divine spiritual light, although the soul thinks not that it has this light, but believes itself to be in darkness, even as we have said of the ray of light, which, although it be in the midst of the room, yet, if it be pure and meet nothing on its path, is not visible" (Saint John of the Cross, *Dark Night*, 59). The account of St. John of the Cross may be too complex

which is believed to be common, and of spirit, which is said to be the portion of the few. Such negative experiences of dispossession may be seen to be part of what John the Baptist referred to as purgation by unquenchable "fire" in Spirit baptism. The Spirit paradigmatically transforms the human spirit by stripping him/her of all-natural desires first, and then spiritual desires. Williams observes that this ascetic practice brings focus to "a *concentration* of desire" after God. He sees a paradoxical logic to these apparently dehumanizing negative experiences. Christ himself is for Saint John "the ultimate touchstone of spiritual 'authenticity,'" especially in his experience of the passive night of the spirit.[58] To me, however, Saint John is perhaps one of those who have gone far to describe the paradigmatic Spirit-spirit transformation journey into dispossession so we may know where we are in this journey and how much further we may have to go.[59]

Readers can also discern contemplation's paradigmatic outcome: the Spirit forms a spiritual person. When readers emerge from this spiritual journey into the greatest and darkest depths of their interiority, they

---

for many readers and I risk using this example too easily. Readers would probably have to read his account many times to appreciate part of what he may be saying. However, I have personally benefited from allowing his account to sit and grow within me in meditation as I read it again and again.

58. Williams observes that while the "night of the senses" is relatively straightforward, the "night of the spirit" is more bitter as it strikes at the roots of human illusions. The latter purifies human spiritual activity, reducing it to one of faith and longing. Here, the passive night is more terrible and costly than the active night. Its significance bears resemblance to that of Jesus carrying his cross. An absolute felt absence of God's presence and consolation hints at God's hostile rejection of sin. St John describes this as the midnight that has to come before the dawn" (Williams, *Wound of Knowledge*, 166–67).

59. Saint Teresa's conception, which represents a point of departure from Saint John's, may be more appropriate for some. For further discussion of Saint Teresa of Avila, see, e.g., Peers, *Mother of Carmel*; Williams, *Teresa of Avila*. Cuthbert Butler reads Saint Teresa to regard the action of God on the soul (to her a sign of supernatural prayer and contemplation) "is not merely a silent working of grace, but an act, of which the soul is sensibly and consciously aware." As well, Saint Teresa "insists that we should not try in prayer to empty the mind of images or silence the faculties as a preparation for contemplation, but let intellect and will go on working in discursive and affective prayer until God stops them and creates the needed silence. But this, again, is entirely counter to St John's attitude: let the first chapter of Book III of the *Ascent of Mount Carmel* be read, and the difference springs to the eye; indeed the active emptying of the mind and the silencing of the faculties is the burden of the whole treatise" (Butler, *Western Mysticism*, xxvi). Kerygmatic hermeneutics recognizes that there is not one or two but several forms of contemplation that can range from acquired to infused or mixed to quasi-quiet to mystical, along which spectrum a kerygmatic reader grows in experience of the divine.

speak incisively and powerfully into the world. These appraise all things with God's wisdom that comes from the spiritual light within (1 Cor 2:6–16). According to Saint John, "this spiritual light is so simple, pure and general" that it "discerns and penetrates whatsoever thing presents itself to it".[60] As well, this spirit that is purged of all its loves takes on the mind of Christ.[61]

5.3.3 Proclamation and witness

Witness to Jesus Christ flows naturally from an experience of life in the Spirit. This is because life in the Spirit *is* a life of witness to Jesus—a life in which the Spirit catches humans up continuously into an encounter with Jesus so we may proclaim him.

This life of witness that the Spirit leads us into is a witness to our encounter with Jesus, in what is happening or has happened to ourselves as much as what had happened long ago or far away. This proclamation comes in speech, life, and power in the Spirit: what we *say* about this realism with regards to God—the fact that God exists apart from any human representation, or whether we believe this or not—*and* how our *lives* have been transformed by this realism in the power of the Spirit. This witness is *not* an extra burden upon the life of faith, because it is the form it inherently takes. That is, to live a life in the Spirit *is* to embody God's *word*—the *Word* in which God proclaims Godself and witnesses to Godself.

In this section, I have shown how these habits in community life are as much a life in the Spirit. These carry all four marks of the Spirit: intoxication, life, participation, and a revelation of truth. In the next chapter, I will be laying out clearly what community practices in kerygmatic praying and kerygmatic reading would look like. For now, I discuss the theological categories underlying these community practices.

---

60. John of the Cross, *Dark Night*, 60.

61. Karl Barth argues for scriptural interpretation to go beyond an exegesis that is an application of historical criticism. He says, "By genuine understanding and interpretation I mean that creative energy which Luther exercised with intuitive certainty in his exegesis . . . The conversation between the original record and the reader moves round the subject-matter, until a distinction between yesterday and to-day becomes impossible" (Barth and Hoskyns, Preface, 7). However, it is not clear what Barth means by this "creative energy" and how it comes to be. It is also not clear how the Spirit would be involved in this interpretive process.

5.4 Community Practices

There are two dimensions to community practices in kerygmatic hermeneutics: the discerning and the performing. The discerning and performing of scriptural truth are inter-dependent—a community is better able to live this out fully and coherently in every situation when it can better discern the Spirit's revelation of truth. It can better discern when it can better apprehend the shape and substance of that truth as it is performed in the Spirit.

This discerning concerns the apprehending of God and his ways in the world. Unlike a grasping of reason or an understanding of a fact, this apprehending of God and his ways is *incomplete* until it is embodied in the Spirit—because it is the Spirit who guides a reader into what s/he ought to say or do in his/her particular context to do the Father's will.[62] It is in performing that readers can *fully* apprehend God and his ways in the world.

I discuss next discerning in the Spirit and performing in kerygma in kerygmatic community practices.

5.4.1 Praying in the Spirit

Praying in the Spirit is that wider experience within which spiritual discernment and scriptural interpretation in the Spirit take place. *Praying in the Spirit* has two elements: *flowing and listening in the Spirit*. These are not mutually exclusive; they may both be happening in the same situation. However, each focuses readers to a different kind of attentiveness in the Spirit.

There is an attentiveness to the Spirit, to what he is saying and doing in engaging humans, as these are caught up in intoxication, *flowing in the Spirit*. Readers experience another kind of attentiveness in *listening in the Spirit*; it is an attentiveness to the situation, the context, when the Spirit speaks by way of multiple human voices (perhaps on various scales: e.g., listening to one's local group, to the whole congregation, to the wider church).

---

62. In one sense, our understanding of God is completed in a specific moment of embodiment: we inhabit fully what God wills for that situation. In another sense, our understanding is always incomplete: there is always more of God to know—a "more" that we will explore but never exhaust as we learn to embody God's word in situation after situation.

One may trust the discernment and scriptural interpretations that emerge from kerygmatic readers the more that readers in community are visibly characterized by *flowing in the Spirit*. Although this realism with regards to God cannot be neatly reduced to visible signs, it will nevertheless show itself in such signs as the community losing itself in wonder, love, and praise, devoting time to prayer and Scripture reading in a willing dedication to devotion.[63] Devotion, as in all relationships, needs investing in and then sustaining.[64] Yet spending time with the One we love is rewarding in itself. Therefore, discernment of one *flowing in the Spirit* can come in visible form—in a committed practice of spiritual disciplines, the setting apart of sacred space and sacred time in a daily encounter with the Holy.[65]

63. Williams talks about how we can trust that others, even when we disagree with them, are part of the one church together with us. He says, "I suggest that what we are looking for in each other is the grammar of obedience: we watch to see if our partners take the same kind of time, sense that they are under the same sort of judgement or scrutiny, approach the issue with the same attempt to be dispossessed by the truth they are engaging with. This will not guarantee agreement; but it might explain why we should always first be hesitant and attentive to each other. Why might anyone think this might count as a gift of Christ to the Church?" (Williams, "Making Moral Decisions," 11).

64. Flowing in the Spirit is recognizably a spiritual experience that transcends the causal factors at work in the natural grain of life. Yet, even after such an experience, this relationship still needs sustaining with personal effort. A reader spends time in the presence of God, without necessarily going away each time with an encounter with God that may be apprehended by the five senses. That is, a spiritual encounter is not necessarily a felt experience.

65. Our discussion up till now, from reader dispositions, community habits to community practices, identifies the necessary predispositions and the engagements that will engender the outcomes that make a difference (or impact) to the world. Each part of this process in the forming of an embodied witness to Christ in kerygmatic readers and communities that will glorify God bears the Spirit's signature in the marks of the Spirit. For example, the work of the Spirit in intensified and perhaps ecstatic devotion and worship in coming together is likely to show itself in various ways beyond this community. his work is likely to carry over into what is perhaps more mundane things of life, like giving more monies and time to address unmet social needs. Here, there may be a more patient expression of love in doing all good. Such expressions in fact constitute part of the testing and evaluation in kerygmatic criticism. That is, discerning such work of the Spirit in the ordinariness of daily living in the world, when kerygmatic readers and communities are not with other believers, is essential even though this is less straightforward. For a full account of the work of the Spirit, discerning the work of the Spirit merely in reader dispositions, community habits and practices is necessary but not sufficient. There is sufficient kerygmatic criticism when discernment in a testing and evaluation includes a dynamic assessment of the

Listening in the Spirit in a community of faith is a form of Spirit-centered informal spiritual direction.[66] This takes humility and effort to be open to the Spirit's work in edifying the body of Christ.[67] Paul teaches in 1 Cor 12–14 that each part of the body of Christ has a distinct role. Therefore, each part is also significant in discerning and performing his/her role. There must be a respect for one another: the scholar needs to respect the blue-collar worker, and the latter has to respect what the scholar has to say. The unity comes about in the learning and correction, in correction and learning. With humility one stands corrected and therefore learns from one another—including one who may not be well schooled but may have the richness of life's experience.

Listening intently to one another in the performing—in one's own and another's narrative of faith—discerns credible voices through whom the Spirit might speak to reveal lies and self-deception.[68] It should be

---

outcomes and impacts of such a practice of kerygmatic interpretation. Even then, untangling these outcomes and impacts from other ecclesial practices may be challenging. For example, there had been big disputes in 16th century when godly people found themselves on both sides of a chasm (over hermeneutics plus other ecclesial issues); it then become difficult to recognize one other as Christians, not to mention godly people. In section 5.7, I will lay out a framework for a testing and evaluation that allows for a composite picture of what may be attributable to the work of the Spirit beyond a discernment within each dimension of his working—in reader dispositions, community habits, practices, outcomes, and impacts—that necessarily reflects what may be seen and heard as true of God in the world beyond the community. Of course, this testing and evaluation come with all the limitations of human discernment and empirical enquiry.

66. Historically, formal spiritual direction of the type referred to by Thomas Merton, has been practiced in monasteries and by ordained clergy (see, e.g., Merton, *Seven Storey Mountain*). Contemporary practice tends to be more informal without predefined programmatic roles for a spiritual director and directee in a one-to-one relationship. *Listening in the Spirit* in a community of faith, for example, is premised on spiritual direction being a way of leading a directee to see, hear and obey the real Director, the Holy Spirit.

67. Here in kerygmatic hermeneutics, kerygmatic leaders who are appointed to grow the small groups or fellowships could serve as informal spiritual directors. This does not preclude a kerygmatic reader from speaking and confronting truth in one another's life in mutual accountability. Again, one would trust the spiritual guidance the more a leader or reader is visibly characterized by a devoted practice of spiritual disciplines and humble learning.

68. This avoids some of the problems when Christian voices disagree, as in the past. The question—Who identifies which voice to heed?—depends on the significance of the (hermeneutical or ecclesial) issue at hand. Consistent with the previous footnote, believers in community presumably have an understanding of some ecclesial accountability structure, as well as communal decision-making process. Ecumenical

listening to voices of past and present Christian readers in a small group, and in the whole congregation, as well as the wider church body. It is also listening in each case to the interpretations that have emerged as these readers lived lives with the text in response to the Spirit.

Praying in the Spirit is the language of revelation. A revelation of God's working when he is doing something new often comes when a reader or community is *praying in the Spirit*, whether in the vernacular, spirit speech or silent contemplation. In whatever form this praying takes, there is a freeing of one's being (spirit, desire, mind, emotion, volition, etc.) in intoxication in the Spirit, with the Spirit directing the prayer wherever the Spirit may lead.

Praying in the Spirit can take different expressions ranging from praying in the vernacular, praying in spirit speech to praying in silent contemplation. Praying in the vernacular is not praying to a set script of prayers or exegetical readings. It is articulating what the Spirit is saying and doing in the present situation. Praying in spirit speech, on the other hand, is an exercise of charismata like tongues, interpretation of tongues, prophecy, wisdom, knowledge, and discernment (1 Cor 12–14).[69] For the edification of the community, though, an interpretation needs to follow the use of public tongue speech. Praying in silent contemplation is akin to the way of, say, Saint John of the Cross. This could probably best catch a pray-er into the presence of God.

5.4.2 Interpreting Scripture in the Spirit

This revelation from *praying in the Spirit*, when mediated by Scripture, may yield a fresh interpretation of a scriptural text. Here, readers direct their attentiveness to Scripture as well. *Interpreting Scripture in the Spirit* is reading Scripture in the light of what the Spirit is saying and doing in the present situation. *Interpreting Scripture in the Spirit* is therefore a kind of attentiveness to the Spirit working with Scripture, to what the Spirit

---

communities, on the other hand, may need to first formulate a common understanding of some communication protocols for communal decision-making before assuming any agenda that may involve contentious hermeneutical questions.

69. Related to this spirit speech, Sarah Coakley uses wordless prayer to mean the Spirit's intercession "with 'sighs too deep for words' transcending normal human rationality" in Rom 8:26–27 (Coakley, "Trinity, Prayer and Sexuality," 225). Coakley argues that this Christian practice and commitment to wordless prayer is inherently Trinitarian in structure (Coakley, "Trinity, Prayer and Sexuality," 223).

is doing and saying in the present with Scripture. Readers listen in each case to the interpretations that have emerged as these readers have lived their lives with the text in response to the Spirit.

What then are the visible signs of the Spirit's revelatory work with Scripture? Presumably, a healthy kerygmatic community will be able to narrate how it has, through the kinds of attentiveness described above, heard challenging and inspiring voices from the world. It then returns to Scripture and to its established pattern of reading in order to re-read. Readers do this to test what they think they have in *givenness*, but also to have their eyes opened to new possibilities to be *found* in their reading.[70] Readers listen for the Spirit in one another in the discerning—what do they read of the Spirit in the history of interpretation of a scriptural text? In tradition? In today's context?[71]

Therefore, a kerygmatic community will be one with a history of evolving reading: it is always serious about faithfulness to Scripture, but always discovering new things in it (and being weaned away from some old ways of reading), rather than a community that sticks with an unvarying pattern of reading. More significantly, *interpreting Scripture in the Spirit* brings conviction for change and correction in a hermeneutical spiral towards a fullness in its humanity.

5.4.3 Proclaiming Christ in the Spirit

A contemplative kerygmatic is heard and seen not in his/her prayer closet but in the world. The integrity of kerygmatic hermeneutics is predicated on the coherence of the work of the Spirit in a kerygmatic reader's lived-out proclamation of the *logos*, God's self-gift in Jesus Christ.

Readers' proclaim Jesus as Lord and Savior in speech, life, and power to the world. This message resonates with that from the

---

70. On the question, 'Is Scripture indeterminate or biblical interpretation indeterminate?' Fowl and Jones argue that "[t]he key lies in difference between Scripture and Bible—significance versus meaning, where meaning remains intact but significance changes with context" (Fowl and Jones, "Scripture, Exegesis, and Discernment," 113). Notwithstanding, I argue that meanings may also change in God's economy, e.g., in Acts 10–15, the apostles re-read Scripture to admit gentiles into the church of Jesus Christ, while scriptural truth does not. Kerygmatic hermeneutics acknowledges the work of the Spirit to inspire new meanings when text is read through the lens of God and his ongoing work in creation.

71. In chapter 6, I address these questions in a proposed practice of kerygmatic interpretation for a community to read Scripture in the Spirit.

non-self-referential Spirit. The same Christ who had borne our sins is the Lord of this created order, this cosmos, this world. This is the most important message that humankind needs to know—to retrieve our identity in God, our Father—so that we can live to the fullness of our humanity. This message is a message of salvation and redemption by Jesus, the Son, who brought us back into fellowship as children of God. This message brings life and transformation in not just the hearer but also the messenger as Christlike children of God.

Jesus Christ is the exemplar of this messenger who spoke with divine wisdom and power into the world. When Jesus walked this world, he spoke into and broke the bonds of human suffering and death that veiled the presence of God in the world. He healed the sick, delivered the spiritually oppressed and possessed and freed the marginalized and outcast. He challenged religious traditions to re-read the Hebrew Scriptures afresh in the Spirit from God's context. He pointed the way to his Father God, a reality that is spiritual yet made concrete in the Son's incarnation. He demonstrated this otherness of God is not a projection of human thought and will. Above all, the resurrected Jesus Christ gave us the Spirit to discern this Other. Therefore, kerygmatic hermeneutics is that voice and act through which the *world may hear and see God* in possibly every dimension of human affairs in our contemporary world—in politics, institutions, family, education, civil society, and the economy.

5.5 Community Outcomes

The outcomes of the Spirit's work in kerygmatic hermeneutics include the forming of kerygmatic readers and kerygmatic communities. Theology calls for the discernment of God and his word in the lives of believers.[72] That is, the lives of believers could help the world to hear and see God and his word. In a similar sense, Moberly argues in his apologetic account to a disenchanted world that the realist claims of the Bible are credible as long as the church, in its diverse forms, as a people of God formed by the Bible, continues to be what can give meaning to those claims.[73] Following

72. For example, Johnson says that "pastoral or practical theology is the research arm of theology" since theology is not theoretical nor speculative (Johnson, *Decision Making*, 51). In this sense, theology is practical, anthropological, and ethnographic.

73. Moberly argues, "The biblical portrayal of human nature and destiny will present itself to consciousness as reality only to the extent that its appropriate plausibility structure, the Christian church in its many forms, is kept in existence" (Moberly, *Bible*, 101).

Rogers, reading the Spirit in community outcomes would also include a reading of narratives about Jesus Christ in kerygmatic readers and communities.[74] That is, looking for the Spirit's work in the community would mean looking for readers' narratives about this person Jesus Christ—how he has been real in the ordinariness of readers' lives, in the midst of sufferings, pains and all good things.

We recognize these readers by their divinized lives: they are *logos* enfleshed, flesh becoming *logos*, the eternal Son. Readers are an embodiment of the Son—and are seen to be Christlike. Christlikeness gives the form of expression; love is the power or force that energizes the act that expresses Christlikeness. This form comes into expression in the act; and the act may be seen in the world in the expressed form.

Here, we recognize the critical role that Scripture plays in readers' transformation into *logos* enfleshed, an embodiment of God's speech witnessing to the world. Moreover, this embodiment is an enactment of this realism that Scripture talks about in life and power. Scripture gives the otherness to a testing and evaluation of readers' ongoing performance of scriptural truth. This life in the Spirit is a life that is gathered around the Bible.[75]

We also recognize a kerygmatic community by a unity of love. The Spirit is love; he fosters unity in communion. This unity is significant because members of a church community tend to be diverse in socioeconomic categories, political orientations, cultures, and ethnicity. Again, this love is the power or force that energizes the act that brings unity in kerygmatic communities.

---

74. Rogers formulates his thesis thus, "To think about the Spirit it will not do to think 'spiritually': to think about the Spirit you have to think materially. 'In the last days God poured out God's Spirit on all flesh' (Joel 3:1; Acts 2:17–18). You might object that 'all flesh' in that passage means 'human flesh': but theological interpreters have taken it both more broadly and more concretely" (Rogers, *After the Spirit*, 56). Moreover, Rogers adds, "And if Hans Frei is right about the difference between person and principle, the Spirit, if a person, cannot be reduced to a principle, because character is represented irreducibly in narrative. If the Spirit is a person, we must turn to narrative to identify her. And yet the Spirit is such, that the narratives *of* the Spirit are narratives *about* Jesus" (Rogers, *After the Spirit*, 71).

75. The sacraments, including the Eucharist, are significant for readers living a life in the Spirit. Given the constraints of this research, I have focused on how the Spirit works with the objectivity or otherness of Scripture (and community), amongst other created causes, to form an embodied witness to Jesus Christ. This silence over the Eucharist and other sacraments is therefore without prejudice to their importance in the forming of kerygmatic worshipers in community.

I next highlight the characterization of kerygmatic readers and kerygmatic communities of faith. These two sections should be read together. Some of the themes in the community section would already have been developed for the individual reader, in which case I will assume this pre-reading. In other cases, there may be new themes that are read at the community level only. As well, there may be some overlap for easy reference, but it is because I want to develop some points in detail in one and not the other.

5.5.1 Characterization of a kerygmatic reader

In this section, I build on the theology of the Spirit in the formation and transformation of a kerygmatic reader. *A kerygmatic reader is born of God's Word (logos) as a new creation in Christ who flows in the Spirit as logos enfleshed and proclaims the gospel of Jesus Christ in speech, in life, and in power.* S/he is a living proclamation of God's Word to the world. Just as the Son revealed his Father to the world, it is now possible for this Son-like child of God who is not yet without sin to do so in the Spirit.

Kerygmatic readers are characterized by a life centered on the Bible; The Bible is an account of God's Word (*logos*). This life in the Spirit is gathered around reading the Bible, studying, meditating, contemplating, and proclaiming it as God's speech so as to embody it. Readers interpret the truth that Scripture talks about, so they know what to say and do in the present. They enact their interpretation of this truth to the world in the power of the Spirit. Specifically, to enact the Kingdom of God in the present, readers proclaim this seed of God, *logos*, in speech, life, and power.

I next consider the various dimensions of the proclamation of this message (*logos*) and their implications for witness to the world.

First, the message *is* the messenger. S/he is Christlike who makes concrete the being, revelation, and knowing of God. As much as Jesus said one would have known the Father if one knows him, the world would have known Christ (and the Father) if it knows one who is *logos* enfleshed (John 14:7–14).

The messenger (*logos* enfleshed) is the message (*logos*) and more. There is, first, the idea that the scriptural truth that the message (*logos*) talks about concerns spiritual things; an explicit teaching of the *logos* can only give a certain level of understanding. Second, there is the idea that the *messenger* being the message would mean that the message could not simply be grasped by taking in explicit teaching. It requires an encounter with the person behind the teaching (faith is not belief in a set of dogma or principles but relating with God in Jesus Christ). Likewise, scriptural truth that is located in God cannot be adequately grasped apart from relating with God himself. Third, there is the idea that the message is inseparable from the *performance*, so that grasping the message (like 'the Kingdom of God is at hand') means encountering, being caught up in, and participating in a stream of activity in the flow of the Spirit. In kerygmatic hermeneutics, I am meaning truth to be a combination of the second and third idea, although such an understanding may be aided by some teaching as in the first idea.[76]

Summarizing, kerygmatic readers are *logos* enfleshed in many senses. It is a participation in divinity—a catching up into a union of grace with God in the proclamation of Christ. This *logos* enfleshed is a representation of God in the abiding indwelling of the Father and the Son. It is an embodiment of Christlikeness, an image in the likeness of God. This *logos* enfleshed is also an embodied enactment of the Kingdom of God, a performance of the *kerygma* in the present. Above all, proclaiming the *logos* and enacting the Kingdom of God to the world are readily observable of kerygmatic readers. In the next section, I highlight the characterization of a kerygmatic community, which bears the characterization of kerygmatic readers and more.

5.5.2 Characterization of a kerygmatic community

A kerygmatic community is a local assembly of kerygmatic readers that is characterized by a unified identity and witness in the Spirit yet without need for uniformity in communal life. A kerygmatic community is characterized by what kerygmatic readers are as individuals and more.[77] That

---

76. Congar presents an idea of "the messenger" being "the message," not from the reception or interpretation perspective but from the revelation perspective. He argues, "The history of salvation is not simply the history of God's revelation of himself. It is also the history of his communication of himself. God himself is the content of that self-communication" (Congar, *I Believe*, 3:12).

77. See Collicut, *Christian Character Formation*, 162–67. Collicut uses social identity theory to explain that while affiliation to a social group contributes to an individual's identity, affiliation also consolidates the group identity. To identify a group's members, identity markers like habits, dressing, beliefs and speech are used to mark who are the "in" and who are "out" (Collicut, *Christian Character Formation*, 163). Therefore, a kerygmatic community may be identified by specific characteristics like

is, it has characteristics that are more than simply an aggregate of those of individual kerygmatic readers; it takes on characteristics that emerge from the structure, relationships, and processes by which these individuals stand.[78]

The Spirit unifies a kerygmatic community because of her differences.[79] To the extent that individual members of a community flows in the Spirit as he directs, the Spirit unifies her. The desired impact of such a witness to the world is that people might believe that Jesus Christ is Son of God.[80] This is because the world is naturally diverse in many ways, the church being its microcosm; yet unity in the world is more often an ideal to be desired than realized. More significantly, this oneness in the Spirit is unnatural because it cannot be engendered by any political manipulation, philosophical argumentation, or social affinity.

A kerygmatic community speaks with the same voice, same clarity, and same coherence as the singularity of message that comes through the Trinitarian communion. There is a singularity of identity and purpose consonant with the scriptural truth located in the Trinitarian communion. The singularity of identity and purpose speaks similarly to the set of relationships and inter relationships among members of the kerygmatic community.[81] In this sense, the church becomes the visible representation of the Godhead in the Spirit, through whom the world sees God. The world sees God in the acts of the church as much as the world had seen God in the Acts of the Apostles.

---

dispositions, habits, and practices that may serve as identity markers.

78. Again, the silence here (given the constraint of this project) on the role of the sacraments, e.g., baptism and the Eucharist, in the forming of a community of God's people is without prejudice to their significance.

79. Augustine, in his struggle against the Donatists, developed more precisely the role of the Spirit in the church. For him, the Spirit is the principle of unity, and there is room in the church to embrace differences in orientations and traditions. See Augustine, *Bibl. August.* 28 (1963) 109–15.

80. See Jesus's intercessory prayer for the disciples in John 17:20–21: that the oneness of the church in her witness may cause the world to believe that Jesus Christ is sent of God.

81. Unity in kerygmatic hermeneutics takes the formulation of a grace-act of human participation in divinity through Spirit baptism, which is uniquely the work of the Spirit (1 Cor 12:13–14). In this sense, unity in the Spirit in kerygmatic hermeneutics finds its essence *within and beyond* the sociological and psychological identification of a community in practices and tradition, and the theological identification of the Spirit with *agape* love. See related discussion in Radner, "Holy Spirit and Unity," 207–20.

The Spirit works works in and through the materiality of readers' lives—their particular flesh, their particular histories—and so in and through that which makes them diverse. Therefore, he works in multicontextual and polyphonic ways that are contingent on the diversity in a community. While the Spirit unifies across traditions and persuasions in the church of Jesus Christ, oneness in lived-out scriptural truth does not equate to uniformity of speech-acts. Like the polyphonic voices heard through the human redactors in Scripture, the Spirit continues to give a consistent self-revelation in the present. There is an analogous idea of a symphony of diverse instruments categorized by strings, brass, percussion, and wind; all have a role to play in an interpretation in the Spirit, each giving a different color to the interpretation. Yet it is the Spirit, who blends the hues of these categories of instruments, both intra-category and inter-category, to give that interpretation that proclaims Christ, the Truth, in the particular. That is, the materiality of readers' lives is the material that the Spirit orchestrates to play the theme of the *logos*.

A kerygmatic community is thus characterized by a communal life that is centered on the Bible in order to enact this theme of the *logos*. This community is identified by its focus on Scripture. This community embodies and enacts its scriptural interpretation because of this identity; this embodiment and enactment in turn form and reinforce its identity.

The Spirit's unifying and intoxicative love can potentially draw and keep various traditions together. It opens up a discourse that is pluralistic, potentially involving diverse traditions of faith like the Eastern Orthodox, Roman Catholic, Lutheran, Anabaptists, Methodist, Anglicans, etc. even as the Pentecostal-charismatic movement has swept through the churches in three waves in the last century. Therefore, the unity into which the Spirit leads exists on three levels minimally. First, there is a local unity; second, there is an ecumenical unity; and third, there is a unity across the Christian tradition, both past and present. A kerygmatic community that seeks the unity of the Spirit is therefore open and sensitive to the Spirit's work not only in one's local community, but also in other church communities and traditions, both past and present.

In formulating kerygmatic criticism, I have systematically traced both the theological characterization as well as the observable representations of the realism with regards to the Spirit that is at work in reader disposition, community habits, community practices and here, outcomes in kerygmatic readers and communities. The unified lived-out proclamation of Christ and enactment of the Kingdom of God, with people responding in faith or rejecting the gospel, are visible and observable.

In the next section, I conclude with the community impacts that kerygmatic hermeneutics engenders. Each of the forms of the Spirit's outworking, individually, and taken together, lends itself to spiritual discernment. This realism with regards to the Spirit may find further support from empirical testing and evaluation—they can help us make an attribution to the Spirit and his working.

5.6 Community Impacts

I have earlier established two propositions concerning kerygmatic hermeneutics. First, kerygmatic hermeneutics is an interpretation of scriptural truth in the Spirit that forms an embodied witness to Jesus Christ. Second, kerygmatic hermeneutics is an interpretation of scriptural truth in the Spirit that brings readers into an encounter with God in the present.

Here, I propose a third claim that may address the question, *how may the world hear and see God?*[82] That is, kerygmatic hermeneutics is *one* of the ways in which the world may hear and see God. This third claim is: kerygmatic hermeneutics is an interpretation of scriptural truth in the Spirit that brings the world into an encounter with God in the present. This third claim takes the work of the Spirit further, so the truth of God may now be heard and seen by even the unbelieving world.

The visible impact of a kerygmatic community is an embodied witness to Jesus Christ, a representation of the Body of Christ that can manifest Christ's likeness and speak grace and truth into an unbelieving world in concrete ways.[83] It brings light and reveals the manifold wisdom

---

82. Williams raised this question: "how is God heard or seen to be present to the human world?" (Williams, *On Christian Theology*, 110). At the end of a rich and thick discourse, Williams concludes, "This essay has been in part an attempt to set out what is involved in some classical and modern theologies of Spirit as interpreter of the Word or agency of inspiration and to question the adequacy of such models for a critical theology. I have, however, no single accessible model to put in their place" (Williams, *On Christian Theology*, 126).

83. See Richard Bauckham for a thorough discussion on glory of God as a key theme in the Gospel of John (Bauckham, *Gospel of Glory*, 43–62). Bauckham highlights an important category of its meaning: visible splendor—"[t]his is what God has when people see his glory. Glory in this sense is always something visible" (Bauckham, *Gospel of Glory*, 44). Bauckham therefore articulates this theme as: that the glory of God is seen in the flesh of Jesus. "The glory is the radiance of the character of God, the grace and truth about which Moses heard, but which the disciples of Jesus have seen in his human person and life . . . The law was grace and truth in words . . . Jesus spoke the words of God's grace and truth, certainly, but he also enacted God's grace and truth" (Bauckham, *Gospel of Glory*, 52). For example, in Luke's account of Jesus

and glory of the Father to the rulers and authorities in the world and the heavens.[84] When the unbelieving world catches this glimpse of Christ's likeness and the Father's glory, people can hear and see God in the present.[85] Those who believe the gospel and the signs come to faith in Jesus Christ and become the new creation.[86] The Spirit then catches these up in participation to form living proclamations of Christ when they too are joined to a kerygmatic community.[87] Therefore, the two sets of dynam-

---

raising a widow's son from the dead, Jesus felt compassion for the weeping widow. He responded in the fullness of his humanity to give her son back to her. The impact of this miraculous act of raising the dead brought fear (of God) to all who witnessed this. The crowd glorified God, saying, "A great prophet has arisen among us!" and, "God has visited His people!" (Luke 7:11–17, NAS). That is, the crowd recognized Jesus as one who spoke and acted for God; the people interpreted Jesus's presence as a visitation from God—Jesus was God in the flesh. Therefore, they believed they saw the glory (or appearance) of God, and they glorified God. Here, there was an undistorted representation of God's grace and truth, a truthful manifestation of the shape and fullness of God in Jesus. In this mode of revelation, people could see a clear attribution of Jesus's presence, speech and act to God himself. Note in this account, it was not mentioned that Jesus made any spoken reference to God. Nonetheless, Jesus had so embodied his witness to God in the ordinariness of life that people could clearly attribute this raising of the dead to God himself.

84. See Eph 3: 9–10. The Church is hence empowered to mediate this revelation of the mystery of God in Christ. Lincoln explains, "To return to Eph 1:22b: κεφαλή is used here to denote Christ's position of rule and authority over all things, and as the one given to the Church, the head is an entity distinct from the body. In the juxtaposition of cosmic and ecclesiological perspectives found in this clause, the writer has taken a confessional formulation about Christ's cosmic lordship and subordinated it to his interest in the Church's welfare. All the supremacy and power God has given to Christ he has given to be used on behalf of the Church. In this way the Church is seen to have a special role in God's purposes for the cosmos" (Lincoln, *Ephesians*, 70).

85. This desired impact of the presence and activity of the Spirit is consistent with Lash's articulation in Lash, *Believing Three Ways*.

86. Bauckham explains, "The most obvious way in which the glory of God is revealed in Jesus's ministry is the miracles, for which John uses the term 'signs' (*sēmeia*) ... The signs are important because, as we have noticed, Jesus was not self-evidently the revelation of the glory of God. He revealed the glory *in the flesh* ... The signs point beyond mere flesh" (Bauckham, *Glory of God*, 55). "Yet, there will be those in the unbelieving world who will prove to be blind to even miraculous signs. For example, the Pharisee said to the man born blind, 'Give glory to God! We now know that this man is a sinner' (9:24). Thus they refuse to see that God has been glorified not despite Jesus, but in his Son, whose glory is revealed in the sign" (Bauckham, *Glory of God*, 57).

87. Finally, the radiant glory of God is visibly seen in the church when believers love one another and be one, as the Father and Son are one (John 17:22). As well, the Father is glorified when disciples bear much fruit (John 15:8) (Bauckham, *Glory of God*, 61–62).

ics in kerygmatic hermeneutics (in participation and proclamation) feed into and reinforce each other in a sustained circularity that glorifies God.

The community impact is therefore a transformation into the *likeness of Christ from glory to glory*. This is grace, a transformation Godward that cannot come by human design or habit. This necessarily takes its life, breath, and shape from God himself, in the fullness of the Father, Son, and the Holy Spirit.

How may humanity become God-like except it is the work of God? And what is the visible form of this likeness of God? Holiness and the likeness of Christ in humankind, though worked out in human processes, are observable only to the discerning eye. We may observe this glory, an aura or glow, on the face—it is hard to describe but we recognize it when we see it, including those who do not know God. When the world looks at this reader, they see something beyond the human. They see holiness.[88] This is the ultimate impact of kerygmatic hermeneutics—a transformation into Son-like children of God in the likeness of God.

I next conclude this chapter by summarizing the various expressions of a life in the Spirit where readers may discern the marks of the Spirit and so make an attribution to his presence and activity in the world.

5.7 Conclusion

In this chapter, I attempt to show that kerygmatic hermeneutics includes self-criticism, in that its realist claims about the Spirit's transformative work can be apprehended two ways, by spiritual discernment and empirical testing of their concrete and visible expressions. I paint this picture of readers being caught up in the Spirit in living out two sets of transformative dynamics, within their interiority and in the world, that form an embodied witness to Jesus Christ. Readers learn to discern and inhabit the shape and fullness of a valid reading of this transforming truth. By doing so, readers are also enabled to discriminate against invalid or distorted readings. Empirical enquiry into these observable expressions further corroborates the presence and activity of the Spirit.

I have described observable expressions of this life in the Spirit in reader dispositions, community habits, practices, outcomes, and impacts

---

88. Maintaining this communion in the Spirit is a moment-to-moment relating. Therefore, this visible glory may just be episodic if this communion cannot be sustained in being caught up God-ward.

(see Figure 1). These culminate in a lived-out interpretation of scriptural truth in the world. Kerygmatic readers and communities represent the Body of Christ that manifest Christ's likeness and radiates God's glory so the world may hear and see God. Therefore, kerygmatic hermeneutics has wider implications for society and social challenges.

Readers learn to discern the marks of the Spirit in their own transformation—intoxication, life, participation, and revelation of truth—and so make attributions to the Spirit.[89] For example, readers may discern signs of intoxication in transformed reader desires, accountability to the otherness of the Spirit and Scripture and an attending and listening to the Spirit and one another in community. They are caught up in a life in the Spirit and make judgments and decisions that confound contemporary wisdom. Readers may observe signs of participation in the Spirit in their kerygmatic devotion. There is a growing sense of self-emptying and self-abandonment in a flow in the Spirit. They read over-against themselves and one another in praying and interpreting Scripture in the Spirit, in a revelation of truth and correction of error. Yet, this learning, unlearning, and relearning are done in a communion of love. Readers in community engender life as they proclaim the logos with works of healings and deliverances, signs and wonders, and all good. The Spirit acts on readers' proclamation of the logos to seed the new creation in Christ. The world can observe an embodied witness to Jesus Christ that stands in unity because of its diversity. This witness is lived out in the world in the ordinariness of life; it speaks wisdom that addresses social challenges and impacts society. Christlike expressions of this life in the Spirit glorify God and bring the world into an encounter with God. Chapters 4 and 5, when read together, constitute kerygmatic theology. In the next chapter, I apply this theology to propose a practice of kerygmatic reading in a Spirit-led church community.

---

89. Recall our discussion on how a reader may discern the four marks of the Spirit in section 3.2.

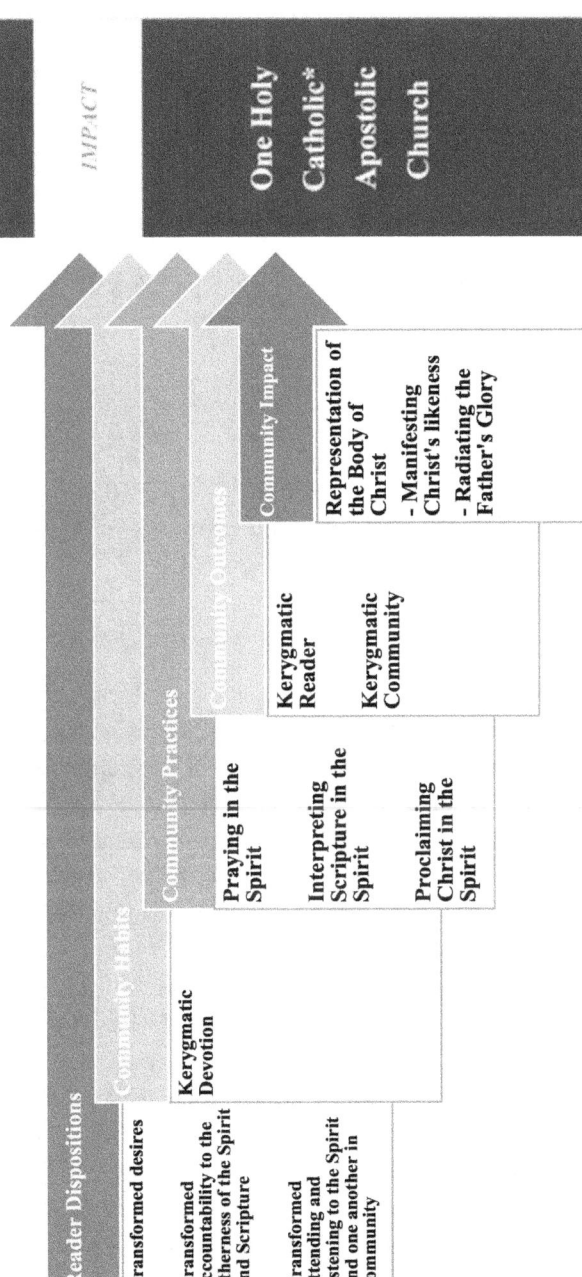

FIGURE 1

*that is, the true Christian church of all times and all places

Kerygmatic Hermeneutics: An Account of the Spirit's Presence and Working in a Kerygmatic Community

6

KERYGMATIC HERMENEUTICS: A PRACTICE

"The wind blows where it wishes and you hear the sound of it, but do not know where it comes from and where it is going; so is everyone who is born of the Spirit." (John 3:8 NAS)

A PRACTICE OF KERYGMATIC interpretation is concerned with seeking to hear from the Spirit how he reads the scriptural text and what he is saying that we should be, say and do in the present. That is, it is concerned with a kerygmatic community adopting a particular exegetical reading of a scriptural text in the Spirit, and more. It is concerned with a community deciding on a scriptural reading against which it holds itself accountable to God and one another. It is about a scriptural reading that guides one's attitude, behavior, thoughts, and speech, which altogether express a community identity. It is also concerned with a scriptural reading that a community proclaims to the world. These are some of what a practice of kerygmatic interpretation yields at the end of this process.

In chapter 3, I drew from extant literature on the presence and activity of the Spirit to formulate the marks of the Spirit. In chapter 4, I formulated a kerygmatic theology, encouraged by empirical evidence from a community practice of praying in the Spirit. Kerygmatic theology claims that the Spirit makes use of Scripture's otherness to reveal scriptural truths and form an embodied witness to Jesus Christ. In chapter 5, I proposed a kerygmatic criticism based on the coherent and observable outworking of the Spirit's transformative work in reader dispositions, community habits, practices, outcomes, and impacts. I thus argued that kerygmatic hermeneutics can bring the world into an encounter with God in the present.

In this chapter, I propose a practice of kerygmatic interpretation for a church community that flows from my formulation of kerygmatic theology and what went before that. Here, I give an example of a church community's practice of praying in the Spirit. I argue that such an example of a practice of reading Scripture in the Spirit in community has theological integrity. Therefore, this practice can speak into the wider Pentecostal-charismatic community without losing any legitimacy to the presence and working of the Spirit.

A practice of kerygmatic hermeneutics involves community habits and practices in kerygmatic devotion, praying in the Spirit, interpreting Scripture in the Spirit, and proclaiming Christ in the Spirit.[1] Community practices, in particular, involve processes and structures that create spaces and times that facilitate a community's patient waiting for the Spirit's free working and speaking through Scripture.[2] I argue that such corporate processes are open to testing in discernment and evaluation in empirical enquiry, which makes kerygmatic hermeneutics self-critical. This means that the results of this practice can corroborate my theological claim that a Spirit-led process is the appropriate context for an interpretation of Scripture that forms an embodied witness to Jesus Christ.

In section 6.1, I draw from my formulation of kerygmatic theology what praying in the Spirit in community may look like and set out in a preamble my presuppositions and their implications for such a practice in a church community. In section 6.2, I draw from extant literature Seah's case study as one such example of a practice that has gone far to

1. Given the purpose and constraints of this research, I will focus on specific habits and practices that are core to a Spirit-led interpretation of Scripture. Of course, the Spirit also works in readers through the church's mediation in rituals and pastoral practices, etc. See, e.g., Ward, *Participation and Mediation*.

2. Prayer features significantly and consistently in a practice of kerygmatic interpretation, both in a reader's habituated practice of kerygmatic devotion as well as community practices of praying and interpreting Scripture in the Spirit. Related to this, Moberly, in his response to a collection of six essays on pneumatic hermeneutic in a discussion-by-essay, observes that prayer, which is central to a life of faith, has not been given a more explicit and central place in pneumatic hermeneutic by those who proclaim the work of the Spirit. Various voices in dialogue generally concur on the significance of prayer in the renewal movement. Some acknowledge, however, that prayer can easily get side-lined through tacit assumption (Spawn and Wright, *Spirit and Scripture*, 160–61, 180–81, and 183–84).

give shape to what this praying in the Spirit in community may look like and how it may lend itself to testing and evaluation.[3] I argue that this is an appropriate example because the practice does not lose focus on the theology that the Spirit's enabling humans to pray—to attend and listen to the Spirit, and to learn and correct in the Spirit—comes with its criticism that allows for discernment in such a practice of praying in the Spirit.

In this account, a church community, challenged for its vision and mission, waited on the Spirit to hear from him. It sought to test what was purportedly said in the Spirit (guarding against self-deception, and perhaps even employing a hermeneutics of suspicion), to discriminate which of these human voices was also that of the Spirit. For an evaluation of the longer-term outcomes of the Spirit's working in the interiority of individuals, Seah also applied socio-scientific empirical enquiry to examine the forming of a community with Spirit-guided purpose, goals, and actions.

Both qualitative and quantitative analyses in Seah's case study yielded evidence that motivated this research. However, for the purposes in this chapter, I will highlight only some findings from Seah's qualitative analyses that evidence the Spirit's revelation of truth. I draw from transcripts of readers' praying in the Spirit that evidence this process of discernment in the Spirit.[4] Moreover, I want to highlight the results of this process of spiritual discernment—a conviction of failure, even of sinful attitudes and practice, and a learning from the Spirit and one another.[5] This testing and evaluation allowed us to make attribution to the presence of the Spirit and his working in this community.

3. Seah, "Spirituality Approach," 178–203.

4. Walter Moberly argues there is a need for critical discernment in the context of discussing what a true knowledge of God is. Moberly observes that this criticism is "the development of the kind of moral and spiritual awareness that enables its possessor to distinguish between the genuine and the counterfeit within human life in its moral and spiritual dimensions. This critical awareness is necessary for a simple reason: there are differing, indeed conflicting, claims on the part of those who speak for God. It is possible to claim to speak for God, and yet do so falsely" (Moberly, *Prophecy and Discernment*, 13).

5. The Spirit's call to repentance also engendered longer-term transformative outcomes. Seah evaluated the results of this practice of praying in the Spirit with quantitative analyses (Seah, "Spirituality Approach," 363–87). He found systemic changes in attitudes and behavior of the PAL participants and in the wider church community (for specific findings of the quantitative analyses, see section 1.1.1 on a practice of praying in the Spirit in search of a theology). However, our discussion in this chapter

In section 6.3, I build on kerygmatic theology and such a community practice of praying in the Spirit to propose a community practice of kerygmatic interpretation—that is, interpreting Scripture in the Spirit in community. Since kerygmatic theology is concerned with the revelation, apprehension, and reception of what God is doing here and now, and what God is asking God's people to do here and now, as mediated by the Spirit and Scripture (viz. chapter 4), its practice also sees the Spirit catching humans up in intoxication, life, and participation in divinity. This means readers may look for the marks of the Spirit (viz. chapter 3) in one another in what results from this practice to find an attribution to the Spirit. Testing and evaluation are not additional projects; they are integral to a practice of kerygmatic interpretation (viz. chapter 5).

In section 6.4, I conclude this chapter by arguing for the theological integrity of kerygmatic hermeneutics. This theological exploration of kerygmatic hermeneutics claims that readers may discern the Spirit at work in their reading in this practice of theological interpretation that forms an embodied witness to Jesus Christ. It also claims that there should be observable effects of the Spirit's transformative work. However, theological integrity demands that we test these claims appropriately for an assessment of the spiritual and observable effects. Here, I argue that spiritual discernment and socio-scientific empirical evaluation can corroborate these realist claims about the presence and activity of the Spirit in forming the one holy catholic apostolic church.

A practice of kerygmatic interpretation develops readers' ability and hones their skills to discern the Spirit. The principle of spiritual discernment undergirds the power and efficacy of kerygmatic readers' apprehension and reception of the Spirit's revelation of truth. This practice can expect results in repentance and correction of errors in a community learning to live lives that are true to God. Evaluation, therefore, addresses the questions if and to what extent this lived-out interpretation of scriptural truth—in reader dispositions, community habits, practices, outcomes, and impacts—visibly bears the marks of the Spirit in a transformed life that is lived true to God. Evaluation informs readers in community if they are indeed transforming (and, fast enough) to become living proclamations of Jesus Christ. Therefore, I claim that this practice

---

focuses more on the Spirit's presence and activity in the revelation, apprehension and reception of truths in individuals, rather than systemic changes at the level of PAL participants and the organization.

of kerygmatic hermeneutics, appropriate to a community's context, has theological integrity.

6.1 Preamble

In this practice of kerygmatic interpretation, I would read Scripture in a kerygmatic community. I seek to formulate a community practice of interpreting Scripture in the Spirit in the present; one that flows from the Spirit's speaking through human voices in a history of revelation and interpretation.[6] This hermeneutical enterprise has the following presuppositions and implications. Firstly, the objective of scriptural interpretation is aimed at transformation at the level of the individual reader as well as that of a community of faith. It is not merely an impartation of God's self-knowledge. Therefore, the outcome of this practice of kerygmatic hermeneutics goes beyond an exegetical reading of a text.[7] Its outcome is an apprehension of scriptural truth for readers' embodiment.

Secondly, the Holy Spirit and Scripture are central in kerygmatic theology and its epistemology. While this transformation involves spiritual disciplines of Bible reading and meditation, prayer and contemplation, proclamation and witness, and praise and worship, this life in the Spirit is gathered around the Bible.[8]

Thirdly, the ancient meaning and background of the text are foundational for reading *how* the Spirit reads in scriptural interpretation in spite of Scripture's underdeterminacy. The spiritual reality that is signified by his first inspiration to the original redactors not only marked out for us what the text did not say, it also located the text in a particular

---

6. This is consistent with how a kerygmatic community lives out the marks of the Spirit in a culture of learning where teachings are open to being challenged, obstacles to change are being recognized and removed, and errors are being acknowledged and corrected. This community is open to learning, from its own history of interpretation as well as that from theologians and scholars who speak from other traditions and practices. What needs to be done is a testing in discernment to tease off the voice of the Spirit from those of humans and other spirits.

7. Exegetical readings serve more as inputs to this transformation process. That is, biblical scholarship and theology making are at the service of the church.

8. This presupposition flows from my formulation of kerygmatic theology (in section 4.2.3). There, the Spirit uses Scripture to reveal truth in three modes—illumination, inspiration, and co-creation—through readers who are caught up in a life in the Spirit.

socio-historical context to give meaning to its original set of audience.[9] The same text, because of Scripture's underdeterminacy, may be read in different contexts over the eras and in the contemporary world to give different meanings to different readers.[10] However, this does not displace the need to go back to the text's ancient meaning and background. Reading a text in its ancient meaning and background helps to inform contemporary readers of how the text may not be read. It also informs readers of the way this text has been read in its history of interpretation.[11]

Finally, spiritual discernment is the key principle and presupposition in this practice. I bring into this practice of kerygmatic hermeneutics pre-knowledge of the spiritual landscape that confronts church leadership in Asia as well as other parts of the world. Various religions and philosophical practices in Asia, for example, are eclectic in nature, and Buddhism, Hinduism, and Chinese religion (comprising a blend of Confucianism, Taoism, and ancestral worship) respectively are sometimes practiced together with the worship of spirits and idols. It is not surprising, therefore, that pagan and other spiritual practices may be brought into churches of various traditions in these countries as a carry-over from members' pre-conversion experiences. This is why apprehending discernment—discerning spiritual phenomena, spiritual things, and spiritual persons—is critical in kerygmatic hermeneutics.

This spiritual landscape has implications for the training of pastors and missionaries in hermeneutics. What Paul (as used conventionally) taught concerning spiritual battle in Eph 6.12 is real existentially and not

---

9. This follows my discussion on how the Spirit uses Scripture's otherness in a revelation of truth (section 4.2.1)—the coherence of Spiritual truths gives tacit *boundary markers* for hermeneutical moves, determining what is permissible and what is not for communities for all times and places.

10. See, e.g., Archer, *Spirit, Scripture and Community*. Among other scholars, Archer traces the works of scholars through the eras and observes that the underdeterminacy of biblical texts allows for a range of "possibilities of future meaning" (Archer, *Spirit, Scripture and Community*, 207).

11. What the Spirit says today through scriptural text has to cohere with what he had said to the apostles and church fathers down the ages. Readers who attend carefully to read a text in its ancient context and in a history of interpretation are likely to apprehend a recurring finding of the same scriptural truth in God and how this has been played out concretely in different situations. Such a practice enriches a reader's apprehension of God and his creative ways in the world. S/he learns to discern a pattern of God's ways in the world. Therefore, this practice can help to give a fuller shape to the enactment of this scriptural truth in the present (see the preamble to kerygmatic theology in section 4.1).

just metaphorically, for apostles, evangelists, prophets, pastors and teachers ministering in these lands that are steeped in occult practices. These have to wage battle against the rulers, the powers, the world forces of this darkness and spiritual forces of wickedness in the heavenly places in wrestling souls from darkness into light besides standing firm themselves. In this context, a training in hermeneutics that is underpinned by spiritual discernment in testing and evaluation is not only appropriate; it is necessary.

6.2 Praying in the Spirit

This section is set up to draw from the extant literature of Pentecostal-charismatic practices what praying in the Spirit in community may look like. From this review, I reference a local church community's practice of praying in the Spirit as one such *example* of a practice that has gone far to give shape to *what* this praying in the Spirit in community may look like. I argue that this is an appropriate example because the practice does not lose focus on the theology that the Spirit's enabling humans to pray—to attend and listen to the Spirit, and to learn and correct in the Spirit— comes with its criticism that allows for a discernment of the marks of the Spirit. I also argue that any reference to this case of a community's practice of praying in the Spirit serves the purpose to demonstrate *how* constructive theology has been applied in re-reading this practice that helped in formulating kerygmatic theology.

On praying in the Spirit, I briefly describe in section 6.2.1 what attending and listening to the Spirit look like in Seah's Participatory Active Listening (PAL) Prayer Method. Then in section 6.2.2, I demonstrate from Seah's case study of a church community how this praying in the Spirit, when mediated by the PAL Prayer Method, attended to the otherness of the Spirit to bring organizational transformation to a church community.[12] This humble attendance to the otherness of the Spirit lent itself to testing and evaluation if and to what extent there had been a transformation in attitudes and behavior at both the individual and organizational levels. Such early evidence that God is truly at work—established by spiritual discernment, empirical enquiry and evaluation—is

---

12. I am deferring a thorough description of the corporate process of PAL praying till the next section 6.2. While I briefly introduce Seah's PAL Prayer Method in this section, I intend more to first evidence the presence and activity of the Spirit in a church community when mediated by the PAL Prayer Method. This would buttress my motivation for this research.

what motivated my pursuit of a theology that accounts for the Spirit's presence and activity in his economy, and in particular, the church.

In the following sections, I present how the PAL Prayer Method models a community's attending and listening to the Spirit, with consequential learning and correction in the Spirit.

6.2.1 Attending and listening to the Spirit

Seah's PAL Prayer Method outlines a process of discerning the Spirit by seeking to patiently hear from him what our community ought to be, say, or do, to be God's people. Through the mediation of the PAL prayer program, the participating church leadership sought to co-create in the Spirit a statement of vision and mission and core values of the church. This reading of the Spirit sought to facilitate a sensemaking and sensegiving that would build identity in the church community over a two-year organizational transformation program.[13]

In its generic form, the PAL Prayer Method is a method that makes operational an attending and listening to the Spirit in a testing of claims to speak for God. It may be adapted for a corporate discourse on any theme—on a corporate issue that may range from a finding of a vision and mission of the church community (as in Seah's case study), or a theological challenge like the role of woman leadership in the church, or scriptural interpretation of any generic text (as in this research). Yet its efficacy does not lie in the method. Rather, its efficacy lies in participants' ability and efficacy in spiritual discernment. Therefore, this testing is as good as participants' spiritual discernment.

The PAL Prayer Method is also a *practice* of discernment in testing in itself, so that participants *learn* to recognize and ascertain what the Spirit is saying for them to do, or what decisions to make. That is, it trains them to tease out from human voices what the Spirit is saying to the community. Moberly frames the discernment problem thus: How does one "distinguish between those words (and action) which are 'merely' human, and those which are *not only human but also from God*".[14] The triune God

13. For clarity, sensemaking is the ongoing making of meaning by fitting new experiences into one's existing plausibility structure, and any consequent adjustment of that plausibility structure. This is often done collaboratively in a community or organization because sensemaking is context-dependent. On the other hand, sensegiving is the ongoing communication of the meaning that one has deciphered and made sense of to the world, through one's articulation and performance.

14. Moberly cites John 7:16–17 and 1 Thess 2:13 as paradigmatic. See R.W.L

has revealed himself through human speech and action, chiefly in the Word enfleshed in Jesus Christ.[15] Whilst there is a perfect consonance of human and divine in Christ, there is an imperfect consonance amongst those who are united to God not by nature but by grace. For this reason, the Apostles, like Paul and John, adjured the churches to discriminate between truth and deceit by testing the spirits (1 Cor 12:1–3; 1 John 4:1). Spiritual discernment between the voice and works of the Holy Spirit, and those of other spirits, including the human spirit, has been the prescribed practice for hearing God speak since the early church days.[16]

In attending to the Spirit to bring organizational transformation to a church, Seah formulated a community practice of praying in the Spirit that purposefully created sacred times and spaces for the Spirit to speak and for leaders to listen. I present the PAL Prayer Method in its diagrammatic form in Exhibit 1.[17]

Moberly, Lecture Handouts on *Biblical Theology*, 2016–2017, Lecture 14: Discernment of God II: God's Word in Human Words. Moberly argues succinctly that the discernment problem needs to be re-articulated in postmodern context. He says, "Thus the task is to conceptualize the relationship between the divine and the human in ways that will not turn the transcendence and immanence of God into the intrusion within the natural order of a large supernatural being who does not belong there; and to be able to articulate how the fulfilment of human nature in God is to be differentiated from imposition upon, or diminution of, true humanity by something extraneous" (Moberly, *Prophecy and Discernment*, 37).

15. See Hermann Gunkel for an account of how God speaks in Old Testament days (Gunkel, *Genesis*). Gunkel observes, "We believe God works in the world as the quiet, hidden, basis of all things. Sometimes, his efficacy can almost be apprehended in particularly momentous and impressive events and persons. We sense his reign in the wondrous interrelationship of things. But he never appears to us as an active agent alongside others, but always as the ultimate cause of all" (Gunkel, *Genesis*, x).

16. See Welker, "Interdisciplinary Perspectives," 221–32. I concur with Welker on the need to discern the source of spiritual things: "The biblical traditions know about good and evil spirits, salvific and demonic powers. The New Testament traditions identify the divine Spirit, the Holy Spirit, as the Spirit of the merciful creator and Spirit of Jesus Christ, which is the divine living and loving power that unites the self-revealing God and connects God and creation in sustaining, saving, and ennobling ways. In science and philosophy, too, we know about deceiving spirits, we know about individual and shared certainties that prove to be wrong, misleading, and distortive. We know devastating forms of consensus that breed dangerous ideologies or stale theories that block insight over ages. Thus the discernment of the spirits is a most important task in all named fields of experience, knowledge, and conviction" (Welker, "Interdisciplinary Perspectives," 230–31).

17. Exhibit 1 is an abstract of Figure 5.1 of Seah, "Spirituality Approach," 185. I am deferring a detailed description of the PAL praying process here because this will be more appropriately discussed in its adapted version for a practice of reading

Exhibit 1

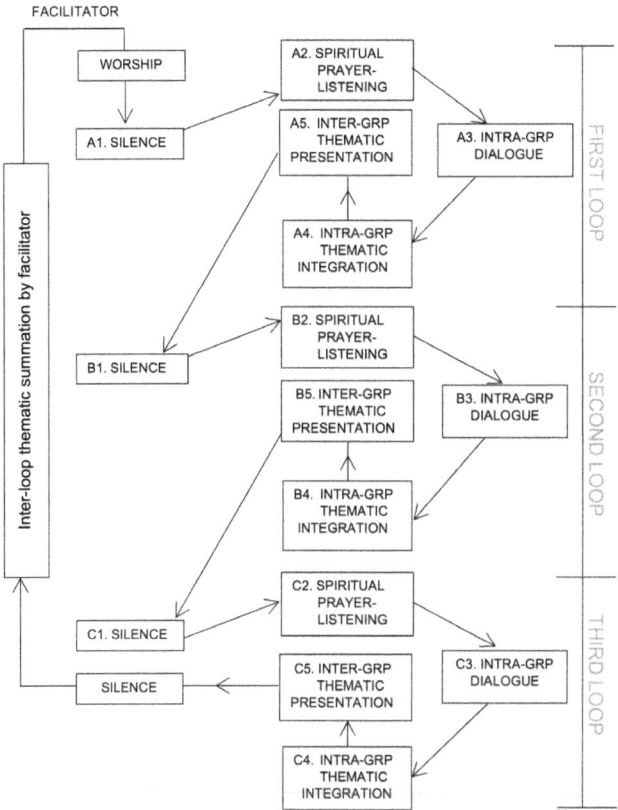

Example of a Prayer Model in Kerygmatic Hermeneutics:
The Participatory Active Listening Prayer Method

Scripture in the Spirit in specific. Put briefly, Seah designs iterative learning loops so participants may learn to listen to the voice of the Spirit for transformative change. He explains, "The Christian spiritual experience involves elements of worship, silence, active listening in prayer, meditation, reflection, and integration. All these elements are integrated into an iterative structure of triple-loop learning cycles ... developed from the literature on action learning ... action research ... and action science ... The PAL Method can attain triple-loop action learning to take into cognizance the broader organizational shared values in which individual values can be embedded ... rendering a third order change attempt at developing organization members' capacity to identify and change their own schemata as they see fit ... The driver for this triple-loop, third order change vests in a theory of religious spirituality to bring about religious spirituality for OT" (Seah, "Spirituality Approach," 10). "OT" is shorthand for "organizational transformation" in this research. In the next section, I will adapt the triple-loop learning cycle (or, a cycle of three learning loops) to interpret Scripture in the Spirit.

Seah explains the operational functioning of the PAL Prayer Method,

> The diagrammatic presentation of the PAL Method in Figure 5.1 represents a complete tri-cycle of prayers and three learning loops per session. Each session begins with a time of worship followed by three prayer cycles, each of which is made up of five components: silence, spiritual prayer-listening, intra-group dialogue, intra-group thematic integration, and inter-group thematic presentation. Following the third prayer cycle, a time of silence ensues followed by a final inter-loop thematic summation by the facilitator. The session then terminates with a short flurry of spontaneous multi-individual worshipful prayers.[18]
>
> The prayer cycle beginning in A1 repeats itself in prayer cycles 2 and 3, commencing with B1 and C1 respectively, except that the level of filtering gets increasingly finer. This means that there is increasingly less dissonance in the spiritual voice and thus the collective voice. Effectively, the whole prayer exercise goes through three learning loops per prayer session.[19]

A devout practice of spiritual disciplines underlies PAL praying. PAL praying involves spiritual disciplines of attending and listening to the Spirit, in prayer and contemplation, and praise and worship. Most significantly, PAL praying is characterized by intermittent silence for attentive and active listening to the Spirit. In moving from this initial practice of praying in the Spirit (in Seah's case study) to my formulating an underlying theology to kerygmatic hermeneutics, therefore, I have formulated kerygmatic devotion (see section 5.3) as a foundational community habit that will now buttress a community practice of praying and interpreting Scripture in the Spirit in this chapter.[20] This means that the

---

18. Seah, "Spirituality Approach," 186.

19. Seah, "Spirituality Approach," 201. Each PAL prayer session has three cycles of prayers in three learning loops. A thematic integration, thematic presentation and a thematic summation means an integration, presentation and summation respectively of a particular theme of the corporate discourse. These thematic components in each prayer cycle, learning loop or session are intended to keep participants focused onto the theme of the corporate discourse.

20. Community habits and practices in kerygmatic hermeneutics interact dynamically. Participants, disciplined individually in their own kerygmatic devotion, learn to become more spiritually discerning and sensitive as they engage in the corporate process of PAL praying. This feeds into an upward spiral in the ability and efficacy of kerygmatic readers' spiritual discernment when community habits in kerygmatic

individual and collective discernment of what is the Spirit's voice, mediated by the PAL Prayer Method, is predicated on participants' consistent personal devotion to attend and listen to the Spirit in both community habits and practices. Depending on the purpose, context, and the theme in question, PAL participants may be drawn solely from senior leaders or a fuzzy set of leadership including leaders-in-training, or even the entire community.[21]

6.2.2 Learning and correction in the Spirit

In this section, I draw from transcripts of readers' praying in the Spirit, mediated by the PAL Prayer Method.[22] These evidenced a *process* of discernment in the Spirit. These also highlight the *results of this process* of spiritual discernment. I focus on negative examples to show what a conviction of failure, sinful attitudes and practice, looked like in PAL praying. On the other hand, what is positive is that there is a learning from the Spirit and one another. These evidenced the fourth mark of the Spirit: a revelation of truth.[23]

To illustrate what such learning and correction may look like, I abstract from Seah's analysis and follow through on his findings in relation to one of the values that emerged from his coding the PAL Transcript—the core value of "commitment".

---

devotion and community praying, interpreting Scripture and proclaiming Christ in the Spirit are practiced habitually.

21. A careful reading of Seah's PAL Prayer Method and the formulation of kerygmatic theology is necessary for an apprehension of the dynamic interactions of reader dispositions, community habits, practices, outcomes, and impacts that will give the power and efficacy of PAL praying or a practice of kerygmatic interpretation. This apprehension also yields wisdom for an adaptation of the PAL Prayer Method for other purposes, contexts, and themes in question.

22. Each weekly discourse of the two-year PAL prayer program was first audio-recorded and then transcribed within the week. The resultant transcript, called the PAL Transcript, is 1,129 pages of single-spaced Microsoft Word document, with 427,442 words and 5,843 paragraphs (see Seah, "Spirituality Approach," 219). This transcript is then coded for key constructs for analysis using both qualitative and quantitative research methods.

23. These observations resonate with my earlier formulation of the fourth mark of the Spirit—a revelation of truth: conviction of sin and correction of error (see section 3.2.4). There, I discussed both the positive side of learning as well as the negative side of conviction and confession.

Here, I abstract some of the negative expressions of commitment (as a value of this community). Firstly, PAL participants discerned that leaders were not rising to do God's work, not because there was a lack of resources, but in spite of God's abundant provisions. This pointed to leaders being tied down with many matters except those concerning God and his work.

> And the Lord gave us many things: people, leaders, building, everything is there. But why are we not joyful? We should be very joyful and ready with all the resources in our hands and *yet we are not doing anything*. In conclusion, it is time to drop our shackles and move on to do the Lord's work . . . (PAL Transcript, 1 Sep 96, p.60)[24]

Secondly, PAL participants discerned and confessed to being lukewarm; and this had hindered the growth and development of the church.

> Basically in our group we shared about frustrations: . . . Secondly, about the problems of the people that there is a *lukewarmness* within the church that does not allow the church to really move forward . . . (PAL Transcript, 14 Sep 96, p.82)[25]

There was also evidence of the Spirit's revelation of truth—truth about the spiritual condition of self and others. In response, the PAL participants (who are leaders) acknowledged their sinful attitude and practice of not rising to the work, and, actually being lukewarm about things they do for God. They confessed to what were revealed in the Spirit as the reasons for their lack of commitment: a fear of doing more and failing, and unwillingness to commit because it is costly.

> Two words: Fear and unwillingness. Fear in the sense of what you have to give up, what you have to take on maybe responsibilities. Unwillingness in the sense that you do not want to give up. (PAL Transcript, 22 Apr 98, p.905)[26]

Together with Spirit's revelation of truth about leaders' own spiritual condition, there was also an apprehension of what the Spirit was saying for leaders to be, to say and to do. Leaders first apprehended God's trust in them notwithstanding their failing him. This apprehension is predicated on participants' relationship with God.[27] Second, they apprehended

24. Seah, "Spirituality Approach," 228.
25. Seah, "Spirituality Approach," 228–29.
26. Seah, "Spirituality Approach," 229.
27. In the same sense, this project on an interpretation of scriptural truth—which

the Spirit's encouragement to trust him to deliver them from all their fears that had led to inaction and non-commitment. Third, leaders apprehended the Spirit's directing them to work as teams in community.

> We see two problems to summarize of all the presentations and two solutions. First of all God trusts us. The two problems are there is fear and apprehension among us and the second problem is that we don't trust ourselves. Primarily we don't trust ourselves because we fear commitment, we fear failure or we lack discipline. The two solutions that the Lord seems to be telling us is one, we need to rely on the Holy Spirit because that is what is going to get us out of our fear and apprehension and bring us to peace and victory. It is the Holy Spirit working in us that is going to be able to cast out all this fear that we have. The other solution the Lord is telling us is that we need to have more teamwork and more community. What we cannot do alone we can do with the encouragement of others around us and we can do together as a team. (PAL Transcript, 22 Jul 98, pp.1104–1105)[28]

The above are some expressions of a lack of commitment at the attitudinal level. I now abstract demonstration of a lack of commitment that is observed at the behavioral level. Late into the third half-year period in this two-year PAL prayer program, the facilitator reprimanded the PAL participants for a consistent lack of punctuality. This is in spite of a declaration of commitment to the PAL prayer program right from its beginning in 1996. This revealed an inconsistency in the collective leadership on their pledge of commitment. This suggests that the attitudinal expression and behavioral display of commitment need not be consonant all the time.

> But don't forget you have committed to be punctual. In fact one of you came in and said, "How come so few people?" And he came in about 7:29 p.m. So while you may think that they don't have to wait, they can probably go ahead, the others are waiting for you. I hope that some of us are not making the habit. More and more of you; more than three-quarters of you actually come after 7:30 p.m. (PAL Transcript, 5 Nov 97, p.705)[29]

Besides a revelation of truth that came in a direct reprimand, the Spirit also uses Scripture's otherness and the charismatic gifts to mediate

---

is the whole of the knowledge of God that God imparts to the world by means of Scripture—may be apprehended by readers who are in relationship with God.

28. Seah, "Spirituality Approach," 245–46.
29. Seah, "Spirituality Approach," 232.

a revelation of truth concerning participants' lack of commitment behaviorally. For example, PAL participants confessed to their lack of focus in prioritizing to do the things of God.

> Two points: The first thing was that there were two visions that point to the people who are busy doing too many things around. (PAL Transcript, 19 Nov 97, p.721)

> The first point was taken from this verse: 2 Tim 2:4 "No soldier in active service entangles himself in the affairs of everyday life so that he may please the one who enlisted him as a soldier." This person shared that he feels he is not effective yet in evangelism because he has many concerns with his work, family and also constantly involves in what is to be done for church activities. So it is a reminder for him that in order for him to be an effective soldier, he has got to set his focus and priorities right. (PAL Transcript, 19 Nov 97, p.722)[30]

The fourth mark of the Spirit—a revelation of truth—has its positive outcome in shaping a learning community. The apprehension and reception of truth that bring a conviction to change in the fear of the Lord was worked through iterative reflection and learning in community. The PAL Prayer Method, with its three cycles of prayers and learning loops, mediated this learning in community.[31]

> *As we reflected upon what we prayed*, we were encouraged to serve without complaints by looking at the leaders' example . . . (PAL Transcript, 1 Sep 96, p.55)

> For the leaders, we thanked God for their dedication, sacrificial service, that they are clean and not corrupt. For the people we thanked God that they love the Lord, that they are committed. *On further reflection* we need to pray that God will grant the leaders a shepherd heart. (PAL Transcript, 1 Sep 96, p.58)[32]

The iterative learning on the development of the core value of commitment over multiple PAL prayer sessions took place over four half-year periods. This summarizes what PAL participants apprehended the Spirit

---

30. Seah, "Spirituality Approach," 232–33.

31. See next section for a detailed description of the PAL Prayer Method and its prayer cycles and learning loops that yield learning and unlearning in interpreting Scripture in the Spirit.

32. Seah, "Spirituality Approach," 233.

revealed for them to be, to say and to do concerning their commitment to this community:

Period 1: Lament on the lack of commitment in the community
Period 2: Agreement on commitment as a core value for the community, and the development of corporate structure
Period 3: Leaders saw themselves as key to create "rippling effect" to stimulate commitment in the wider church community
Period 4: Leaders agreed to demonstrate this commitment and be evaluated for this in their efforts and outcomes in soul-winning. Leadership shared their fears and struggles while remaining positive about commitment.[33]

In this section, I have abstracted both positive and negative examples of learning and correction respectively that are consistent with the Spirit's revelation of truth. Through PAL praying, we find evidence of the Spirit standing over-against readers in their wayward ways and even self-deception. Moreover, the Spirit upholds what is truth for everyone, rather than just my truth or your truth. Iterative collective learning dialogues like these help foster a culture that openly admits failures hence paving the way for constructive devotion for corporate spiritual growth. These accounts of learning and correction evidence the apprehension and reception of the Spirit's revelation of truth. In the next section, I will describe what a community practice of kerygmatic interpretation may look like.

6.3 Interpreting Scripture in the Spirit

In this section, I demonstrate how kerygmatic theology feeds back to help me refine a practice of reading Scripture in the Spirit. I propose a practice of kerygmatic interpretation. This practice is built on a community practice of praying in the Spirit, which in turn, is built on a community habit of kerygmatic devotion that is sustained by transformed reader dispositions.[34] The Spirit works through reader dispositions, community habits and practices to make an embodied witness to Jesus Christ.

---

33. Seah, "Spirituality Approach," 235.
34. In this section, I am moving from my formulation of kerygmatic theology in

I now illustrate what a community practice of kerygmatic interpretation looks like reading a generic text, using the PAL Prayer Method. To make operational a community practice of kerygmatic interpretation, I have made three moves. First, I have designed a Program—the PAL Scriptural Interpretation Program. This outlines a process of interpreting Scripture in the Spirit that forms an embodied witness, using the PAL Prayer Method. On the appropriateness of exegetical methods and historical criticism for scriptural reading, Webster argues, "Judgements about the appropriateness of methods rest upon prior judgements about the ends of interpretation, the proper social and institutional locations of interpretation, and the proper dispositions of interpreters."[35] Therefore, the design of an appropriate hermeneutical method or process for my purpose is also a discernment issue. Since kerygmatic hermeneutics is a Spirit-led approach that is underpinned by spiritual discernment, I am cautious to design a process that incorporates suspicion of hidden conflicting and self-serving agendas that explicitly or implicitly make claims to speak in the name of God. The accounts of learning and correction that were mediated by the PAL praying (in section 6.2) evidenced the apprehension and reception of the Spirit's revelation of truth to a community leadership. This supports the claim that the PAL Prayer Method can be efficacious in making discernment operational, by testing claims of attribution to the Spirit in human voices. Through iterative learning loops and prayer cycles, PAL praying was efficacious in teasing out God's voice from human and other voices.

These iterative learning loops and prayer cycles also pay cognizance to the need for a reader to read Scripture in a community that is specifically located with particular socio-cultural and ecclesial context. The iterative reading and re-reading of the same verse (or text) in the light of *other* readers' interpretations and embodied witnesses allows a reader to navigate in a to-ing and fro-ing between general claims of God and the patterns of his actions in the world and the community, and, the embodiment of these general claims in the concrete particularity of contemporary living in one another.[36] Therefore, I argue that the PAL Prayer Method is appropriate for my purpose.

---

chapters 4 and 5 to adapt a community practice of praying in the Spirit for the reading of a generic scriptural text.

35. Webster, *Holy Scripture*, 103.

36. That is, the PAL Prayer Method, by design, could be open to managing this tension in what kerygmatic hermeneutics is saying, between insisting that an interpretation yields something general (the unchanging, constant truth of God) and saying

Second, I consider how this practice of interpreting Scripture in the Spirit relates to historical criticism.[37] Kerygmatic hermeneutics acknowledges that historical criticism is helpful without losing sight of the fact that "Scripture's clarity is neither an intrinsic element of the text as text nor simply a fruit of exegetical labour; it is that which the text *becomes* as it functions in the Spirit-governed encounter between the self-presenting savior and the faithful reader. To read is to be caught up by the truth-bestowing Spirit of God."[38] Therefore, a practice of kerygmatic interpretation, that focuses on attending and listening to what the Spirit has been, and is saying and doing with Scripture, is first open to a history of its interpretation in tradition.[39] This practice is also open to other valid readings that are gleaned from historical-critical scholarship.[40]

---

that it yields something particular (the embodiment of God's truth in specific circumstances) (see section 4.1on a preamble to kerygmatic hermeneutics).

37. I refer us to the discussion in chapter 2 on how locating this project of scriptural reading in the Spirit within the church and for the purposes of God relates to historical criticism and to critical readings.

38. Webster, *Holy Scripture*, 95.

39. I acknowledge the issue of how some 2,000 years of Christian tradition would have created assumptions and expectations about what a good and bad biblical reading may be. This recognizes that the issue deserves more serious consideration although the emphasis in this research has been for contemporary readers (who operate within plausibility structures that are likely to account for their own Christian tradition) to read scriptural truth by moving between the text and the present in a Spirit-led interpretation.

40. Sandra Schneiders explains what a valid reading is. She says, "Meaning, appropriated as and in understanding, is always *meaning for* someone, not some body of objective intellectual data. This means that it is located, limited and partial. Whether the scholar is interpreting to increase the understanding of the text, the pastor to foster the faith of the community, or the individual believer for personal growth in commitment, the reading process is a particular and limited engagement with transcendent reality through a mediating text susceptible of a wide range of valid interpretations. There is no one 'right' interpretation, although there may well be wrong ones. The ideal is not to achieve a dominant interpretation, which will exclude all other possibilities, but to achieve a valid interpretation which commands conviction by virtue of its explanatory power, its fidelity and/or healthy challenge to the tradition, and its potential for transformative influence in the world. No interpretation is final, definitive or irreformable, although the progress of the community in interpretation is, in some matters, irreversible (e.g., its realization that Eph 6:5–8 cannot be used as a justification for slavery)" (Schneiders, *Gospels and the Reader*, 116). Moreover, Luis Alonso Schökel argues that author's intention is not the only and exclusive hermeneutical principle. He says, "According to author-hermeneutics, the meaning of a text is adequately defined by the author's intention; the interpreter should strive to an ideal of objectivity and precision. This type of hermeneutics runs the risk of falling into neutrality, distance and minimalism of content and maximalism of conjectures" (Schökel,

Third, I formulate a practice that models the dynamics in a three-way interaction of the Spirit, Scripture, and readers. God freely chooses to work by means of Scripture; and Scriptures need the Spirit to open the eyes of readers and communities to apprehend scriptural truth, else they remain like any other classical texts. As well, kerygmatic readers need Scripture to stand *over-against* them in an ongoing process of teaching, reproof, correction, and training in righteousness.[41] These readers also need to learn to walk in the Spirit to embody this scriptural truth. This Program therefore accounts for the Spirit working with Scripture in a progressive transformation of kerygmatic readers in community.[42] This Program will not be an exercise in producing a body of objective data on the prescribed text. Instead, it entails an extended period of engagement of readers with the Spirit and the scriptural text so readers may embody and perform the truth that the Spirit reveals through the text.[43]

For a practice of kerygmatic interpretation, I would propose for church leadership to first draw Program participants from the qualified and experienced teaching leadership, who may then go on to instruct others in the community.[44] Church leadership then identifies a couple of

---

From Author-Hermeneutics to Text-Hermeneutics, 34).

41. Amos Yong raises the challenge and research question, "How does one engage spirit conceptually and empirically since something that can mean so much can also mean nothing?" (Yong, "Ruach," 183–204). This Program may be seen to be an attempt that addresses this conceptual and empirical question—*how* one may manage the delicate tension between a suspicion against the tyranny of a universal realism ("that can mean so much") and that against the nihilism of communitarian pragmatism ("that can also mean nothing").

42. Recall our earlier discussion in section 4.2.3—kerygmatic hermeneutics is ordered three-way—on how individual and ecclesial discernment in testing a scriptural reading relate dynamically and reciprocally. A reader's individual learning to discern an illumination, inspiration or co-creation in a kerygmatic interpretation feeds back to engender a sharper ecclesial reading collectively, progressively stripping away possible self-deception within the community in a testing of suspicion, A sharper ecclesial reading in turn works at transforming individual readers for a sharper performance in an embodied witness of Jesus Christ to the world.

43. This practice of an embodiment of scriptural truth reflects what is central to kerygmatic theology (see our discussion on community outcomes in section 5.5). There, I argue that a consistent practice of kerygmatic hermeneutics in the three-way dynamics of Spirit-Scripture-Readers forms and gives fullness to a kerygmatic reader and a kerygmatic community.

44. Leadership may pre-qualify participants in a kerygmatic interpretation by discerning, among other criteria, the four marks of the Spirit in readers. This discernment in a testing and evaluation may be more or less stringently applied depending on the purpose of the kerygmatic reading. The discernment is more generously applied if the

hermeneuticians from those Program participants who are also trained in biblical scholarship and theology.[45] Leadership also appoints a facilitator among these participants, one whom she discerns to have the spiritual gift of discernment, discerning spiritual phenomena, spiritual things, and spiritual persons.[46]

I lay out a proposed 6-month Program to read a generic text (see Figure 2).[47] This Program has two components: pre-PAL and PAL. The pre-PAL Program includes a pre-Program activity that yields exegetical readings of the text using both etic and emic approaches.[48] I plan for the Pre-PAL Program and PAL Program to extend over four and two months respectively.

---

purpose is, say, a training in discernment for leadership development. In this case, those who have been newly baptized in the Spirit may even qualify. On the other hand, this discernment would be more stringently applied if this is an ecclesial reading, say, of contemporary debates like sexual practice.

45. A community leadership could benefit from academic resources on philology, biblical scholarship, etc., especially in cases of difficult texts. In some cases, the community may not be disposed to produce its own theological interpretation. What is critical then is for the community leadership to conduct a thorough evaluation of all the valid readings in the light of the dispositions and preferences of those scholars and theologians, and the contextual challenges that they are addressing. This critical review of valid readings could then form the basis for the kerygmatic community's scriptural interpretation.

46. Besides qualification in biblical scholarship and experience in teaching leadership, spirituality and spiritual discernment are also key principles in a practice of kerygmatic interpretation. Therefore, church leadership would pay attention to reader dispositions (section 5.2) and a habitual practice of kerygmatic devotion (section 5.3) to pre-qualify participants in the PAL Program.

47. The proposed duration of the Program is contextually determined. It depends on the length of the scriptural text, the complexity of the text and related readings, the spirituality, qualification, and experience of biblical scholars and theologically trained participants in reading the Spirit and interpreting Scripture in the Spirit. Therefore, this programming serves merely as an illustration to a process of interpreting Scripture in the Spirit. In the programming in Figure 2, I am assuming this generic text has three verses. This helps to give a sense of the minimum scale of such a Program. As most units of analysis of scriptural text tend to be longer, the duration of each component of the Program generally grows with the length of the scriptural text.

48. In this research, I mean an etic approach as one that attempts to take an 'outsider' reading of a scriptural text that evaluates a reading with lenses that are also open to other preferences, cultures and traditions. On the other hand, an emic approach attempts to take an insider reading, especially when a community intends to hold itself accountable to what a scriptural reading says for it to be, say and do. An emic approach will also draw on a text's history of interpretation within a community's tradition.

Figure 2

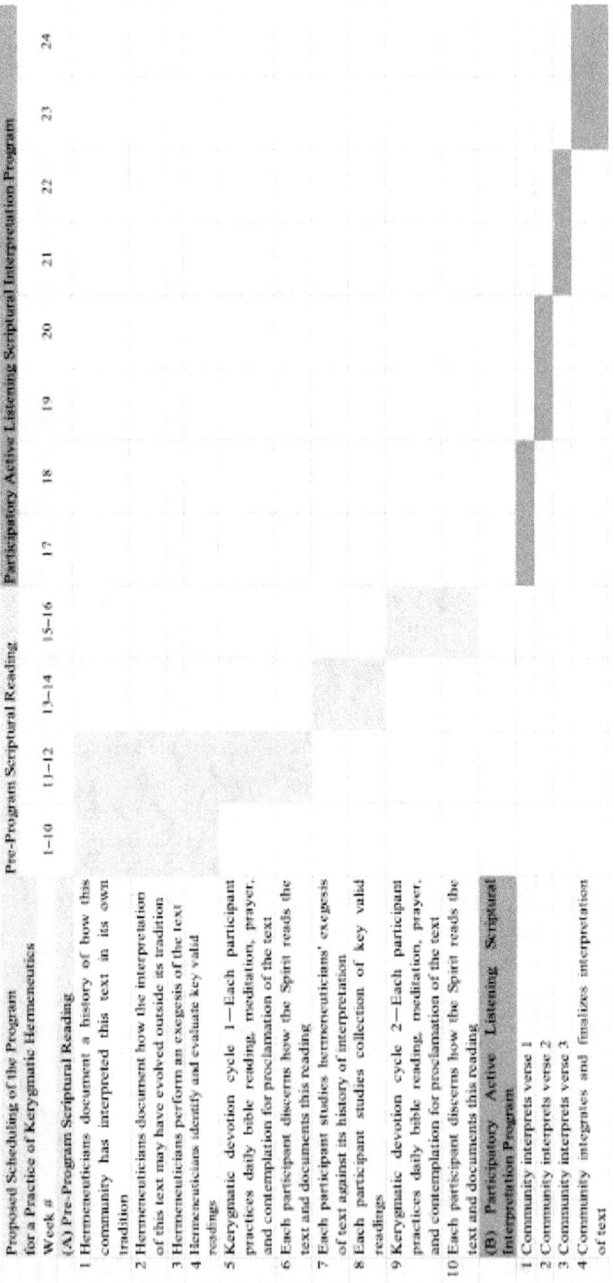

Structuring a Scriptural Interpretation Program with the Participatory Active Listening (PAL) Prayer Method

6.3.1 Pre-PAL Scriptural Interpretation Program

Participating hermeneuticians engage in reading and studying the text to produce a reader that comprises exegetical readings of the text using both etic and emic approaches.[49] These first assemble a history of how this community has interpreted this text in its own tradition. They also document how this scriptural interpretation may have evolved over time. Hermeneuticians then prayerfully craft an exegesis of the text read in the community's context in the present against its own history of interpretation. These also identify and evaluate other valid readings of the text, whether from other traditions or the academy. These hermeneuticians preface each reading with a short annotated biographical account of the author—his/her tradition, motivation, and possibly what questions s/he is responding to—to provide insights into the author's disposition, pre-understanding, social and institutional location, and contextual challenges. All Program participants receive this reader before the commencement of the PAL Program.

Concurrent to this, participating leaders start cycle 1 of kerygmatic devotion using the prescribed scriptural text in their own daily devotion.[50] There is a daily practice of Bible reading, meditation, prayer, contemplation, and proclamation. In this first cycle, readers read the text *devotionally* to discern how the Spirit interprets this text. This cycle extends over a period. Readers work, through the daily disciplines of kerygmatic devotion—to read, memorize, reflect, study, meditate, pray, and contemplate over the weeks so to ingest the *logos*. They then "proclaim" or "preach"

---

49. There are various ways of managing this etic-emic tension in a practice of kerygmatic interpretation. This question calls for discernment of a community leadership: What should be the relative significance that my community places for readings that use etic and emic approaches respectively? For the very established traditions, the clergy board, or equivalent ruling body, may rule that only the tradition's history of interpretation may be admitted for any re-reading of significant scriptural texts. Younger churches, which are in the early days of establishing a tradition, may be more open to voices from other traditions as spiritually discerned in the Spirit. In such cases, readers are provided with a collection of these other readings, together with the participating hermeneuticians' annotated comments on authors' biographical accounts. Kerygmatic readers may be just as open to the Spirit speaking to them through these other readings as those in a history of interpretation from its own tradition.

50. This practice follows my formulation of kerygmatic devotion, with daily disciplines of Bible reading, meditation, prayer, contemplation, proclamation, and witness (see section 5.3).

the text in the Spirit, with reference to only the Bible as they speak.[51] Readers attempt to tease out the Spirit's voice from their own.[52] Cycle 1 of kerygmatic devotion allows participants to first try to hear for themselves what the Spirit is wanting to say and do in the present through the text before other human voices are added to the discourse.

After the dissemination of the reader, participants take extended time to first read and study the hermeneuticians' exegesis of text read from the community's context in the present against its own history of interpretation. Participants may spend another extended period reading and studying other valid readings.[53] In this phase, participants read sensitively to tease out the Spirit's voice from the human voices in those readings. Readers are sensitive to the dispositions, pre-understanding and contextual challenges of these individual redactors, scholars and theologians. They attend to discern the marks of the Spirit as lived out in their lives and their writings. They seek to discern to what extent each exegetical reading signifies the scriptural truth that the Spirit is revealing in the present for this community.

Readers next commence kerygmatic devotion cycle 2 after they have completed their own critical study of the exegetical readings of the text. In this second cycle, readers read the text critically in the Spirit, drawing from disciplined use of philology, biblical scholarship, and theology, to discern how the Spirit illumines and inspires the text in the present. Participants each produce their own exegetical readings in the Spirit in cycle 2, after having studied its history of interpretation and the collated valid readings, and reflected, prayed, and contemplated on the text in the Spirit. Again, this includes a daily practice of Bible reading, meditation, prayer, and contemplation until readers can "proclaim" the text in the Spirit. Cycle 2 allows participants to hear for themselves how the Spirit reads the text, and what the Spirit is wanting the community to be, say,

---

51. Readers devote full attention to hear the Spirit "open up" the text to them; they do not include any post-biblical interpretive categories in cycle 1 reading. Readers "proclaim" the text aloud. The key idea here is that this reading is devotionally based, one that is born out of a reader spending time in reading, reflecting, praying, and contemplating on a scriptural text.

52. Readers pay attention to what is being "proclaimed" as the logos is articulated, to discern what is not only his/her own voice but also the Spirit's. This devotional-based proclamation is a practice in flowing in the Spirit and discerning the Spirit's voice in a daily discipline.

53. Recall various discussions on valid, invalid and distorted readings (see, e.g., sections 4.2.1, 4.3.1, 5, 5.1 and various parts of sections 6.3 and 6.4).

and do in the present through the text, when read against what he had spoken through past voices, and perhaps even present voices outside the community's own tradition.

6.3.2 PAL Scriptural Interpretation Program

In this phase of the Program, participants gather weekly as a church community to discern together how the Spirit reads a designated text. Participants come to these 90-minute weekly sessions to apprehend corporately what the Spirit is illuminating and inspiring the text to say, and what the Spirit is wanting readers to be, say, and do through their scriptural reading. Participants understand that they will hold themselves accountable to the Spirit and one another to perform this Spirit-led interpretation of the text.

For illustration purposes, I plan the PAL Program to extend over 2 months, with a reading of *each* verse being tested over two weeks minimally. A community may need more time to test a reading of a problematic text or verse and hear clearly from the Spirit. I schedule the testing of an integrated reading of the text over at least another two weeks. This Spirit-led scriptural reading goes beyond documenting an exegetical reading; it involves readers apprehending how the Spirit reads the text and what he says for a community to be, say, and do in the present.

For the purpose of clarity, I refer us to Exhibit 1 on the PAL Prayer Method again even as I adapt PAL praying for how a community may pray in the Spirit to interpret Scripture.[54]

The Program facilitator begins the 90-minute prayer session with a time of worship. This brings a sense of the immediacy of the Spirit. Each session consists of three prayer cycles in three learning loops. Each learning loop is designed to filter off the dissonances of human voices with increasing sharpness, so participants distil to hear more clearly the Spirit's voice. After the third learning loop ends in silence, the facilitator closes the session with a thematic summation of the community's scriptural interpretation. S/he dismisses the meeting after a burst of spontaneous individual worshipful prayers.

---

54. In section 6.2 above, I reviewed how praying in the Spirit is made operational using the PAL Prayer Method. For a detailed process that makes operational the three learning loops of PAL, please see Seah, "Spirituality Approach," 185–202.

To start each prayer session, the facilitator organizes participants randomly into small groups of no more than four persons. Each group then appoints its own leader. The facilitator asks the questions, "How is the Spirit interpreting this text (of the week)? What is he saying that we should be, say, and do as a community?"[55] At the end of the three learning loops, the facilitator closes the session with his/her thematic summation of the community's reading of how the Spirit interprets this verse (or text) and what the Spirit said through the text for us to be, say, and do as a community.

I now adapt each of these prayer cycles for reading Scripture in the Spirit. I briefly give an account of a prayer cycle's five components: silence, spiritual prayer-listening, intra-group dialogue, intra-group thematic integration, and inter-group thematic presentation.

Participants contemplate the exegetical questions in prayerful *silence*. Readers, trained in kerygmatic devotion, are disciplined to flow in the Spirit from worship into silent and patient attending and listening to the Spirit speaking through the text. Silence is one mode of praying in the Spirit to hear him speak.[56] Participants still themselves as the Spirit catches them up in the Spirit in a detachment from self. This prepares them for spiritual prayer-listening.

Participants exercise spiritual discernment in *spiritual prayer-listening*. Praying in silence heightens participants' spiritual discernment that enables prayer-listening.[57] Here, readers attend to the Spirit, and how and what he is saying through the Scripture that is being read and studied. Readers also listen to one another beyond the spoken words. They discern the marks of the Spirit as signs of the presence and activity of the Spirit in one another, as each takes a turn to interpret the scriptural text, and argue for his/her particular reading (against all other valid readings

---

55. The scriptural text is projected on screen throughout the weekly meeting for easy recall. Participants also have the text, in either hard or electronic copy, on them.

56. Recall praying in the Spirit (in section 5.4.1) can take different expressions ranging from praying in the vernacular, praying in spirit speech, to praying in silent contemplation. The latter may draw from the way of, say, Saint John of the Cross.

57. Unlike silence, prayer-listening is not silent. Here, each reader takes a turn to argue his/her case while others pray and listen to the Spirit for discernment. Seah says, "In spiritual prayer-listening, both the listeners and the speakers must practice selfless openness, objectivity, and detachment. This is to allow the spirit of the individual to speak through the individual speakers, and, as much as it is, for the listeners in the group to allow the spirit of the speaker to speak to the listeners" (Seah, "Spirituality Approach," 195).

on the table).⁵⁸ There is a commitment to grow together with a genuineness to mutual love and care. Readers discern both human voices as well as that of the Spirit in human voices.

Set in this atmosphere of attentive spiritual prayer-listening and mutual love, participants engage in reading how the Spirit interprets the text in *intra-group dialogue*.⁵⁹ The four participants (including the leader) in each small group take turns to present and argue for where they locate their exegesis of the text against the other valid readings while the rest

---

58. We may review our discussion in section 3.2 on discerning the marks of the Spirit to better appreciate what readers may be looking for in testing for these marks. For intoxication, readers may discern if one behaves as if s/he has fallen in love with God, like one stupefied or drunk with love. There would be attitudes and behaviors that may appear to be non-rational (not conforming to human reasoning). However, s/he is not irrational or deranged. For life, readers may look for people whom this one has brought to faith or helped to grow in faith in Christ Jesus. That is, there would be fruits of discipleship. Besides signs of spiritual life and growth, readers may also look for evidence of the fruits of the Spirit in a restoration of wholeness in all dimensions of humanity. For participation, readers look for signs of divinity mediated by contemplation, communion and flowing in the Spirit. There could be evidence of one's manifesting the gifts of the Spirits in knowledge and wisdom, signs and miracles, healings and deliverances. And, for revelation of truth and correction of errors, readers look for an ongoing learning, unlearning, and relearning in one's journey of transformation in holiness and wholeness. Certainly, readers may discern in one both the positive signs of learning as well as the negative signs associated with a call to repentance. What is more significant, given the dynamism of kerygmatic hermeneutics, is whether such a one is becoming more and more open and sensitive, attitudinally and behaviorally, to being taught of the Spirit. See also the concluding section 5.7 on discerning the marks of the Spirit in various dimensions of a reader's life of transformation in the Spirit. This transformation culminates in a lived-out proclamation of Christ to the world that would have impact on society and social challenges.

59. On "dialogue" Seah adopts the sense of a "discourse of a more conversational character" (Vine, *Vine's Expository Dictionary,* 308–9), meaning it to be a collective conversation for the attainment of understanding (Seah, "Spirituality Approach," 197). In Seah's formulation, the intra-group dialogue stands as a continuation of spiritual prayer-listening. He explains, "first, team members in the multiple small prayer groups must all participate in deep listening, intuitively in heart and spirit, and keep faith to trust each other in the performance of this function; second, both the listeners and the speakers must prudently respond from the position of stillness and silence, both to listen and to speak beyond the spoken words, even to the discerning of the inner voices; third, after all have spoken, and every listener has spoken in response, the collective voice in dialogue is received in positive spirit, without judgement, and the whole discourse is then carried on to the next stage, which is termed intra-group thematic integration" (Seah, "Spirituality Approach," 199–200).

listens attentively and takes notes. The leader, working with the group, then lays out the top reading(s) of the verse for evaluation.[60]

The leader guides the conversation in a group dialogical form, with participants questioning a reading and a presenting member responding, always maintaining the atmosphere of attentive spiritual prayer-listening in deference to one another in love. When appropriate, the leader may bring the group back into contemplative silence and spiritual prayer-listening to discern and apprehend the scriptural truth of the text, before calling on the next presenter. Participants are ever conscious that the Spirit also speaks through the other and they can learn from others who are more spiritually discerning.

At the end of all presentations, the leader facilitates an *intra-group thematic integration* of participants' readings of the text.[61] Participants take turns to pray aloud in spirit speech (as in *glossalalia* or speaking in tongues). This brings an immediate experience of the Spirit. There is a freeing from personal encumbrances and preferences to an embracing of a collective mind of the Spirit's reading of the text. Other participants listen silently and attentively for the Spirit to give an interpretation of the tongue speech. An interpretation of a tongue can come in an inaudible voice, a vision, a thought, or an emotion. Participants may keep their eyes open, close their eyes, write down what they 'hear' for a particular participant, or just remember what has been revealed to them by the Spirit.

The leader then facilitates group sharing of participants' interpretation in the Spirit. Starting with any participant, s/he shares his/her interpretation of his/her own tongue first, then followed by others one after another sharing their interpretations of that same participant's tongue. Participants may pass at any time even as each discerns a collective voice of the Spirit as mediated by the exercise of charismata. Here, participants

60. Depending on whether this is a difficult text, there could be more than four valid readings in the collection of valid readings, drawn from the community's history of interpretation as well as those outside its own tradition, or the academy. Each small group of, say, four participants, argues for where it locates itself in its top three or four readings in this collection. In the limit, there is convergence and consonance of discernment when all participants could agree on one valid reading in this intra-group dialogue.

61. Seah explains, "In integrating the thematic concern(s) and substantive area of concern(s), the individual member's concern is subsumed under the group's focal concern, whereby "I" gives way to "we," such that the thematic concern(s) is expressed in terms of "our thematic concern(s)." This is done by way of an unbusied silence of conversational discourse, being mindful of the dialogical co-presence of God and the person-in dialogue, who are the image of God" (Seah, "Spirituality Approach," 200).

may exercise diverse gifts like prophecy, tongues, interpretation of tongues, word of wisdom, word of knowledge, and discernment of spirits. The leader works with the group to determine the collective mind of the group on a reading of the text. S/he summarizes this group integration of a Spirit-led interpretation of scriptural truth. S/he also summarizes what the group discerns to be what the Spirit is saying through the text for the community to be, say, and do in the present.

The Program facilitator next re-assembles all participants for an *inter-group thematic presentation*. Leaders of each small group take turns to present his/her group integration at the community level. At this level, all group presenters use the plural pronouns like "we" and "our," without making personal references. The group presentations by all the group presenters thus surface the key valid readings of the text across groups. A Program with six participating small groups, say, will therefore yield six or fewer key valid readings. The Program facilitator lays out each key valid reading as a leader presents it. S/he then re-classifies similar readings, when appropriate, with the community's endorsement. We can expect easier convergence of a Spirit-led scriptural interpretation when we start with fewer key valid readings at the inter-group thematic presentation in the first prayer cycle.

For the inter-group thematic presentation in the first prayer cycle, however, participants do not attempt to discern the collective mind. Neither do they give any response to the group presenters. Instead, individual participants practice spiritual prayer-listening and take notes of each group presentation and the resulting key valid readings. After experiencing the immediacy of the Spirit in intra-group thematic integration, there is an increasing sense of individual self-emptying where "I" gives way to "we" as participants attend to other groups' reading of the text. The inter-group thematic presentation completes the first cycle of the PAL Method.

This opening up of individual participants' spiritual senses to hear from the Spirit and others flowing in the Spirit (in intra-group thematic integration and inter-group thematic presentation) leads participants into an increasing sense of the Other in one another. Participants look for the marks of the Spirit—intoxication, life, participation, and revelation of truth—in each other's lives to find an attribution to the Spirit in the prayer-listening throughout the intra-group dialogue, intra-group thematic integration, and inter-group thematic integration. Each evaluates all readings in the Spirit afresh as presented and argued at the session level. This sets the stage for the next two prayer cycles.

The second prayer cycle begins with *silence* in continued self-emptying that sustains a flowing in the Spirit. The learnings from the inter-group thematic presentations now provide the materials for *spiritual prayer-listening* as well as for the *intra-group dialogue*. The first prayer cycle would possibly have yielded a small set of valid readings (out of the original collection of readings) for all participants' prayerful re-reading. There is a sort of "re-setting" of one's discerned choice with each prayer cycle. That is, individual participants are free to move away from their personal readings of the text to consider those that emerged from the inter-group thematic presentation. Individual participants practice spiritual prayer-listening and locate themselves in one of the readings in this new set. Again, the leader lays out the top reading(s) to which this group subscribes.[62] These readings could be similar to or different from that/those that the group evaluated in the first prayer cycle. The process repeats with the *intra-group thematic integration* that again brings an immediacy to the Spirit in yielding the best argued readings in an integrated scriptural interpretation for each group.

The second prayer cycle ends in an *inter-group thematic presentation* that is likely to see some convergence of the groups' reading of the text. Again, the Program facilitator lays out and re-classifies the key valid readings for participants' discernment in testing and evaluation in the third prayer cycle. The final *inter-group thematic presentation* brings to a close the tri-cycle of prayers.

The Program facilitator brings a time of *silence* to allow for personal reflection, learning and resolution. S/he provides an *inter-loop thematic summation* of the session's prayer discourse. This final thematic summation crystallizes the Program's thematic concern—a Spirit-led interpretation of scriptural truth of a text and what the Spirit is saying to the community in the present. The Program facilitator then closes the prayer session with worshipful prayers, in a mixture of the vernacular and *glossolalia*.

Each weekly prayer session is audio-recorded.[63] A transcriber produces a transcript for circulation to all participants for their prayerful

---

62. In both the second and third prayer cycles, participants may freely argue for what s/he discerns in the Spirit as the most valid reading that has been presented in the inter-group thematic integration, even though this may not be his/her own group's integrated reading, or this may be one s/he argued against in the previous prayer cycle. We expect convergence with each prayer cycle.

63. The audio recording is done at the session level, not at the group level.

reading before they return the following week. Participants may then bring up any criticism of the previous session's inter-group thematic summary to the Program facilitator or the church leadership. The Program facilitator starts the following week's PAL praying with the inter-loop thematic summary of the previous week's reading.

This Program ends with a couple of prayer sessions to finalize a Spirit-led interpretation of the text, and to account for, and if necessary, to collectively pray through any remaining criticism that has been brought up during the Program.[64] The facilitator also integrates what the Spirit has said to the community through the text for it to be, say or do in the present. Participants subsequently confirm in writing this reading of the text.[65] In this sense, this Program summation is genuinely corporately owned. Participants commit to be held accountable to the community and one another in this scriptural reading.

The PAL Program is designed to tease out the Spirit's voice from human voices. Through the PAL Prayer Method, kerygmatic readers in community practice kerygmatic criticism in a testing and evaluation. It teases out the Spirit's voice from voices of the PAL facilitator, individual participants, redactors, scholars or theologians who gave the valid readings, or even the hermeneuticians who together prayerfully crafted an exegesis of the text read in the community's context in the present, or its earlier versions in a history of interpretation in the community's tradition.

The PAL prayer process is intended to safeguard against possible self-deception. Seah's qualitative analysis of PAL transcripts documented evidence of community learning from self-deception and correction of attitudes and behavior.[66] Such empirical evidence lends support to the claim that the PAL Prayer Method might be efficacious in safeguarding against self-deception. This could yield a Spirit-led interpretation of

---

64. If necessary, the facilitator, with the concurrence of church leadership, may extend the Program if what is deemed needed is more time for PAL participants to come to a consensual reading that each is convicted of and committed to.

65. Where there is perhaps real tension between the individual and the community in any particular meeting, the facilitator would attempt to intervene to take this dispute offline without interrupting the flow of the prayer program. Where there remains any unresolved strong objection at the end of the Program, especially in cases of difficult texts, the church leadership may take this up for a final review. This smaller circle of senior leaders follows a similar corporate process of reading Scripture in the Spirit until a consensual reading may be achieved.

66. See abstracts of these findings on learning and correction in the Spirit in section 6.2.2

scriptural truth where there is a reduced possibility of manipulating the community because of the corporate testing of the emerging discernment. Therefore, the PAL Prayer Method may make operational a community reading of scriptural truth in the Spirit.[67]

This practice is premised on the otherness of the Spirit and Scripture; the Spirit works with Scripture to reveal truth. The corollary is, kerygmatic readers, in created grace, have all-natural capabilities, potentialities and powers to discern and test what is truly of the Spirit. These apprehend and receive the Spirit's revelation of scriptural truth as authoritative in the otherness of God.

6.4 Theological Integrity

In section 6.3, I have proposed a practice of kerygmatic interpretation that consists in praying and interpreting Scripture in the Spirit.[68] This practice is in part shaped by the kerygmatic theology I formulated (in chapters 4 and 5) and in part shaped by my experience of the PAL Prayer Method (see sections 1.1 and 6.2). This practice flows from kerygmatic theology and has an element of self-criticism within it. This self-criticism is one thread of kerygmatic theology—its kerygmatic criticism—which I have discussed in chapter 5. Therefore, this self-criticism is part of the

---

67. In this section, I make a move from kerygmatic theology to inform on a practice of kerygmatic interpretation. As the proposed PAL Scriptural Interpretation Program that makes this operational is yet untested (even though the PAL Prayer Method has been tested in Seah's study), this process is subject to review and refinement when this is finally implemented in any church community. Moreover, I anticipate challenges from reading difficult texts. A practice of kerygmatic interpretation could benefit by drawing credible resources born of discipline from the academy for what is otherwise not readily accessible to a church community. However, when scholars may also stumble over difficult texts, these would probably be beyond what a typical church leader can handle. In these instances, church leadership may more appropriately draw the targeted participants in the PAL Scriptural Interpretation Program from the community's hermeneuticians who are also biblical scholars and theologians. The PAL prayer processes are designed to keep unfettered the spirit of discernment in a testing and evaluation of multiple valid readings to bring convergence to what is also the Spirit's in human voices. Therefore, a spiritually discerning church leadership is ultimately critical in apprehending the fluidity that surrounds the Spirit and his working in the world, including the church. To some extent, the structures and processes of a kerygmatic community would reflect this fluidity.

68. Proclaiming Christ in the Spirit is also central to a practice of kerygmatic interpretation. I have motivated this embodied witnessing to Christ throughout this research. Therefore, I will not further discuss this here.

way in which this practice reflects that theology. I conclude this chapter by addressing the question of theological integrity.

I argue that kerygmatic hermeneutics displays theological integrity. My claim is that a pursuit of a practice of kerygmatic interpretation will allow a community to discern what the Spirit is saying to the church in the present. This claim can be, and indeed, should be tested and evaluated with criticism, against a possibility of rejection. If the design of this practice were informed by good theology, we should be able to test whether this claim is in fact true.

This process of testing and evaluation takes two forms. Firstly, testing takes the form of an ongoing spiritual discernment. This is a prayerful testing for what is not only human voices but also that of the Spirit in guiding readers in community in what to be, say, and do in the present. Secondly, evaluation takes the form of empirical investigation. This may take on qualitative and/or quantitative analysis that evaluate if and to what extent this practice results in readers and communities visibly bearing the marks that I earlier proposed are the marks of the Spirit. This evaluation tests whether the transformation outcomes and impacts are as kerygmatic theology claims they should be—in an attribution to the Spirit.

For my purposes (and this is Williams's agenda), what matters for theological integrity is that these claims about realities that kerygmatic hermeneutics talk about are accessible or visible not only to those who believe in them. These are claims about realities that are to some degree visible to those outside the community. Williams argues that the theologian does not have a uniquely privileged task of establishing truth in a religious claim. Instead, a theologian has this hope of a possibility of knowing God.[69] That is, others might see things that theologians have

69. Williams critiques the adequacy of theological language in casting a normative response to God without being suspicious of the administration of religious power. He says, "Theology of this sort . . . is willing to learn from non-theological sources something about the mechanisms of deceit and control in language. It is there to test the truthfulness of religious discourse, its fidelity to itself and its openness to what it says it is about; but it does not do this by trying to test the 'truth' of this or that religious utterance according to some canon of supposedly neutral accuracy. Establishing the truth of a religious claim is a matter of discovering its resource and scope for holding together and making sense of our perceptions and transactions without illusion; and that it is a task in which the theologian *as* theologian has a role, but not a uniquely privileged one (as if he or she alone were free enough from the heavy clay of piety to see between the words of believers into the life of God)" (Williams, *On Christian Theology*, 14).

not seen, but which they need to be open to and take account of even though they do not accept that these others will have a comprehensive or neutral view of these realities. Therefore, while the theological exploration of kerygmatic hermeneutics claims that there should be observable effects of the Spirit's work, theological integrity demands that we allow this claim to be tested by methods appropriate for the assessment of such observable effects.

I argue that a practice of kerygmatic interpretation incorporates a process of testing whereby individual acts of spiritual discernment are tested against one another in the Body of Christ. This testing of spiritual discernment is predicated on God's self-gift so that it is possible for created agencies to know, hear, and see God in the Spirit in a work of grace. Participants, flowing in the Spirit, yield natural capabilities, potentialities, and powers, including that of language, to God. The exercise of charismata, in a diversity of spiritual gifts, edifies and unifies the Body of Christ.[70] PAL praying in a church community, by design, brings convergence towards a form of Spirit talk that is not easily manipulated by participants or leaders. Therefore, this practice of kerygmatic hermeneutics is internally protected against the waywardness of personal preferences.

The claims to objective real-world effects of kerygmatic hermeneutics are also open to empirical evaluation. I argue that qualitative research methods can make sense of religious discourses and evaluate the attendant lived-out responses of a kerygmatic community of faith.[71] Quantitative research methods may also be appropriate if a researcher wishes to evaluate if there has been any systematic change in attitudes and behaviors that is attributable to the Spirit's transformative work.[72] That is, socio-scientific empirical evaluation can validate the anticipated outcomes of kerygmatic hermeneutics in the forming of kerygmatic readers and community.[73]

---

70. My review of the discourse on the Spirit and Church, and, Spirit and Transformation in sections 3.1.4 and 3.1.5 respectively suggests that this work of the Spirit is at least in part mediated through the activities of the church. That is, the transformation of individual disciples is an ongoing work, enabled by the Spirit's charisms and mediated through all other members of the Body for the building up of the whole.

71. See, e.g., Swinton and Mowat, *Qualitative Research*.

72. Williams clarifies, "Theology can be no more and no less (and not otherwise) 'systematic' than the processes of faith to which it is answerable, and if it is confident of itself in ways divorced from this, it loses its integrity" (Williams, *On Christian Theology*, 14).

73. In section 3.1, I reviewed the Holy Spirit and his work, and how the Spirit

Kerygmatic theology underpins the claim that a Spirit-led process is the proper context for an interpretation of Scripture that forms an embodied witness of Jesus Christ. Recall how Figure 1 (in section 5.7) gives a visual representation of this Spirit-led process in kerygmatic hermeneutics. This Spirit-led transformation is worked through reader dispositions, community habits, community practices, community outcomes, and community impacts. Kerygmatic criticism also demands that the same coherence of scriptural truths should be seen in the visible representation of communities of faith in the Spirit's making the one holy catholic apostolic church.

The integrity of kerygmatic theology then involves a testing and evaluation of its claims; this testing and evaluation has been built into such a practice of kerygmatic interpretation. Therefore, this testing and evaluation is kerygmatic theology's self-criticism.[74] What is being tested and evaluated in kerygmatic criticism is whether we may discern if this entire account of *how* the Spirit catches them up to make an embodied witness bears the marks of the Spirit—intoxication, life, participation, and revelation of truth. That is, what is being tested and evaluated is an attribution of the transformation results to the Spirit. These marks thus help us to discern critically when and to what extent a performance of Scripture is taking place in the Spirit. Similarly, what is being empirically evaluated in kerygmatic criticism is when and to what extent this performance of Scripture in the Spirit that forms an embodied witness to Jesus Christ is getting better and better.[75]

Kerygmatic hermeneutics is this account of the Spirit's working whose end and purpose is the making of an embodied witness to Jesus Christ so the world may hear and see God. We can discern the impact

---

works in transformative ways with people. He works visibly; his work is mediated by human bodies, dispositions, habits and practices. The invisibility of the Spirit does not necessitate the invisibility of the Spirit's effects. The effects of the Spirit's work are in fact observable and describable. They may even be measurable, provided we are careful enough in specifying what we are looking for. To believe that empirical evaluation is somehow inappropriate is to deny the visibility of the real-world effects of the Spirit's working.

74. Kerygmatic theology claims that the results of a practice of kerygmatic interpretation may be attributable to the presence and activity of the Spirit. For our easy reference, kerygmatic criticism is the name I give to the discerned testing and reasoned evaluation of the realist claims about the work of the Spirit in reader dispositions, community habits, practices, outcomes, and impacts.

75. Practical theology using ethnographic, qualitative, and quantitative research methods can develop this thread of future research.

of the Spirit' working when the Body of Christ is transformed into the likeness of Christ and radiates the Father's glory. Framed with reference to this desired end, a practice of kerygmatic interpretation yields a hermeneutical gap that is teleological. This hermeneutical gap is the 'distance' between what speech (vocalized *kerygma*) and patterns of action (performed *kerygma*) *should be* when the Body of Christ transforms into Christ's likeness and radiates the Father's glory, and, what speech and patterns of action actually are in the reader's world.[76] That is, kerygmatic hermeneutics bears theological integrity to the extent that readers in community can discern and confess to this hermeneutical gap, and, attitudinally and behaviorally, work towards the desired impact of a representation of Christlikeness and the Father's glory. This is how the world may know that a practice of kerygmatic interpretation reflects its theology. Therefore, to the extent that kerygmatic hermeneutics bears theological integrity, it can speak into the Pentecostal-charismatic and perhaps even the wider church community.

In the next chapter, I conclude with a discussion of contributions, implications, and limitations of my general argument, with directions for future research.

---

76. I note my use here is atypical. "Hermeneutical gap" is normally used to describe the "distance" between the reader's present patterns of thought, feeling, and expectation, and the patterns of thought, feeling, and action that were around in the contexts in which Scripture was first produced and received. It is atypical because I am explaining the present kerygma in a teleological manner with reference to its end and purpose, instead of a historically contextual manner as it is normally used.

7

CONCLUSION

But He answered and said to them, "When it is evening, you say, 'It will be fair weather, for the sky is red.'"

And in the morning, 'There will be a storm today, for the sky is red and threatening.' Do you know how to discern the appearance of the sky, but cannot discern the signs of the times?" (Matt 16:2–3 NAS)

THE SPIRIT CATCHES PEOPLE up to become living proclamations of Jesus Christ. The interpretation of Scripture is one of the means by which the Spirit drives this process. This Spirit-led process is therefore the proper context for the interpretation of Scripture. In this research, I attempted to provide an underlying theology for this process of interpretation and the specific practices that are part of it. "Kerygmatic hermeneutics" is the name I have for this account of scriptural interpretation in the Spirit for the making of an embodied witness to Jesus Christ.

The Spirit (and his working) is mysterious, unpredictable, and extraordinary. He is mysterious because he is hidden; his ways are elusive and fluid. His working is unpredictable because he works in different ways with different people and in different contexts. His working is also extraordinary because the outcome is a communion with God rather than a re-arrangement in worldly affairs.

The Spirit's work of catching people up to become living proclamations of Jesus Christ is remarkable. The Spirit is not self-referential: he proclaims Christ and glorifies the Father. As the Spirit of truth, he guides humans into the truth of Christ; he convicts them of sin, righteousness, and judgment; he makes humans holy with the word that sanctifies; he enables humans to remain at one with God and another. His working is Christocentric. Such living proclamation takes a communal shape as the Spirit makes an embodied witness to Jesus Christ in the Church for all times and places.

This, therefore, is the Spirit's work. It is the work that the Spirit does by animating and guiding human practices and processes—including the practices and processes that I call kerygmatic hermeneutics. Such human processes can genuinely participate, in some way, in the Spirit's work. Members of this community that the Spirit is creating are involved in discerning and working in tune with the Spirit's work. This then raises the question of discernment.

Challenges of discernment naturally arise in kerygmatic hermeneutics in all its human processes and practices. Here, the mysterious, unpredictable, and extraordinary working of the Spirit is bound up in complex yet concrete ways with the attitudes and activities of the people of God: their dispositions, disciplines, locations, and situations in life. There is therefore the unavoidable challenge of discerning or discriminating what is not only human but is also attributable to the Spirit. There are two distinct purposes to this discernment or discrimination. There is a discerning for testing *what is to be done* (in order to follow the Spirit's lead and participate in the Spirit's work). There is also a discerning for evaluating *what has been done* (to assess whether it was indeed of the Spirit).

True to the Spirit's working, kerygmatic hermeneutics includes processes for its own self-criticism, in relation to the marks of the Spirit. These marks of the Spirit give us the standard by which we can criticize, test and evaluate. These marks indicate the differences that the Spirit makes in human life. We can look for these marks in the Spirit's outworking in kerygmatic hermeneutics. They serve as a way of judging or assessing to what extent an interpretation is aligned with the Spirit. Therefore, these marks of the Spirit can help address the challenges of discernment in kerygmatic hermeneutics.

My account of kerygmatic hermeneutics has been an exercise in constructive theology. That is, one that is not intended to yield a static, systematic hermeneutical theory. It is, rather, a guide to an ongoing process of Spirit-led revelation and transformation. The Spirit leads humans into knowing God, revealed in Jesus Christ. In this knowing of God, the Spirit opens their eyes and unveils the truth in Jesus Christ. The Spirit shapes those who are open to knowing Christ to become his embodied witnesses. They become holy as they are caught up in the Spirit in a participation in divinity. Therefore, this is also a guide to an ongoing process of proclaiming Christ as they are led into an ongoing encounter with him. That makes this account an exercise in practical theology as well. In this research, I attempted to show what concrete dispositions, disciplines, and practices Christian readers in community might need to pursue in the knowing, becoming, and proclaiming of God. In this exploration in practical theology, I have engaged in conversation with organizational studies in management because kerygmatic hermeneutics has implications for the way in which a community of readers can be organized, the structures and processes it can employ and the forms of self-evaluation it can pursue.

Summarizing, this account of kerygmatic hermeneutics makes ordinary and concrete the extraordinary and mysterious work of the Spirit. At the same time, it also makes apparent what is the extraordinary and mysterious in the ordinariness of human living.

Kerygmatic interpretation, in dynamically forming a kerygmatic reader and community in the one holy catholic and apostolic church, addresses the question: How may the contemporary world hear and see God? This dynamism of the Spirit's work in God's economy in a to-ing and fro-ing between revelation and apprehension, and the proclamation of scriptural truth demands discernment from a kerygmatic reader and community.[1] I argue that discernment has been a constant enterprise for humankind in the knowing of its Creator-Other. This enterprise is not the monopoly of theology, but theology is the lens through which truth gleaned from all disciplines are interpreted to reveal a self-giving God. Therefore, the corollary question to which kerygmatic hermeneutics is an answer is, how may one discern God to speak and act in the human world? This question has two senses. For a participating reader, it would read, how may one discern God and so speak and act in the human world (that is, this reader is the one speaking and acting). For a third-party reader looking on an interpretive act, it would read, how may one discern

1. This unity of truth may be diffused because what can be seen could be refractions of the "treasure in earthen vessels," where truths may appear distorted or even shrouded (2 Cor 4:7). It is therefore understandable that Thiselton raises his skepticism, "I can fully understand why for many Pentecostals Cox's book seems to hover between very cautious approval in its recognition of *worldwide numbers and relevance* to our age, and ambiguity or even skepticism for its *pragmatic and phenomenological* stance, as over against a genuine theological one" (Thiselton, *Holy Spirit*, 452).

God speaking and acting in the human world (that is, God is the one speaking and acting through a human interpretive act).

Kerygmatic hermeneutics is not a method or a model for a hermeneutic of various genres of Scriptural texts. Kerygmatic hermeneutics is not method-centric; i.e., it does not propose the kind of process that, when readers faithfully followed would make possible a re-construction (historically or otherwise) of the meaning of a text. Instead, kerygmatic hermeneutics is Spirit-centric and *logos*-centric; i.e., it proposes that when readers are led by the Spirit to read Scripture in disciplined living in community, they reveal truth and point to Christ in active witness wherever and whenever they are. Kerygmatic readers, in transformed communities, give shape and fullness to the Body of Christ. These flow in the Spirit to reveal a likeness of Christ and the glory of the Father, consonant with Lash's account of *Believing Three Ways*. These transformed communities can evidence the mystery of God and his divine action in the world—in the making of the one holy catholic apostolic church. To this end, a Spirit-led process is the proper context for an interpretation of Scripture that makes for this embodied witness to Jesus Christ.

7.1 Contributions of this Research

My contribution in this research is the seriousness with which I account for the Spirit's presence and activity in a community of faith. There is also a seriousness about the role of the otherness of Scripture in forming an embodied witness to Christ. What is distinctive here is that I am taking this strong account of the captivation, intensity, and efficacy of the work of the Spirit, and putting it *together with* a strong account of the otherness of Scripture. What underlies these moves is the serious acknowledgement that interpreting Scripture in a community of faith and for the purposes of God is not a human enterprise; it is God's self-gift of grace.

This research takes its shape from stepping back in a first move from a church community's practice in praying in the Spirit to a fresh formulation of theological interpretation, and in a second move, for an underlying theology of kerygmatic hermeneutics to inform on its practice. This research has contributions to theology, ecclesial practice as well as methodology.

Concerning theology, kerygmatic hermeneutics can contribute to varying extents towards discourses on theological interpretation,

Pentecostal-charismatic hermeneutics, epistemology, theology proper and pneumatology, and ecclesiology and ethnography. I have attempted to answer some of the hard questions on discernment in relation to the testing and evaluation of realist claims in theology that span these discourses, with especial challenges in the post-modern and post-liberal periods.

I also argue that kerygmatic hermeneutics has theological integrity. Kerygmatic hermeneutics can hold in tension a unity of truth that addresses both the world (in a proclamation that witnesses to Jesus Christ) and the church (in an ecclesiastical use in teaching and a refutation of heresy). It can hold in tension a critical reading of what is universally true of God ("scriptural truth") and what is read as true for a particular community of faith in the Body of Christ (in its own history of interpretation). It can also hold in tension what is abstract and spiritual and what is concrete and existential.

Finally, while kerygmatic hermeneutics is as fallible as any human reader, structure, system, or process, it is potentially "self-correcting" because the Spirit uses Scripture (and other media) to read over-against its readers and communities. That is, I attempt to show that kerygmatic hermeneutics remains theologically coherent and valid even when sin and error are expected, and aberrations are observed in this participation in divinity. That this transformative practice is allowed to take its time is also a continued gift of God's grace.

Concerning ecclesial practice, kerygmatic hermeneutics advances kerygmatic devotion as a model for religious reading in a kerygmatic community. Community practices of praying and interpreting Scripture in the Spirit can directly contribute to ecclesial decision-making, while that of proclaiming Christ in the Spirit is central in missionary works. A practice of kerygmatic hermeneutics may also contribute to training and development in spiritual leadership and discipleship, and church growth and missions. Above all these, a practice of kerygmatic hermeneutics is a practice of flowing in the Spirit in the Spirit's making of *logos* enfleshed, which gives shape and fullness to the Body of Christ, the embodiment of Truth to the world.

Concerning methodology, kerygmatic hermeneutics employs a constructive theological approach that locates this hermeneutical enterprise as a narrative of the Spirit's presence and activity in God's economy set in the particularity of a community of God's people. This approach minimizes reductionist tendencies that typical hermeneutical categories (e.g. tradition, Scripture, reason, experience) may bring to the table.[2] More importantly, this constructive theological approach allows the Spirit to freely choose any, or some, or all of these hermeneutical categories, together with human efficacies enabled by his charismata, to mediate a revelation, apprehension, and proclamation of scriptural truth in the contingency of each situation.

Since these realist claims to the Spirit's presence and activity have real world effects in human communities, the kerygmatic theology thus formulated lends itself to be critically tested and evaluated.[3] That is, this theological interpretation enterprise can exemplify how practical theology may be open to inter-disciplinary analysis in testing and evaluation. I next highlight three key contributions.

7.1.1 A theology of a Spirit-led hermeneutics

In this research, I propose a theology of a Spirit-led hermeneutics. These address some of the key challenges in theological interpretation and Pentecostal-charismatic hermeneutical discourse. While many scholars in biblical studies and theology would unreservedly assent to the claim that the Spirit of Christ reveals, many understandingly have reservations going down this path in hermeneutics. To date, a Spirit-led hermeneutics is possibly received with skepticism, if not rejection, even in theological interpretation circles. Kerygmatic theology attempts to advance this discourse by addressing some of these challenges.

I recall for us four main challenges to a Spirit-led hermeneutics. Firstly, the Spirit's fluidity and unpredictability mean that readers cannot

---

2. Kerygmatic hermeneutics, examined in its various perspectives, can account for Wesley's quadrilateral (Scripture, Tradition, Experience, and Reason) as well as the "Spirit-Text-Community" interpretive model. Each hermeneutical category—Scripture, tradition, experience, and reason—taken on its own with any particularly strong emphasis, tends to become reductionist (see discourse in Spawn and Wright, *Spirit and Scripture*). In this research, however, I have taken a constructionist approach in formulating kerygmatic hermeneutics. This accounts for how the Spirit makes an embodied witness to Jesus Christ, mediated by human hermeneutical principles like Scripture, tradition, experience, reason and all human efficacies, in an act of grace.

3. In this approach, I did not formulate the process of reading Scripture in the Spirit as the goal of the research. Instead, this process takes its appropriate place in God's economy to engender concrete, real world outcomes and impacts beyond the production of an exegetical account of a text. In this sense, kerygmatic hermeneutics lends itself to self-criticism even to a secular world.

readily discern the truth of any realist claims about his revelation of scriptural truth. Secondly, even if readers can make claims to the charismata of discernment, it remains for readers to discriminate, in themselves and one another, what is not only human voices but also God's voice. That is, such a hermeneutic has to make an attribution of a scriptural reading to the Spirit. Thirdly, this attribution has to stand up to criticism, and perhaps even suspicion. Lastly, a Spirit-led hermeneutic needs to account for how the Spirit may relate to other hermeneutical categories, e.g., tradition, Scripture, reason, and experience. I have attempted to account for each of these challenges in my formulation of kerygmatic theology.

7.1.2 A practice of a Spirit-led hermeneutics

Proponents of a Spirit-led hermeneutics have generally not gone far enough to show how any theological or philosophical account of scriptural interpretation in the Spirit may translate into a systematic practice in a community. A practice of kerygmatic hermeneutics is an embodied interpretation of scriptural truth that witnesses to Jesus Christ. I demonstrated what this embodiment—of reader dispositions, community habits, practices, outcomes, and impacts—would look like in a community.[4] Scriptural truth that is abstract and spiritual is lived out in the concrete existentially. Scriptural truth that is universal is apprehended for the contingency of every situation. In this habituated practice, kerygmatic readers are transformed into *logos* (i.e., God's seed for new life in Christ) in the flesh even as the Spirit catches them up in intoxicated sensibilities in a participation in divinity.

Kerygmatic hermeneutics contributes to ecclesiology by proposing a type of religious reading that may help to sustain and grow the church and her vision and mission in the unity of the Spirit. Kerygmatic devotion is an account of a Spirit-filled community's daily spiritual discipline practiced in moments of reading, meditation, praying, contemplation,

---

4. Recall a diagrammatic presentation of kerygmatic hermeneutics as an account of the Spirit's presence and working in a kerygmatic community (see Figure 1, section 5.7). In this account, I gave shape to a community habit of kerygmatic devotion, in daily disciplines of reading, meditation, prayer, contemplation, proclamation, and witness. I also set out how this community may practice praying and reading Scripture in the Spirit, using the PAL Prayer Method. Readers flow in the Spirit as he illumines and inspires Scripture afresh; readers also co-create with the Spirit in working his charismata to give and restore life. Central to a practice of kerygmatic hermeneutics is the proclamation of Christ in the Spirit.

and proclamation in the Spirit. Kerygmatic devotion is a discipline that grows the efficacy of Spirit-filled readers to live a life in the Spirit.

The efficacy of a practice of kerygmatic hermeneutics lies in the efficacy of kerygmatic readers. Readers are transformed into *logos* enfleshed, into wholeness and holiness as they proclaim Christ. As *logos* enfleshed, they co-create in the Spirit to give life, both physical and spiritual, in turn. However, this life in the Spirit may also embrace negative experiences of falling back into sinful and idolatrous living. In this research, I demonstrated, using the PAL Prayer Method, how readers in community may pray and read Scripture in the Spirit to reveal and confess truth, about themselves and one another. That is, I showed how such a practice of kerygmatic hermeneutics could be efficacious when readers in community can confess to a hermeneutical gap (what speech and action, dispositions, attitudes and behaviors they are falling short of) and devote themselves to learning and correction to close this gap.

7.1.3 A criticism of a Spirit-led hermeneutics

In this research, I have attempted to address the challenge of how humans may make an attribution to the Spirit's presence and activity in what is concrete and observable in this world. Kerygmatic criticism is the name I give to the discerned testing and reasoned evaluation of the realist claims about the work of the Spirit in reader dispositions, community habits, practices, outcomes, and impacts. Kerygmatic readers exercise discernment in testing and evaluation of what is not only human but also of the Spirit by looking for the marks of the Spirit—intoxication, life, participation, and revelation of truth.

Kerygmatic criticism holds kerygmatic theology and its practice in tension. Kerygmatic theology informs a practice. A practice of kerygmatic hermeneutics opens up its theology to a testing and evaluation of its theological integrity. Kerygmatic hermeneutics is self-critical if testing and evaluation follow disciplined processes that are open to discovery, learning, and correction. These processes do not confirm self-preferences and biases. A practice of kerygmatic hermeneutics grounds kerygmatic theology to give it a context, and kerygmatic criticism provides a structure that informs on the shape and fullness (whether valid, distorted or invalid) that such a practice has taken in this context. Kerygmatic criticism thus helps build self-learning and self-correcting kerygmatic communities.

Summarizing, kerygmatic hermeneutics' contributions may be presented in its three frames—theology, practice, and criticism. I further discuss their implications for epistemology and theology.

7.2 Implications for Epistemology and Theology

Kerygmatic hermeneutics is an account of transformed human efficacy in the *knowing* of God who is not knowable apart from what he reveals in a self-gift of grace. Kerygmatic hermeneutics is not a humanly conceived method where following systematic rules would yield a knowledge of the Other. Therefore, this enterprise locates more naturally in theology than in epistemology.

In kerygmatic hermeneutics, the Spirit uses Scripture's otherness and leads readers into a discovery of the mind of God in the particular. With the Spirit working with Scripture, a kerygmatic reader navigates in a to-ing and fro-ing between general claims of God and the patterns of his actions in the world and the embodiment of these general claims in the concrete particularity of contemporary living. This dynamic (instead of a two-step sequential) to-ing and fro-ing yields a revelation, apprehension and reception of God and his ways that shapes an embodied witness to the world.

This dynamic to-ing and fro-ing draws a continuum of reader responses that reflect readers' discovery of the whole of the knowing of God that he reveals. Yet there are distinct characteristics and transition points in this journey of discovery that line up with God's revelation of scriptural truth through illumination, inspiration, and co-creation. Readers move from an initial questioning of "What is *my* response here?" to taking a step back and asking, "What are *You* doing here?" to discerning "What new things do *You* want to do here through *me*?" These transformed reader responses reflect a knowing of God and his patterns of action in the world that yields transformed reader dispositions—transformed desires (that flow from a transformed mind, emotion, and volition), a transformed accountability to the otherness of the Spirit and Scripture, and a transformed attending and listening to the Spirit and one another in community.

Kerygmatic readers are trying to understand and, more than that, to embody this truth. Putting this another way, to embody this truth is to be united to God or to be imprinted with God's character and to act in every situation with the mind of Christ. Humans, as free acting agencies, become a way of God's working in the world. That is, humans can co-create with God, in signs and wonders, healings and deliverances, and doing all good in the fullness of humanity as free acting agencies. Yet, this whole process of co-creation happens within the providential will of God. Readers have not *performed* kerygmatic hermeneutics if they merely *state* what this truth of God is. An exegetical statement is not sufficient. Readers need to embody this truth in their particular circumstances; and this embodiment will be context-specific and particular.

Kerygmatic hermeneutics is thus an invitation to participate in divinity in both the concrete as well as the mystery of God. It puts in tension the concrete knowing of God as *logos* enfleshed and the acknowledgment that the inexhaustible God may only be apprehended in part even if made accessible in Spirit experience. This paradigmatic knowing of the mystery of God invites the fear of the Lord with a keen awareness of the fallibility of human knowing.

Kerygmatic hermeneutics offers a way of reading supernatural and ecstatic phenomena not merely as exuberant mountaintop experiences. Readers discern these phenomena as signs that God is working out his work through us. Kerygmatic hermeneutics thus holds in tension the ordinariness of Christian living and the mysterious revelation of God, the silent listening, patient waiting, and the joyful celebration in the Spirit, the disciplined reading and meditation, kenotic prayer and contemplation, and the co-creative proclamation with miraculous healings and dramatic deliverances—in a transformation that spirals toward divinity. This makes ordinary the supernatural and reads grace into mystery.

How can one talk about this participation in the mystery of God in the developed Western world when theology may not speak of the metaphysical foundation of wholeness in reality, evil in demonic possession, good in healings and deliverances, mystery in signs and wonders?[5] By

5. Such workings of the mystery of God in the non-Western world may more readily be observed in social anthropological accounts. For example, see Robbins, "Dispossessing the Spirits" and Robbins, *Becoming Sinners*. In Robbins's anthropological study of Christianity, he constructs theoretical models of radical cultural change. In his primary fieldwork in Papua New Guinea among the Urapmin, all of the members converted to charismatic Christianity in the late 1970s even though they were never directly missionized by Westerners. Robbins offers one of the richest available anthropological accounts of Christianity as a lived religion in the Spirit. He documents collective salvation and hunger for the Word in the Urapmin community accompanied by manifestations of Spirit possession (Spirit *disko*), tongues, healings, and deliverances, and spiritual experiences. In the rapid and extensive changes in Urapmin culture and social life following the conversion experience, changes included

failing to engage with knowing this mystery of God, theologians may risk relegating what lies at the heart of the Christian faith to the side-lines. Kerygmatic hermeneutics provides a way for readers to testify to their encounter with the metaphysical foundation of wholeness and holiness in God in the ordinariness of faithful living. Therefore, in this discovery journey of knowing God, kerygmatic hermeneutics addresses the main concern of theology: knowing the mystery that God is.

Can the theology that has been developed in this research inform on how other Spirit-led communities may read Scripture in the Spirit? In the last chapter, I have argued that kerygmatic theology possesses theological integrity. Therefore, kerygmatic theology, in its general claim of God and the patterns of his actions in the world, can inform Spirit-led readers' life in the Spirit in general and their reading Scripture in the Spirit in specific.

However, individual Spirit-led readers may face limitations in the practicing of kerygmatic hermeneutics, depending on the extent to which their own communities practice a reception of the Spirit's presence and activity in communal life. Minimally, Spirit-led readers could attempt to make their own formulations of how this theology may translate to a practice in their particular contexts—how they may create spaces and times for his working in their lives. While a practice of kerygmatic hermeneutics is formulated to grow reader efficacy in a Spirit-filled community, readers who do not enjoy the benefits of learning in bodily life in the Spirit, may still practice kerygmatic devotion to grow personal efficacy in flowing in the Spirit.

7.3 Directions for Future Research

Kerygmatic criticism offers a frame to read communities or ecclesiological movements critically.[6] Cox observes, "The most amazing thing

---

abandoning an elaborate traditional system of strict gender separation in almost all areas of life. Therefore, Robbins advances how anthropology can construct theories that at once account for the highly structured nature of most social life and at the same time its potential for radical transformation. Here we observe an example of a unity in diversity that brings reconciliation of gender and socio-economic differences in, not merely a mystical or even sacramental unity, but a concrete living out of a Spirit-filled life in community. If church communities in the Western world may open themselves up more for the Spirit's creative surprises, we may then hear more of the multiphonic voices of the Spirit's renewal work.

6. See examples of communities and Pentecostal-charismatic movements in Kay and Dyer, *Pentecostal and Charismatic Studies*; Kay, *Pentecostalism*.

about the runaway divisiveness in the young Pentecostal movement is that while the spats and squabbles continued, so did its spread. The more Pentecostals fought, the more they multiplied . . . The pattern of division and proliferation continued apace."[7] Kerygmatic criticism, that provides this structure to discriminate what a valid, distorted or invalid reading may look like, may account for this apparent contradiction; it helps readers to discern what, if any, of their own communities is attributable to the Spirit against human acts of sin and error. In this sense, kerygmatic readers may help the world hear and see God in such movements in spite of all dissonances.

Where else can we look for the movements of the Spirit that may help the world hear and see God? In the postmodern and postliberal world, we can increasingly hear and see more of such movements, ironically, outside the ambit of theology in the developed Western world.[8] Keener is one of the few theologians who takes on an anthropological perspective to eye-witness accounts in the New Testament Gospels and Acts of the Apostles. Keener argues that "spirit-possession claims . . . are a fairly widespread cross-cultural experience.[9] Anthropologists like Fennella Cannell, Matthew Engelke and Emma Cohen have offered critical accounts from grounded research of Spirit possession experiences in the non-Western world where many theologians would not tread.[10] If contemporary Christian theologians would not be open to hear and see the work of the Spirit in all his mystery in concrete living, then perhaps we may look to scholars in other disciplines who may be more open to knowing this mystery of God that theology purportedly seeks to reveal.

Looking into the future, Daniel Castelo observes,

> Contrary to its North transatlantic condition, Christianity is flourishing widely in the global South. The epicentre of Christianity's future has changed . . . What are those of us who are in the North to make of what is happening in the South? Or in terms of other directional locators, what are those of us in the West willing to learn and hear about Christianity from those in the East? . . . A dogmatic point of consideration within such conditions is the person and work of the Holy Spirit, for one

---

7. Cox, *Fire from Heaven*, 77–78.
8. See, e.g., Anderson et al., *Studying Global Pentecostalism*.
9 Keener, "Spirit Possession," 215–36.
10. See, e.g., Cannell, *Anthropology of Christianity*; Engelke, *Problem of Presence*; Cohen, "What is Spirit Possession?" 1–25; Keener, "Spirit Possession," 215–36.

persistent mark of global Christianity repeatedly raised by observers is its 'charismatic' character: often, those places and environments in which Christianity is flourishing today are ones that implicitly and explicitly operate out of sensibilities inclined to the pneumatic dimensions of the Christian life.[11]

Therefore, there remains much patient listening and attending to the Spirit. Kerygmatic readers read in a to-ing and a fro-ing from these variegated contexts to scriptural texts for an apprehension and reception of what the Spirit is saying and doing in the world, until they are gripped in the flow of the Spirit to discern what new things God wants them to do here and now.

---

11. Castelo, "Editorial," 124.

BIBLIOGRAPHY

Abbott, T. K. *A Critical and Exegetical Commentary on the Epistles to the Ephesians and to the Colossians*. International Critical Commentary on the Holy Scriptures of the Old and New Testaments. New York: Scribner, 1897.

Alford, Henry. *The New Testament for English Readers*. 4 vols. London: Rivingtons, 1866.

Anderson, Allan, et al., eds. *Studying Global Pentecostalism: Theories and Methods*. London: University of California Press, 2010.

Archer, Joel. "Against Miracles as Law-Violations: A Neo Aristotelian Approach." *European Journal for Philosophy of Religion* 7 (2015) 83–98.

Archer, Kenneth J. *A Pentecostal Hermeneutic: Spirit, Scripture and Community*. Cleveland, TN: CPT, 2009.

———. *A Pentecostal Hermeneutic for the Twenty-First Century: Spirit, Scripture and Community*. London: T. & T. Clark, 2009.

———. "Pentecostal Hermeneutics: Retrospect and Prospect." *Journal of Pentecostal Theology* 8 (1996) 63–81.

Archer, Kenneth J., and L. William Oliverio, Jr., eds. *Constructive Pneumatological Hermeneutics in Pentecostal Christianity*. New York: Palgrave Macmillan, 2016.

Arrington, French L. "Hermeneutics, Historical Perspectives on Pentecostal and Charismatic." In *Dictionary of Pentecostal and Charismatic Movements*, edited by Stanley M. Burgess and Gary B. McGee, 382–84. Grand Rapids: Zondervan, 1988.

Ayres, Lewis. *Augustine and the Trinity*. Cambridge: Cambridge University Press, 2010. https://www-cambridge-org.ezphost.dur.ac.uk/core/books/augustine-and-the-trinity/epilogue-catching-all-three/9E24C0AAF5D6F32D36C65D03A07ACCA4.

Badley, J.-A., and K. R. Badley. "Slow Reading: Reading Along Lectio Lines." *Journal of Education and Christian Belief* 15 (2011) 29–42.

Barr, James. *The Semantics of Biblical Language*. London: Oxford University Press, 1961.

Barrett, C. K. *The Acts of the Apostles. A Critical and Exegetical Commentary*. The International Critical Commentary 2. Edited by J. A. Emerton et al. Edinburgh: T. & T. Clark, 1998.

Barth, Karl. *Church Dogmatics*. Edited by G. W. Bromiley and T. F. Torrance. Edinburgh: T. & T. Clark, 2009.

———. *Church Dogmatics*. 1st ed. Vol. 4. Edited by G. W. Bromiley and T. F. Torrance. Edinburgh: T. & T. Clark, 1969.

———. "Revelation." In *God in Action*. Edinburgh: T. & T. Clark, 1936.

Barth, Karl, and Edwyn Clement Hoskyns, Sir. *The Epistle to the Romans*. Oxford: Oxford University Press, 1933.
Bauckham, Richard. *Gospel of Glory. Major Themes in Johannine Theology*. Grand Rapids: Baker Academic, 2015.
Beasley-Murray, G. R. *John*. Word Biblical Commentary 36. Edited by Bruce M. Metzger et al. Grand Rapids: Zondervan, 1999.
Bonk, Jonathan J., ed. *Encyclopedia of Missions and Missionaries*. New York: Routledge, 2007.
Boone, R. Jerome. "Pentecostal Worship and Hermeneutics: Engagement with the Spirit." *Journal of Pentecostal Theology* 26 (2017) 110–24.
Borgen, Peder. "Logos Was the True Light. Contributions to the Interpretation of the Prologue of John." *Novum Testamentum* 14 (1972) 115–30.
———. "Observations on the Targumic Character of the Prologue of John." *New Testament Studies* 16 (1969) 288–95.
Brown, Raymond E., SS. *The Community of the Beloved Disciple*. New York: Paulist, 1979.
Bruce, F. F. *The Book of the Acts*. Grand Rapids: Eerdmans, 1988.
———. *The Canon of Scripture*. Downers Grove, IL: InterVarsity, 1988.
Butler, Cuthbert. *Western Mysticism*. 2nd ed. London: Constable, 1926.
Cannell, Fenella, ed. *The Anthropology of Christianity*. Durham, NC: Duke University Press, 2006.
Cargal, Timothy B. "Beyond the Fundamentalist-Modernist Controversy: Pentecostals and Hermeneutics in a Postmodern Age." *Pneuma: The Journal of the Society for Pentecostal Studies* 15 (1993) 163–87.
Carruthers, M. *The Craft of Thought: Meditation, Rhetoric, and the Making of Images*. Cambridge: Cambridge University Press, 1998.
Carson, Donald A. *Showing the Spirit*. Grand Rapids: Baker, 1987.
Cartledge, Mark J. "Charismatic Spirituality." In *The Bloomsbury Guide to Christian Spirituality*, edited by Richard Woods and Peter Tyler, 214–25. London: Bloomsbury, 2012.
Castelo, Daniel. "Editorial." *International Journal of Systematic Theology* 16 (2014) 124–25.
———. *Pneumatology. A Guide for the Perplexed*. London: Bloomsbury, 2015.
———. "What If Miracles Don't Happen? Empowerment for Longsuffering." *Journal of Pentecostal Theology* 23 (2014) 236–45.
Coakley, Sarah. "Does Kenotic Christology Rest on a Mistake?" In *Exploring Kenotic Christology*, edited by C. Stephen Evans, 246–64. Oxford: Oxford University Press, 2006.
———. "Living into the Mystery of the Holy Trinity: Trinity, Prayer and Sexuality." *Anglican Theological Review* 80 (1998) 223–32.
Cohen, Emma. "What Is Spirit Possession? Defining, Comparing, and Explaining Two Possession Forms." *Ethnos* 73 (March 2008) 1–25.
Cole, Casey S. "Taking Hermeneutics to Heart: Proposing an Orthopathic Reading for Texts of Terror Via the Rape of Tamar Narrative." *Pneuma* 39 (2017) 264–74.
Collicut, Joanna. *The Psychology of Christian Character Formation*. London: SCM, 2015.
Colón-Emeric, Edgardo A. *Wesley, Aquinas, and Christian Perfection. An Ecumenical Dialogue*. Waco, TX: Baylor University Press, 2009.
Congar, Yves. *I Believe in the Holy Spirit*. Translated by David Smith. New York: Crossroad, 1983.

Coulter, Dale M., and Amos Yong. *The Spirit, the Affections, and the Christian Tradition.* Notre Dame, IN: University of Notre Dame Press, 2016.

Cox, Harvey. *Fire from Heaven: The Rise of Pentecostal Spirituality and the Reshaping of Religion in the Twenty-First Century.* Cambridge, MA: Da Capo, 1995.

Dawson, John D. *Christian Figural Reading and the Fashioning of Identity.* London: University of California Press, 2002.

Delatte, Paul. *Commentaire Sur La Règle De Saint Benoît* Translated by Justin McCann. Paris: The Abbey of Saint-Pierre de Solesmes 1948.

Dunn, James D. G. *The Baptism in the Holy Spirit. A Re-Examination of the New Testament Teaching on the Gift of the Spirit in Relation to Pentecostalism.* London: SCM, 1970.

———. "Baptism in the Spirit: A Response to Pentecostal Scholarship on Luke-Acts." *Journal of Pentecostal Theology* 3 (1993) 3–27.

———. *The Baptism of the Holy Spirit.* 2nd ed. London: SCM, 2010.

Engelke, Matthew. *A Problem of Presence. Beyond Scripture in an African Church.* London: University of California Press, 2007.

England, Doctrine Commission of the Church of. *We Believe in the Holy Spirit.* The Westminster Confession of Faith. London: Church House, 1991.

Evans, C. Stephen. *Exploring Kenotic Christology. The Self-Emptying of God.* Oxford: Oxford University Press, 2006.

Fee, Gordon D. *God's Empowering Presence. The Holy Spirit in the Letters of Paul.* Peabody, MA: Hendrickson, 1994.

———. "Hermeneutics and Historical Precedent. A Major Issue in Pentecostal Hermeneutics." In *Gospel and Spirit. Issues in New Testament Hermeneutics,* 83–104. Peabody, MA: Hendrickson, 1991.

Ferguson, Everett. *The Rule of Faith. A Guide.* Eugene, OR: Wipf & Stock, 2015.

Foder, Jim, and Mike Higton. "Scripture, Devotion and Discipleship." In *Routledge Companion to the Practice of Christian Theology,* edited by Mike Higton and Jim Foder, 123–40. London: Routledge, 2015.

Foster, D. *Reading with God. Lectio Divina.* London: Continuum, 2005.

Fowl, Stephen E. *Engaging Scripture: A Model for Theological Interpretation.* Oxford: Blackwell, 1998.

———. "How the Spirit Reads and How to Read the Spirit." In *The Bible in Ethics: The Second Sheffield Colloquium,* edited by John W. Rogerson, Margaret Davies, and M. Daniel Carroll R., 348–63. Journal for the Study of the Old Testament Supplemental Series 207. Sheffield: Sheffield Academic, 1995.

———. *The Theological Interpretation of Scripture: Classic and Contemporary Readings.* Malden, MA: Blackwell, 1997.

Fowl, Stephen E., and L. Gregory Jones. "Scripture, Exegesis, and Discernment in Christian Ethics." In *Virtues and Practices in the Christian Tradition. Christian Ethics after Mcintyre,* edited by Nancey Murphy et al., 111–31. Harrisburg, PA: Trinity, 1999.

Gardner, Rex. "Miracles of Healing in Anglo-Celtic Northumbria as Recorded by the Venerable Bede and His Contemporaries: A Reappraisal in the Light of Twentieth-Century Experience." *BMedJ* 287 (1983) 1927–33.

Geisler, Norman L. *Signs and Wonders. Healiings, Miracles and Unusual Events.* Matthews, NC: Bastion, 2019.

Green, Chris E. W. "Beautifying the Beautiful World: Scripture, the Triune God, and the Aesthetics of Interpretation." In *Constructive Pneumatological Hermeneutics in*

Pentecostal Christianity, edited by Kenneth J. Archer and L. William Oliverio Jr., 103–19. New York: Palgrave Macmillan, 2016.

Green, Joel B. *Practicing Theological Interpretation. Engaging Biblical Texts for Faith and Formation*. Grand Rapids: Baker Academic, 2011.

Grey, Jacqueline. *Three's a Crowd: Pentecostalism, Hermeneutics and the Old Testament*. Eugene, OR: Pickwick, 2011.

Gunkel, Hermann. *Genesis*. Macon, GA: Mercer University Press, 1997.

Hauerwas, Stanley, and William H. Willimon. *The Holy Spirit*. Nashville: Abingdon, 2015.

Hays, Richard B. *Echoes of Scripture in the Gospels*. Waco, TX: Baylor University Press, 2017.

———. *Echoes of Scripture in the Letters of Paul*. New Haven, CT: Yale University Press, 1989.

———. *Reading Backwards*. London: Baylor University Press, 2014.

Heisler, Greg. *Spirit-Led Preaching: The Holy Spirit's Role in Sermon Preparation and Delivery*. Nashville: B & H, 2007.

———. "The Spirit and Our Preaching: Why We Are Desperate for the Spirit's Illumination." In *Holy Spirit: Unfinished Agenda*, edited by Johnson T. K. Lim, 197–202. Singapore: Genesis, 2014.

Higton, Mike. *Christian Doctrine*. SCM Core Text. London: SCM, 2008.

———. *Difficult Gospel. The Theology of Rowan Williams*. London: SCM, 2004.

———. "Incarnation." In *The Cambridge Dictionary of Christian Theology*, edited by Ian A. McFarland et al., 235–37. Cambridge: Cambridge University Press, 2011.

Hollenweger, W. J. "The Contribution of Critical Exegesis to Pentecostal Hermeneutics." *Spirit and Church* 2 (2000) 7–18.

Holmes, Stephen R. *Holy Trinity. Understanding God's Life*. Milton Keynes: Paternoster, 2012.

Hume, David. *An Enquiry Concerning Human Understanding*. 2nd ed. Edited by L. A. Selby-Bigge. Oxford: Oxford University Press, 1902.

Israel, Richard D., et al. "Pentecostals and Hermeneutics. Texts, Rituals and Community." *Pneuma. The Journal of the Society for Pentecostal Studies* 15 (1993) 137–61.

Jacob, Alan. *A Theology of Reading. The Hermeneutics of Love*. Oxford: Westview, 2001.

Jenson, Robert W. "The Holy Spirit." In *Christian Dogmatics*, edited by Robert W. Jenson and Carl Braaten, 105–8. Philadelphia: Fortress, 2011.

John of the Cross, Saint. *Dark Night of the Soul*. Translated by E. Allison Peers. Edited by C. D. P. Silverio de Santa Teresa. Mineola, NY: Dover, 2003.

Johns, Cheryl Bridges. "Grieving, Brooding and Transforming: The Spirit, the Bible, and Gender." *Journal of Pentecostal Theology* 23 (2014) 141–53.

Johnson, Bob L., Jr., and Rickie D. Moore. "Soul Care for One and All: Pentecostal Theology and the Search for a More Expansive View of Scriptural Formation." *Journal of Pentecostal Theology* 26 (2017) 125–52.

Johnson, David. *Hume, Holism and Miracles*. Ithaca: Cornell University Press, 2018.

Johnson, David R. *Pneumatic Discernment in the Apocalypse: An Intertextual and Pentecostal Exploration*. Cleveland, OH: CPT, 2018.

Johnson, Luke T. *Decision Making in the Church*. Philadelphia: Fortress, 1983.

Kärkkäinen, Veli-Matti. *One with God. Salvation as Deification and Justification*. Collegeville, MN: Liturgical, 2004.

---. "Pentecostal Identity." In *Pentecostals in the 21st Century: Identity, Beliefs, Praxis*, edited by Corneliu Constantineanu and Christopher J. Scobie, 14–31. Eugene, OR: Cascade, 2018.

---. *Pneumatology. The Holy Spirit in Ecumenical, International, and Contextual Perspective*. Grand Rapids: Baker Academic, 2002.

Kay, William K., ed. *Pentecostalism*. London: SCM, 2009.

---. "Philosophy and Developmental Psychology: Relevance for Pentecostal Hermeneutics." In *Constructive Pneumatological Hermeneutics in Pentecostal Christianity*, edited by Kenneth J. Archer and L. William Oliverio, Jr., 267–78. New York: Palgrave Macmillan, 2016.

Kay, William K., and Anne E. Dyer, eds. *Pentecostal and Charismatic Studies*. London: SCM, 2004.

Keener, Craig S. *Acts. An Exegetical Commentary*. Grand Rapids: Baker Academic, 2014.

---. *Miracles. The Credibility of the New Testament Accounts*. Grand Rapids: Baker Academic, 2011.

---. "Pentecostal Biblical Hermeneutics/Spirit Hermeneutics." In *Scripture and Its Interpretation: A Global, Ecumenical Introduction to the Bible*, edited by Michael J. Gorman, 270–83. Grand Rapids: Baker Academic, 2017.

---. *Spirit Hermeneutics. Reading Scripture in Light of Pentecost*. Grand Rapids: Eerdmans, 2016.

---. "Spirit Possession as a Cross-Cultural Experience." *Bulletin for Biblical Research* 20 (2010) 215–36.

Kelsey, D. H. *Eccentric Existence. A Theological Anthropology*. Louisville, KY: Westminster John Knox, 2009.

Kilby, Karen. "Perichoresis and Projection: Problems with Social Doctrines of the Trinity." *New Blackfriars* 81 (2000) 432–35.

Lash, Nicholas. *Believing Three Ways in One God: A Reading of the Apostles' Creed*. London: SCM, 1992.

---. "Performing the Scriptures: Interpretation through Living." *The Furrow* 33 (1982) 467–74.

---. *Theology on the Way to Emmaus*. Eugene, OR: Wipf & Stock, 2005.

Levering, Matthew. "The Holy Spirit in the Trinitarian Communion: 'Love' and 'Gift'?". *International Journal of Systematic Theology* 16 (2014) 126–42.

Lewis, C. S. *Miracles*. London: William Collins, 2012.

Lightfoot, J. B. *The Acts of the Apostles. A Newly Discovered Commentary*. The Lightfoot Legacy Set 1. Edited by Ben Witherington, III and Todd D. Still. Downers Grove, IL: InterVarsity, 2014.

Lincoln, Andrew T. "Ephesians." Word Biblical Commentary 42, edited by David A. Hubbard and Glenn W. Barker. Dallas: Word, 1990.

Lindbeck, George. *The Nature of Doctrine: Religion and Theology in a Postliberal Age*. London: SPCK, 1984.

Magrassi, Mariano, OSB. *Praying the Bible. An Introduction to Lectio Divina*. Translated by Edward Hagman, OFM Cap. Collegeville, MN: Liturgical, 1998.

Martin, Lee Roy, ed. *Pentecostal Hermeneutics: A Reader*. Leiden: Brill, 2013.

Mather, Hannah R. K. *The Interpreting Spirit*. Eugene, OR: Pickwick, 2020.

McFarland, Ian A., et al. *The Cambridge Dictionary of Christian Theology*. Cambridge: Cambridge University Press, 2011.

McGuckin, John Anthony. *St. Cyril of Alexandria. The Christological Controversy: Its History, Theology and Texts.* Leiden: Brill, 1994.

McLean, Mark D. "Toward a Pentecostal Hermeneutic." *Pneuma: The Journal of the Society for Pentecostal Studies* 6 (1984) 35–56.

Menzies, Robert P. "Luke and the Spirit: A Reply to James Dunn." *Jounal of Pentecostal Theology* 4 (1994) 115–38.

Menzies, William W. "The Methodology of Pentecostal Theology: An Essay in Hermeneutics." In *Essays on Apostolic Themes: Studies in Honor of Howard M. Ervin*, edited by Paul Elbert, 1–14. Peabody, MA: Hendrickson, 1985.

Merton, Thomas. *The Seven Storey Mountain*. London: SPCK, 1949.

"Miracles." In *Christian Classics Ethereal Library*, Jan 11, 2021. https://ccel.org/entity/miracles?queryID=-1&resultID=miracles.

Moberly, R. W. L. *The Bible in a Disenchanted Age. The Enduring Possibility of Christian Faith*. Grand Rapids: Baker Academic, 2018.

———. *Prophecy and Discernment*. Cambridge Studies in Christian Doctrine. Cambridge: Cambridge University Press, 2006.

Moltmann, Jürgen. "God in the World—the World in God: Perichoresis in Trinity and Eschatology." In *The Gospel of John and Christian Theology*, edited by Richard Bauckham and Carl Mosser, 369–81. Grand Rapids: Eerdmans, 2008.

———. *The Spirit of Life: A Universal Affirmation*. Minneapolis: Fortress, 1992.

Moo, Douglas J. *The Letters to the Colossians and to Philemon*. Cambridge: Eerdmans, 2008.

Moore, Rickie D. "Altar Hermeneutics: Reflections on Pentecostal Biblical Interpretation." *Pneuma* 38 (2016) 148–59.

Moschella, Mary Clark. *Ethnography as a Pastoral Practice. An Introduction*. Cleveland, OH: Pilgrim, 2008.

O'Collins, Gerald. *Christology: A Biblical, Historical and Systematic Study of Jesus*. 2nd ed. Oxford: Oxford University Press, 2009.

Ochs, P. *Another Reformation: Postliberal Christianity and the Jews*. Grand Rapids: Baker Academic, 2011.

Oliverio, L. William, Jr. *Theological Hermeneutics in the Classical Pentecostal Tradition: A Typological Account*. Global Pentecostal and Charismatic Studies. Leiden: Brill, 2012.

Olson, Mark K. *John Wesley's Theology of Christian Perfection. Developments in Doctrine and Theological System*. Vol. 2. Fenwick, MI: Truth in Heart, 2009.

Osmer, Richard R. *Practical Theology. An Introduction*. Grand Rapids: Eerdmans, 2008.

Peers, E. Allison. *Mother of Carmel. A Portrait of St Teresa of Jesus*. London: SCM, 1961.

Peters, John L. *Christian Perfection and American Methodism*. Nashville: Abingdon, 1956.

Peterson, E. H. *Eat This Book: A Conversation in the Art of Spiritual Reading*. Grand Rapids: Eerdmans, 2006.

Pinnock, Clark H. *Flame of Love. A Theology of the Holy Spirit*. Downers Grove, IL: InterVarsity, 1996.

———. "The Work of the Holy Spirit in Hermeneutics." *Journal of Pentecostal Theology* 2 (1993) 3–23.

———. "The Work of the Spirit in the Interpretation of Holy Scripture from the Perspective of a Charismatic Biblical Theologian." *Journal of Pentecostal Theology* 18 (2009) 157–71.

Polkinghorne, John. *Faith in the Living God: A Dialogue*. London: SPCK, 2001.

Quash, Ben. *Found Theology. History, Imagination and the Holy Spirit.* London: Bloomsbury, 2013.
Radner, Ephraim. "The Holy Spirit and Unity: Getting out of the Way of Christ." *International Journal of Systematic Theology* 16 (2014) 207–20.
———. *Time and the Word. Figural Reading of Christian Scriptures.* Grand Rapids: Eerdmans, 2016.
Robbins, Joel. *Becoming Sinners: Christianity and Moral Torment in a Papua New Guinea Society.* London: University of California Press, 2004.
———. "Dispossessing the Spirits: Christian Transformations of Desire and Ecology among the Urapmin of Papua New Guinea." *Politics of Culture in the Pacific Islands Ethnography* 34 (1995) 211–24.
Robeck, Cecil M. Jr., and Amos Yong. *The Cambridge Companion to Pentecostalism.* Cambridge: Cambridge University Press, 2014.
Rogers, Eugene F., Jr. *After the Spirit. A Constructive Pneumatology from Resources Outside the Modern West.* London: SCM, 2006.
Root, Andrew. *Christopraxis. A Practical Theology of the Cross.* Minneapolis: Fortress, 2014.
Schnackenburg, Rudolf. *Ephesians. A Commentary.* Edinburgh: T. & T. Clark 1991.
Schneiders, Sandra M. "The Gospels and the Reader." In *The Cambridge Companion to the Gospels*, edited by Stephen C. Barton, Chs. 97–118. Cambridge: Cambridge University Press, 2006.
Schökel, Luis Alonso. *From Author-Hermeneutics to Text-Hermeneutics: A Manual of Hermeneutics.* Edited by Luis Alonso Schökel. Sheffield: Sheffield Academic, 1998.
Seah, David J. H. H. "A Spirituality Approach to Organisational Transformation." PhD diss., University of South Australia, 2005.
Searle, John. *The Construction of Social Reality.* New York: Simon & Schuster, 1995.
Seitz, Christopher R., and Kent Harold Richards, eds. *The Bible as Christian Scripture. The Work of Brevard S. Childs.* Atlanta: Society of Biblical Literature, 2013.
Spawn, Kevin L., and Archie T. Wright. "Cultivating a Pneumatic Hermeneutic." In *Spirit and Scripture: Exploring a Pneumatic Hermeneutic*, edited by Kevin L. Spawn and Archie T. Wright, 191–98. London: T. & T. Clark, 2012.
———. *Spirit and Scripture. Exploring a Pneumatic Hermeneutic.* London: T. & T. Clark, 2012.
Stendahl, Krister. "Selections from 'Biblical Theology, Contemporary.'" In *Theology, History, and Biblical Interpretation: Modern Readings*, edited by Darren Sarisky, 239–52. London: Bloomsbury, 1962.
Stibbe, Mark W. G. "The Theology of Renewal and the Renewal of Theology." *Jounal of Pentecostal Theology* 3 (1993) 71–90.
———. "This Is That: Some Thoughts Concerning Charismatic Hermeneutics." *Anvil: An Anglican Evangelical Journal for Theology and Missions* 15 (1998) 181–93.
Stronstad, Roger. *The Charismatic Theology of St. Luke.* Peabody, MA: Hendrickson, 1984.
———. "Pentecostal Experience and Hermeneutics." *Paraclete* 26 (1992) 14–30.
———. "Some Aspects of Hermeneutics in the Pentecostal Tradition." In *Pentecostals in the 21st Century: Identity, Beliefs, Praxis*, edited by Corneliu Constantineanu and Christopher J. Scobie, 32–58. Eugene, OR: Cascade, 2018.
Stylianopoulous, Theodore. *The New Testament: An Orthodox Perspective. Vol. 1: Scripture, Tradition, Hermeneutics.* Brookline, MA: Holy Cross Orthodox, 1997.

Swinton, J., and H. Mowat. *Qualitative Research and Practical Theology*. London: SCM, 2006.
Synan, Vinson. *The Century of the Holy Spirit. 100 Years of Pentecostal and Charismatic Renewal, 1901–2001*. Nashville: Thomas Nelson, 2001.
Tanner, Kathryn. *God and Creation in Christian Theology: Tyranny or Empowerment?* Oxford: Basil Blackwell, 1988.
———. *Jesus, Humanity and the Trinity. A Brief Systematic Theology*. Minneapolis: Fortress, 2001.
———. *Theories of Culture: A New Agenda for Theology*. Minneapolis: Fortress, 1997.
Tennant, F. R. *Miracle and Its Philosophical Presuppositions: Three Lectures Delivered in the University of London 1924*. Cambridge: Cambridge University Press, 1925.
Tesafaye, Leulseged Philemon. *Pneumatic Hermeneutics: The Role of the Holy Spirit in the Theological Interpretation of Scripture*. Cleveland, TN: CPT, 2019.
Thiselton, Anthony C. *The Holy Spirit. In Biblical Teaching, through the Centuries, and Today*. London: Society for Promoting Christian Knowledge, 2013.
———. *New Horizons in Hermeneutics. The Theory and Practice of Transforming Biblical Reading*. London: Harper Collins, 1992.
———. *Two Horizons. New Testament Hermeneutics and Philosophical Description*. Grand Rapids: Eerdmans, 1980.
Thomas, John Christopher. "Women, Pentecostals and the Bible: An Experiment in Pentecostal Hermeneutics." *Journal of Pentecostal Theology* 5 (1994) 41–56.
Thompson, Marianne Meye. *John. A Commentary*. Louisville, KY: Westminster John Knox, 2015.
Tillich, Paul. *Systematic Theology. Three Volumes in One*. Chicago: University of Chicago Press, 1967.
Torr, Stephen C. *A Dramatic Pentecostal/Charismatic Anti-Theodicy. Improvising on a Divine Performance of Lament*. Eugene, OR: Pickwick, 2013.
Twelftree, G. H. "The Historian and the Miraculous." *Bulletin for Biblical Research* 28 (2018) 199–217.
Van Inwagen, Peter. *God, Knowledge and Mystery: Essays in Philosophical Theology*. Ithaca, NY: Cornell University Press, 1995.
Vanhoozer, Kevin J. *Is There a Meaning in This Text? The Bible, the Reader, and the Morality of Literary Knowledge*. Grand Rapids: Zondervan, 1998.
Vine, W. E. *Vine's Expository Dictionary of New Testament Words*. Iowa Falls, IA: Riverside, 1952.
von Rad, Gerhard. *Genesis*. London: SCM, 1972.
Vondey, Wolfgang. *Beyond Pentecostalism: The Crisis of Global Christianity and the Renewal of the Theological Agenda*. Grand Rapids: Eerdmans, 2010.
———. *Pentecostal Theology: Living the Full Gospel*. London: T. & T. Clark, 2017.
Waddell, Robby, and Peter Althouse. "An Editorial Note on the Roundtable Dialogue of Craig S. Keener's *Spirit Hermeneutics: Reading Scripture in the Light of Pentecost*." *Pneuma* 39 (2017) 123–25.
Ward, Pete. *Participation and Mediation. A Practical Theology for the Liquid Church*. London: SCM, 2008.
———, ed. *Perspectives on Ecclesiology and Ethnography*. Grand Rapids: Eerdmans, 2012.

Ware, Kallistos. "Salvation and Theosis in Orthodox Theology." In *Luther Et La Réforme Allemande Dans Une Perspective Oecuménique*, edited by W. Schneemelcher, 167–84. Geneva: Editions du Centre Orthodoxe, 1983.

Webster, John B. *Holy Scripture: A Dogmatic Sketch*. Cambridge: Cambridge University Press, 2003.

———. "Illumination." *Journal of Reformed Theology* 5 (2011) 325–40.

———. "'In the Society of God': Some Principles of Ecclesiology." In *Perspectives on Ecclesiology and Ethnography*, edited by Pete Ward, 200–22. Grand Rapids: Eerdmans, 2012.

———. *Word and Church: Essays in Christian Dogmatics*. Edinburgh: T. & T. Clark, 2001.

Welker, Michael. "The Spirit in Philosophical, Theological, and Interdisciplinary Perspectives." In *The Work of the Spirit: Pneumatology and Pentecostalism*, edited by Michael Welker, 221–32. Cambridge: Eerdmans, 2006.

———. *The Work of the Spirit: Pneumatology and Pentecostalism*. Grand Rapids: Eerdmans, 2006.

Williams, Rowan. "Making Moral Decisions." In *The Cambridge Companion to Christian Ethics*, edited by Robin Gill, 3–15. Cambridge: Cambridge University Press, 2011.

———. *On Christian Theology*. Oxford: Blackwell, 2000.

———. "The Spirit of the Age to Come." *Sobornost: The Journal of the Fellowship of St. Alban and St. Sergius* 6 (1974) 613–26.

———. *Teresa of Avila*. 2nd ed. London: Continuum, 2000.

———. "The Theology of Vladimir Nikolaievich Lossky: An Exposition and Critique." PhD diss., Oxford University, 1975.

———. *The Wound of Knowledge*. 2nd ed. London: Darton, Longman & Todd, 1990.

Wright, Andrew. *Christianity and Critical Realism: Ambiguity, Truth and Theological Literacy*. New York: Routledge, 2013.

Wright, N. T. "How Can the Bible Be Authoritative." *Vox Evangelica* 21 (1991) 7–32.

———. *The Resurrection of the Son of God*. Minneapolis: Fortress, 2003.

Yong, Amos. *The Hermeneutical Spirit: Theological Interpretation and Scriptural Imagination for the 21st Century*. Eugene, OR: Cascade, 2017.

———. "Ruach, the Primordial Chaos, and the Breath of Life: Emergence Theory and the Creation Narratives in Pneumatological Perspective." In *The Work of the Spirit: Pneumatology and Pentecostalism*, edited by Michael Welker, 183–204. Cambridge, MA: Eerdmans, 2006.

———. *Spirit-Word-Community: Theological Hermeneutics in Trinitarian Perspective*. Eugene, OR: Wipf & Stock, 2002.

Yung, Hwa. "The 21st Century Reformation: Recover the Spiritual." *Christianity Today* 54 (2010) 32–33.